A
BEHAVIORAL
APPROACH
TO
HISTORICAL
ANALYSIS

A

BEHAVIORAL

APPROACH

TO

HISTORICAL

ANALYSIS

ROBERT F. BERKHOFER, JR.

THE FREE PRESS, NEW YORK

COLLIER-MACMILLAN LIMITED, LONDON

To my Clio

Like so many other books, this too started out as quite another one. Some of the thoughts contained in these pages began in my attempts to teach and to write about American social and cultural history in general and the American frontier in particular. The specific impetus was an attempt to write an introductory section for a social interpretation of American history. I felt I had to provide some theoretical underpinnings for what I hoped would be an example of the so-called "new history." The introduction soon grew to this book-length essay.

The traces, or scars, if you will, of this evolution exist in the examples I use to illustrate my arguments. They are primarily from American history and frequently from social and cultural history. The preponderance of American illustrations, however, should not cause the reader to assume that this volume is addressed only to historians of the United States' past. Despite the provincialness of examples, the book deals with problems I believe common to the entire historical profession.

To write a book of this sort demands heavy dependence upon authorities in many disciplines. My foremost acknowledgments must therefore be to the authors with whom I agree and disagree in the following pages. Perhaps those authors who aroused me to the staunchest opposition deserve the greatest thanks, even though I may have reserved the harshest words for them. My intellectual indebtedness is only feebly indicated by the footnotes and, in a few cases, by my gratitude for permission to reprint excerpts.

On the level of personal acquaintance, my acknowledgements are large in number and great in satisfaction. Although they may not realize it, Robin Williams, Jr., Allan R. Holmberg, and Lauriston Sharp influenced the direction of my thinking many years ago as a graduate student. More recently, my colleagues in Project Social Studies at the University of Minnesota stimulated many thoughts by their persistent requests for a defense of history as a discipline useful to elementary and secondary school students. Theta Wolf, Allan Spear, my colleagues in the History Department Colloquium, and members of the Social Science Colloquium at Cleveland State University offered comments upon portions of the manuscript they read or heard. Lee Benson, Allan Bogue, J. Rogers Hollingsworth, and Ernest May read the whole manuscript and attempted to save me from the wrath of my readers-to-be by urging more examples and a wider variety of approaches. I have followed their advice whenever the suggestions did not lengthen the book or challenge my convictions. Fred Lukermann and Homer Mason gave me the benefit of views from outside the discipline of history, and Byron Marshall and David Kopf did the same from within the discipline but with a viewpoint critical of Western civilization and its ethnocentrism. Edith West, Mary Turpie, Mary Young, and my wife, Genevieve, not only improved the substance of this essay but also its phrasing by their criticism. Delores Dolan produced a typed manuscript from my wretched handwriting, and Martin Dolan helped me and her by reading that manuscript.

All these people tried to save my ego in the long run by bruising it in the short run. I hope the reader feels the benefit as much as I do. Needless to say, the final content of this book is my responsibility and conviction.

The Graduate School of the University of Minnesota hastened the appearance of this volume by providing my salary during a quarter's leave. I thank the Dean and the selection committee for their faith.

Minneapolis   R. F. B.

CONTENTS

A
BEHAVIORAL
APPROACH
TO
HISTORICAL
ANALYSIS

To issue a clarion call for his- **INTRODUCTION**
torians to adopt a behavioral
approach to their subject
may seem as up-to-date and exciting as last month's newspaper, for it is the academic fashion today to argue the
utility of social science theory in the writing of history.
Books and articles issue forth from the presses in seeming
profusion advocating and even occasionally demonstrating
such an approach. Yet these many pages fail in three significant ways to accomplish the end they nominally espouse
and which I urge.

First, if they are not specific instances of specific uses
of some concept or theory, they are mere compendia of
techniques or concepts that are passed off as social theory.
If the book or article really talks about theory, the larger
framework of which the theory was a part is neglected.
Social theories today are not shreds and patches but attempts at integrated sets of hypotheses, concepts, and
generalizations. Our sister disciplines offer us structured
theoretical frameworks. If pieces of these frameworks are
haphazardly removed from the larger context, as they
are in most historical writing, then further implications are
obscured at the least or the isolated elements are distorted
or inaccurate at the worst.

This confusion about the nature of social science theory points to a second caveat: The profusion of pages does
not provide clues to the heated controversies over the
fundamental approaches to man's behavior that rage in
the various social science disciplines today. Disputes over
systems analysis, functionalism, dynamic versus static analysis, consensus versus conflict models of society all show the
great unresolved rift between structure and process in
studying man's behavior. Yet these debates have not even
found their way into historical circles, though these prob-

lems and their solutions are as crucial, if not more so, to understanding past behavior as they are to understanding present behavior.

Third, social scientists are seeking and achieving a more precise and rigorous analysis of their subject matter because they are reading modern philosophers of science who stress criteria for valid explanation. As a result of this cross-disciplinary aid, social scientists are probing their presuppositions, examining their theories, and framing their studies more carefully than ever before. This concern has directed social scientists' attention to methodology as well as to method, or to the philosophy of the procedures as well as to the procedures themselves. For this reason they have gone to the philosophical journals for clarification. Again any attempt by working historians to borrow modern social theory must include this quest of behavioral scientists for analytical rigor and explanatory precision.

Thus far I have seemed to imply that the social scientists have a neat package of theory and concept that the bumbling historian can easily borrow. Nothing is further from the current state of affairs in those disciplines. The complaints about jargon, from both within and without the behavioral science disciplines, are but one indication of the true state of theory in those areas. The squabbles over terminology—or jargon, if you will—are far from mere arguments over semantic niceties; rather, these debates represent basic conflicts over the very nature and explanation of social phenomena. Even economics, the most theoretically developed of the social sciences, is not entirely exempt from the intramural pastime of debates over the vocabulary applicable to fundamentals of the subject. If this is the case in economics, then the situation is far worse in the other social sciences, because their theoretical frameworks are less agreed upon, hence less codified than that of their senior sister.

Given this situation in the social sciences, historians who borrow theories and concepts must also accept the disputes over their meaning, whether they want to or not. Thus the reader is warned that any terminology in those disciplines is burdened with long disputes over its definition and the nature of the fundamental social reality the terms represent. This intellectual baggage of past and present argument is not solely a disadvantage, however, for it forces one to be definite about what is meant by a term and therefore obliges one to perform the task of clarification. To borrow at all requires one to choose sides, therefore, in the arguments over the nature of behavioral reality as it is viewed today, but this is desirable for the historian because it promotes consciousness of his assumptions about behavioral reality in the past. In these circumstances, modern philosophy again aids the would-be borrower by its emphases on the nature of explanation, verification, and general analysis.

At the same time as most historians have neglected the philosophy of science when appropriating social theory, they have given almost as little notice to the latest developments in the modern philosophy of history. Wearied by the irrelevance to their work of the older theorizing about the grand meaning of history that called itself philosophy of history, many historians have similarly rejected, or so it seems, the newer work of the critical, or analytical, philosophers of history writing today. Most historians know of Hegel, Marx, or Spengler, but have they heard of Patrick Gardiner, William Dray, or Arthur Danto? These latter men with others probe the logical nature of the connections that the historian asserts in linking together his facts. Thus they, too, contribute to the more complex approach to the past demanded by contemporary behavioral knowledge by clarifying what needs to be understood and whether and how what we know contributes to that understanding. These men also explore anew the age-old questions about history as science or art, as objective or subjective, and as story or analysis and come forth with interestingly different answers, but again historians have paid little heed.

But here, unlike the material in the social sciences, the work of the philosophers cannot be appropriated as it appears in the pages of their journals and books. There they argue these issues as central to philosophers' concerns and not to historians' interests, so therefore "translation" is necessary. Second, philosophers are no more agreed upon many topics pertinent to historians' concerns than are the social scientists. They may argue their differences more precisely than do the behavioral scientists, but they differ no less. So once again the historian must be aware of or even choose sides in the debates if he would benefit from those newest developments in philosophy relevant to his goal of writing history.

Although I advocate liberal borrowing of social science theories, concepts, and techniques, such loans need not make the practice of history a social science; they are meant only to make it scientific. In short, what I urge in this book is not the abandonment of goals traditional to the historical profession for ones espoused by the social scientists or philosophers but rather the incorporation of sophisticated social theory and precise explanation into the writing of history in order to achieve a more complex representation of past reality than hitherto found in the subject. I suggest, and hope to prove, that these other disciplines can alert us as historians to a previously unachieved appreciation of the complexity of the past through their more sophisticated conceptions of man and logic.

The fundamental assumptions of my essay are that the subject of the historian concerns the past of man; that man individually and collectively is complex; that to study man in sufficient complexity requires social science concepts and theory; that man can only be studied as an analytical entity through some conceptual framework; and that once a knowledge of human behavior is gained, then other aspects of historiography fall into their proper sphere. History is its own discipline, but it needs to be enriched by borrowing from other disciplines for its own purposes. Thus the question becomes not whether to use social science knowledge, but what to use. In my opinion, the approach denominated behavioralism today offers the best answer to this question, for it incorporates the new knowledge of man's behavior derived from the basic social sciences of psychology, sociology, and anthropology with a rigorous and self-conscious methodology for the acquisition and application of that knowledge derived from the philosophy of science.

Though fashionable in other disciplines, the term behavioralism is rarely used by historians. Those few who do use it refer usually to methods of quantification and statistical techniques. Although these methods and techniques are part of the approach and can be useful to the historian, I believe the broader meaning of behavioralism is more basic to historical research and writing. Behavioralism not only means the recent advances in data collection and analysis but also the significant developments in theory formulation and testing as well as a new orientation to the study of man's behavior. According to these latter developments, behavioralism is a more complex approach to human action than the mere quantifying of variables and the collection of data, important as these may be, because it signifies new conceptions of variables and hence new types of data. In fact, behavioralism in the narrow sense so often used can only produce results when employed in conjunction with broader behavioral approaches. Quantified data can never be better than the hypotheses that frame the search for evidence, and theories of human behavior provide these indispensable foundations for any research into present or past human activities.

Since historians have already started borrowing behavioralism as techniques, this book concentrates rather upon the theoretical side of the approach. In reality, there is no *one* behavioral approach, only approaches, because of the many arguments over the fundamental interpretations of human behavior. Until a "paradigm" of agreed-upon model problems and solutions, to use Thomas Kuhn's useful conception, exists for the behavioral sciences as for the physical and biological sciences, there can be no one behavioral approach. In these circumstances each behavioral approach must be a personal one to some extent and must build anew from the very foundation elements of definitions and concepts. Furthermore, theory can only be used in a loose sense, but however meager it may be in content, the formulation and testing of theory is an integral part of the approach. For all these reasons, my book tends to explore basic theoretical orientations more than applied social science or techniques in the hopes of moving toward a "paradigm" of historical analysis for our time. Thus one could say this book is an essay more in methodology than in method.

THE DIFFICULTY OF STUDYING MAN IN PAST TIME

Rigorous analysis and precise explanation are difficult in any discipline, yet they seem beset with even more perplexity in the social than in the natural sciences. Some people even argue that the disciplines studying human behavior so lack analytical precision and explanatory results that they cannot be called scientific at all. The lack of results, however, does not prove that they cannot be scientific, only that it is very difficult for them to be so.

The source of the difficulty, all agree, is the peculiar nature of the subject matter of the social sciences, namely, man himself. Natural scientists are not concerned with the motives or intentions of atoms, clouds, or even frogs or mice, but social scientists believe motivation and intent to be at the core of their studies. Social scientists believe that men have an "inside" component of behavior as well as the "outside" manifestations; something always seems to intervene between external stimulus and external response. Whether this should be studied or how it can be studied is a matter of great dispute, but that it exists few deny.

The problem with studying mankind, then, to paraphrase Alexander Pope, is man. To the extent that both historians and social scientists study human behavior, they have a common concern and shared problems in handling their subject matter. Given the historian's aim to understand man's behavior in past time, the very complicated problem of studying man is made even more difficult. Before we can understand the additional complications of the historical analysis of human behavior, we must examine briefly the difficulties involved in its study in the present.

Since man is both the object of study and the observer doing the study, the relationship between the analyst and his subject matter is an important consideration in the social sciences. While this relationship is rarely discussed in the natural sciences, the distinction is so crucial in the social sciences that it is at the center of the controversy over methodology and explanation in the study of human behavior. The basis of the problem lies in the possibility of studying the internal component of human action as opposed to the mere external manifestations.

At the very least, the existence of an internal component as well as external behavior means that man can be and has been studied in two different ways. Some analysts argue that only behavioral manifestations can be observed empirically, hence social science should abandon the unverifiable hypotheses that constitute the supposed analysis of the internal component. By examining empirical evidence only, these people propose to follow the lead of the natural scientists as they conceive of their fellow scholars' goals. Other analysts maintain that man's external behavior is explained meaningfully only when discussed in terms of such constructs as motives, intentions, and even ideals and feeling. In the first case, the analysis is purely the observer's interpretation of the observed actions. In the second instance, it is the observer's attribution of the internal component that produced the observed actions; it is supposedly the actor's interior state causing the behavioral manifestation.

This distinction between the observer's construct and the actor's conceptions or other internal state is an essential one in talking about social theory and analysis. It adds a necessary difficulty that does not exist in the natural

8

sciences. Thus every theory and every concept about human behavior must be examined as to just what it purports to be in relationship to this distinction. Does the evidence adduced really demonstrate what the analyst says it does in this connection? The philosophical question of whether it ever can is quite another problem.[1]

Those who believe that the internal component may be studied explore the actions of man for clues to the scheme they postulate exists "inside his skin." Some argue that symbolic behavior, for example, particularly talking and writing, constitute important data as to the attitudes, beliefs, intentions, and other elements comprising the interior state. In fact, communication in the broadest sense is presumed by these analysts to be the chief means used by human beings to cope with each other and to raise their offspring in the ways of their society. The categories of language and symbolization are seen as important indicators of men's conceptualization of their environment in the most comprehensive sense. Thus these theorists contend that such data yield valid information about the internal state of man. Such an hypothesis has important implications for documentary analysis, as we shall see later.

Although symbolic behavior may reveal aspects of the internal component of human action, it must never be assumed that it is the only or even the chief clue to the interior condition of man. Verbal espousal of certain ideals and practices, for example, does not mean that they are truly held or manifested by those individuals professing

[1] Two excellent modern introductions to the philosophical problems of the social sciences are Peter Winch, *The Idea of a Social Science, And Its Relation to Philosophy* (London, 1958), and Quentin Gibson, *The Logic of Social Enquiry* (London, 1960). Anthologies of readings on the same subject are Maurice Natanson, ed., *Philosophy of the Social Sciences* (New York, 1963), and May Brodbeck, ed., *Readings in the Philosophy of the Social Sciences* (New York, 1968).

*THE DIFFICULTY
OF STUDYING MAN
IN PAST TIME*

them. Thus the ideal and the real beliefs that compose the ideational—to use a term for the conscious[2] internal component of human action—and the actual behavior must be examined separately in each case to see if they coincide or not. Elaborate safeguards have been worked out in interviewing, participant observation, and other procedures for behavioral study to circumvent, if possible, these problems. The historian, too, we shall see, must be on guard in a different way about these distinctions.[3]

The undeniable existence of an internal component intervening between stimulus and response in human action introduces a difficulty, even an indeterminacy, into the study of human behavior. On one hand, the very problem of determining this component raises philosophical questions bordering upon the unanswerable in the eyes of many current theorists. Even those favorably disposed to the study of an inner component feel wary of accepting external manifestations as the clues to the internal mechanisms they postulate as producing those manifestations. Their opponents say such a procedure is a mere vicious circle of unreason. On the other hand, the very presence of the observer among the human beings he observes as subjects may change the behavior under investigation. Natural scientists can study their subjects without worrying whether those subjects will change their behavior upon reading the research report. This feedback, as it is called

[2] The specific degree of consciousness I leave to a later chapter.
[3] Different insights into the nature of communication as presented here may be obtained from Susanne K. Langer, *Philosophy in a New Key* (Cambridge, Mass., 1942); Harry Hoijer, "The Relation of Language to Culture," in Alfred Kroeber, ed., *Anthropology Today: An Encyclopedic Inventory* (Chicago, 1953), 554–73; John B. Carroll, ed., *Language, Thought, and Reality: Selected Writings of Benjamin Lee Whorf* (New York, 1956); Hugh D. Duncan, *Communication and Social Order* (New York, 1962); and Dell Hymes, ed., *Language, Culture, and Society: A Reader in Linguistics and Anthropology* (New York, 1964).

A BEHAVIORAL APPROACH
TO HISTORICAL ANALYSIS

today, makes for another kind of indeterminancy that even those postulating internal components must admit happens often in the social sciences.[4]

Historical study of human behavior frees the historian from one of these problems and at the same time increases all the others. Certainly, his subjects cannot change their behavior during and after investigation, because they are dead. Yet at the same time that the social scientist's presence in the observational situation causes the problem of indeterminancy, it also affords him one great convenience denied the historian: The latter can never examine his subject's behavior at first hand in all its complexity. This luxury of research the historian is forever denied. As a result, the historical analysis of human behavior poses special perplexities.[5] The historian cannot immediately see the distinctions between the observer and the actors, let alone the inner and outer components of human action. To understand this problem as well as others peculiar to the study of man in past time, let us examine the assumptions behind the process of producing written history.

Since time is irreversible, the historian knows the past only by the remains left over. These traces are presumed valid evidence of the past, although just what they indicate is interpreted variously and disputed vigorously by

[4] All books on the philosophy of the social sciences must deal with these problems in some sense. On the question of indeterminancy, see the Preface to Karl R. Popper, *The Poverty of Historicism* (3d ed., London, 1961). The role of the observer in relation to his subject is treated briefly by Jurgen Reusch, "The Observer and The Observed: Human Communication Theory," in Roy R. Grinker, ed., *Toward a Unified Theory of Human Behavior* (New York, 1956), 36–54. The reaction of people in communities studied to the published studies of their community is seen in Arthur J. Vidich, Joseph Bensman, and Maurice Stein, eds., *Reflections on Community Studies* (New York, 1964).

[5] For another position, see the brief comment by Leon J. Goldstein, "Evidence and Events in History," *Philosophy of Science*, XXIX (1962), 183.

THE DIFFICULTY
OF STUDYING MAN
IN PAST TIME

historians. But in the end, historians do not doubt that a part of the past can be known *and* must be known, or at least postulated, from this evidence.

The only history therefore is historiography. What we call history is in reality only an image or hypothetical conception of the actual past. Historical facts are really only propositions about the past based upon the remaining evidence and how these propositions fit into a general interpretative scheme already postulated. The historian, unlike the social scientist, can never check his conclusions against a personally inspected, complex living reality, only against the fragmentary remains of that once living reality.

Yet his goal is the understanding of that past living reality, for the foundation of his discipline is the idea of a once existent past to be comprehended. No historian questions this basic working assumption, though he may well argue with his colleagues about the nature of that past. Historians believe that the past possessed an objective reality independent of their own consciousness of it, although they may wonder how or even if they can know such a reality. Thus they believe this past must be reconstructed, not created, that history writing must be factual, not fictional. For some men at some time, they argue, the past existed as their complex and real present. This assumption throws the spotlight of historiography upon the actors of the era under examination.[6]

[6] The best references among many on these topics are *Ibid.*, 175–82; William P. McEwen, *The Problem of Social-Scientific Knowledge* (Totowa, N.J., 1963), 261–66; Carl Becker, "What are Historical Facts?" reprinted in Hans Meyerhoff, ed., *The Philosophy of History in Our Time* (Garden City, N.Y., 1959), 120–37; Raymond Aron, "Evidence and Inference in History," in Daniel Lerner, ed., *Evidence and Inference* (Chicago, 1959), 19–47; and Gustav J. Renier, *History: Its Purpose and Method* (Harper ed., New York, 1965). Compare the contrasting views of two contemporary philosophers about whether or not

The emphasis upon man places the historian in the same position as the social scientist in explaining human behavior. He, too, must cope with distinctions between the observer and the subjects and between the inner and outer components of human actions. At the same time, he cannot usually even observe, let alone talk to, the actors he studies. He must depend upon physical remains of past behavioral manifestations as the evidence of that and other behavior and what these indicated about the ideational and the internal state in general of the actors producing that behavior.

To the trained eye and mind, remains can reveal a great deal. A vase, for example, can give clues to past life by a scene on it, can provide an actual example of the aesthetics and technology of a bygone era, and can suggest the economic network of the period by its location. A diary can reveal social rules, ideals, personality quirks, social groupings, governmental organization, family life, and many other things about a man and his times. A newspaper can reproduce laws, provide statistics, print political speeches, and editorialize about problems believed common to the society of which it was part; it in itself can demonstrate the technology and business organization of the period in which it was printed.[7] Yet no matter how much is found from the past and no matter how much it reveals,

the past can be said to exist and whether it can be studied: Arthur C. Danto, *Analytical Philosophy of History* (Cambridge, Eng., 1965), 27–111, and Jack W. Meiland, *Scepticism and Historical Knowledge* (New York, 1965).

[7] Vernon K. Dibble, "Four Types of Inference from Documents to Events," *History and Theory*, III (1963), 203–21, is the best treatment of the subject mentioned in its title. Consult also Allen Johnson, *The Historian and Historical Evidence* (New York, 1926). Compare Folke Dovring's treatment of sources in *History as a Social Science: An Essay on the Nature and Purpose of Historical Studies* (The Hague, 1960), 21–36, with mine.

THE DIFFICULTY
OF STUDYING MAN
IN PAST TIME

the historian can never observe most of his subject matter in the flesh. He can only check his hypotheses about it by reference to other surviving evidence and its place in his hypothetical system.

To note that the writing of history is limited by the amount of surviving evidence and the inability to observe the past as a living reality is not to lament these limitations as some historians have done. In fact, these limitations provide the strength of history as a study. At the same time that historians cannot inspect personally the whole of the past they study, they do possess a knowledge of the outcome of human ideas and actions that the actors could never possess. This knowledge of past men's futures more than compensates for present men's inabilities to relive the past. Furthermore, even if the historian could reconstruct or re-create the total past, as many historians would at first seem to wish, he would still need to select from this melange the facts he would present in his history of it. Complete re-creation would just mean the historian's job was yet to be done once again.[8]

From the behavioral viewpoint, these limitations, regardless of their necessity or their desirability, do make the job of the historian in distinguishing between the observer and the actor far more difficult than it is for the social scientist. The very ambiguity of the word "history" shows this obfuscation by meaning both a past reality and the hypothetical reconstruction of it in the present.

To the extent that the historian's goal of studying past human action demands that he interpret the evidence of the past through the eyes of the producer, then his task is no different from that of the cultural anthropologist who attempts to understand another society on its own terms.

[8] Thus the arguments of Danto, *op. cit.*, 112–15, 183–200.

A BEHAVIORAL APPROACH
TO HISTORICAL ANALYSIS

The historian is merely trying to do in time what the anthropologist does in space. The anthropologist by living with his subject matter can see and feel the distinction between actor and observer; the on-going process of life reminds him constantly of the difference between him and others. The distinction is not so clear to the historian as he sits in a library or a museum. The separation between the observer and the actor in time is purely his mental construction. He must re-create the "climate of the times" or the "spirit of the age" in order to understand the on-going process that produced the evidence he sees. To accomplish this feat, he has only his reading of other evidence and the historiography of his time to guide him.

Far too often the historian collapses the distinction between the observer and the actor and becomes present-minded, as they say. He reads the evidence in terms of his own time rather than of the postulated past time. Thus, for example, the ideas and actions of Jefferson or Jackson are seen as forerunners of those of Franklin Delano Roosevelt, to the distortion of all three men.[9] This trend is encouraged all too often by the historian's tendency to use moral judgment as an organizational theme. All too frequently past ideas and actions are combined with the moral prejudices of the historian to produce a work that distorts past reality in an attempt to praise or to castigate the past and to lecture the present. Much writing of the so-called "revisionist" schools on the Civil and First and Second World Wars seems to be of this genre.[10]

[9] An example notorious in the profession is Arthur M. Schlesinger, Jr., *The Age of Jackson* (Boston, 1945). On the changing interpretations of Jefferson and Jackson, see Merrill D. Peterson, *The Jefferson Image in the American Mind* (New York, 1960), and Charles G. Sellers, Jr., "Andrew Jackson Versus the Historians," *Mississippi Valley Historical Review*, XLIV (1958), 615–34.
[10] Analysis of and bibliographical references to revisionist positions are

THE DIFFICULTY
OF STUDYING MAN
IN PAST TIME

That the simple distinction between observer and actor has important implications for historical analysis was demonstrated at one convention of the American Historical Association in a session devoted to ante-bellum Southern slavery. At the end of the session a debate arose on the floor about the profitability of slavery. Some scholars maintained it could not have been profitable, because they had found references in diaries and periodicals by Southerners that pointed out the lack of profit. On the other hand, others argued that Black bondage was indeed profitable, because they had examined the actual ledgers of plantation owners. The two sides should never have continued to argue because clearly they were resorting to different levels of evidence. The account-book examiners chose to use the observer's construction of reality whereas the diary readers were arguing in terms of the actor's conception of that

found in Thomas J. Pressly, *Americans Interpret Their Civil War* (Collier ed., New York, 1962), chap. 7; Warren I. Cohen, *The American Revisionists: Lessons of Intervention in World War I* (Chicago, 1967); Wayne S. Cole, "American Entry into World War II: A Historiographical Appraisal," *Mississippi Valley Historical Review*, XLIII (1957), 596–617; Ernest May, *American Intervention: 1917 and 1941*, American Historical Association pamphlet no. 30 (Washington, D.C., 1960); and Louis A. Sears, "Historical Revisionism Following the Two World Wars," in George L. Anderson, ed., *Issues and Conflicts: Studies in Twentieth Century Diplomacy* (Lawrence, Kans., 1959), 127–46. This didactic function of history was explicitly espoused by Thomas A. Bailey during the Second World War in the Preface to *Woodrow Wilson and the Lost Peace* (New York, 1944), v, when speaking of the Paris Peace Conference of 1919:

But so costly have been our blunders, and so strong is the likelihood that we shall run through the same tragic cycle of disillusionment and isolationism, that I regard it as a solemn duty to rise above the inhibitions of false modesty and call spades by their right names. I happen to be among those who believe that history has lessons for those who will read, and that the Paris Conference of 1919 presents many striking illustrations of what to avoid. Every generation of apes begins where the previous generation began, because apes can hand down no record of their experience. Man leaves a record; but how much better is he than the apes if he does not study it and heed its warnings?

A BEHAVIORAL APPROACH TO HISTORICAL ANALYSIS

reality. There are, of course, ways of reconciling these two positions but not until each side recognizes the simple distinction between the observer and the actor.[11]

Because the nature of historical data conceals the difference between observer and actor, it also obscures the distinction between the ideational and the behavioral, or what the actor thought and what he did. The historian must postulate in this case what the social scientist can readily observe. Documentary and other evidence from the past are all the product of external behavior, but do they tell us more about the ideational or the actual behavioral manifestations of the actor? The subjective origin of most documents veils the actual behavior in favor of what the actor thought. As E. H. Carr reminds us,

No document can tell us more than what the author of the document thought—what he thought had happened, what he thought ought to happen or would happen, or perhaps only what he wanted others to think he thought, or even only what he himself thought he thought.[12]

In many ways, his words apply also to statistics, books, and poems among other things, although creative works offer special problems of their own when used as historical evidence. Such objects as vases, machines, and houses do reveal actual behavior insofar as they are products of it, but the historian is still left with the important question of their actual role in past societies. All in all, the documentary evidence available to historians tells them more about the subjective states of the actors than about their actual be-

[11] Compare, for example, the statements of fact and the methods of proof in the following: Ulrich B. Phillips, *Life and Labor in the Old South* (Boston, 1929), 173-87; Kenneth M. Stampp, *The Peculiar Institution: Slavery in the Ante-Bellum South* (New York, 1956), 383-418; and Alfred H. Conrad and John R. Meyer, "The Economics of Slavery in Ante-Bellum South," *Journal of Political Economy*, LXVI (April, 1958), 95-122. We shall return to this debate in later chapters.
[12] E. H. Carr, *What is History?* (New York, 1963), 16.

havior, other than the production of the document itself, and physical objects as such reveal more about themselves as objects than they do attitudes about their role in past life or their actual place in past behavior.

For these reasons, the historian is forced to fall back upon implicit or explicit hypotheses in order to discover the actual behavior the social scientist can see in person. Since the historian can never see the real actions of his subjects, he must derive behavioral manifestations from the subjective documents he reads according to some theoretical scheme that postulates that relationship. All the facts asserting historical behavior, therefore, except the actual physical manifestations that remain as traces of the past, are only propositions about past human actions based upon a theory connecting the ideational contents of documents with their presumed behavioral results, of which we have no direct evidence in almost all cases. In other words, the historian has already used a great deal of theory just to arrive at a point where most social scientists start to build theory. The behavioral evidence that the social scientist can observe and use to test a theory about the internal and external components of human action must, for the historian, be constructed using a theoretical scheme already answering the question he is researching in at least one way. Thus, for the historian, the analysis of evidence in the first place is as dependent upon behavioral theory as is the interpretation of the behavioral activity uncovered by that analysis. He must use his theory of the relationship to discover what the relations were so that he can talk about the relationship between such internal aspects as intention and motivation and external behavioral activity. If the historian must use so much theory just to discover behavioral activity, how much more theory must he apply to connect that action to the supposed internal states, whether ideational or otherwise, that presumably produced it? Given this double circularity of analysis, it would seem that the historian should be twice as careful as the social scientist in stating explicitly the theoretical premises upon which he bases his explanation of human behavior. Surely, such circularity shows that he needs explicit rather than implicit theory about the ideational-behavioral relationship, let alone about the deeper causative processes described as unconscious, to avoid more viciousness than necessary in the circular reasoning process.

To demonstrate the relation between ideation and behavior, let us examine briefly some examples, to which we will refer at greater length in later chapters, of the possible connections between ideas and practice. Two current controversies in colonial American history revolve about this relationship. One dispute concerns the extent to which the Puritans practiced the ideals they preached. If they did, then they should have lived in communal agricultural villages, eschewing the isolated farm and the practice of a commerce unregulated by religious ideals. This is just the picture that Darrett B. Rutman denies ever existed in early Boston and the surrounding area. From the reconstruction of actual behavior, he concludes that the living arrangements of the society from the very beginning refute the idea of a closed religious community.[13] In another controversy, American historians are debating whether or not democracy existed in the eighteenth-century colonies. Those who argue that democracy did indeed exist point to, among other things, the widespread practice of suffrage. Those who take the other side argue that democracy was

---

[13] Darrett B. Rutman, *Winthrop's Boston: Portrait of a Puritan Town, 1630-1649* (Chapel Hill, N.C., 1965). For his statement of the issues in the dispute, see Darrett B. Rutman "Mirror of Puritan Authority," in George A. Billias, ed., *Law and Authority in Colonial America* (Barre, Mass., 1965), 149-67.

not espoused as an ideal at the time.[14] In both instances, we find historians arguing their cases either from the point of view of ideals or from that of practice. One side compiles statistics and evidence of practice; the other side depends on sermons and pamphlets for the espousal of ideals. Rarely does a historian point out that somehow there must be a relationship between ideation and behavior.

If we add to the preceding problems of theory facing the historian that of the paucity of evidence surviving from the past, we see what a complicated task historians have set themselves. They possess but few traces of all the possible evidence that must have been produced. From that little they must infer a great amount if they aim at producing very much of what they call a history of man's past. Quite obviously they must fall back upon theoretical considerations to patch out the relatively few fragments they possess in order to write the history of a past society. In fact, the less evidence they possess from an era, the more they must utilize some theories about man and his relation to his social and physical environment in order to compose a history of that period. The scarcity of evidence therefore only compounds the other problems, demanding even more theory, so that the few scraps of evidence can be assumed complete enough to allow work on the other problems and, for that matter, any writing.

With the completion of our discussion of the general problems of studying human behavior, past and present, we can turn to the implications of these arguments for the writing of history as traditionally practiced today. The presumed process of producing history involves essentially

[14] This controversy among others is presented in J. R. Pole, "Historians and the Problem of Early American Democracy," *American Historical Review*, LXVIII (1962), 626–46, and in Michael Kammen, ed., *Politics and Society in Colonial America: Democracy or Deference?* (New York, 1967).

A BEHAVIORAL APPROACH
TO HISTORICAL ANALYSIS

two steps: (1) the analysis of surviving evidence to produce facts, and (2) the synthesis of those facts into a written form, again called *history*. The ideal relationships in the process as seen by many historians may be represented by the direction of the arrows in Figure 1–1.

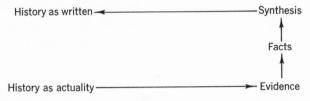

Figure 1–1

Much of the preceding discussion applies quite obviously to the first step of deriving facts from evidence. The subjective origins of documentary evidence obscure the distinction between the ideational and the behavioral. Physical objects considered as evidence do not tell the role they played in the society that produced them. The historian must therefore reconstruct the behavioral and the ideational by reference to theories about human behavior. At the same time he must separate the actor and the observer through conscious and constant wariness and by again resorting to a hypothetical system in order to see the evidence as it should be interpreted according to his professional ideal of not imposing the present upon the past. If present-day historical methods books are of any aid to the historian, it is in this first step.[15]

Theoretical considerations apply also to the second step of synthesizing facts into written history. Frequently these syntheses are called interpretations. More often than not, the theoretical underpinnings of an interpretation or

[15] Compare, for example, Parts 2 and 3 in the well-known methods book of Louis Gottschalk, *Understanding History: A Primer of Historical Method* (New York, 1950).

THE DIFFICULTY
OF STUDYING MAN
IN PAST TIME

synthesis are implicit, but they are nevertheless necessary, in spite of many historians' claims to the contrary. Among other considerations, the historian must have some criteria for the selection of the facts he wishes to include in his synthesis. Although he cannot hope to derive all the possible facts about the past, still he must select even from those he does produce. Upon what grounds does he choose to include and exclude facts in his synthesis? Furthermore, how should he arrange those facts once they are derived and selected? To what extent must the historian depend upon theories of explanation for synthesizing the facts? Is he sure his facts really prove his overall interpretation? These questions are all related and are all answered at one time in the process of writing a history. They all also depend upon explicit or implicit theory. At this stage modern methods books, unlike the classic ones that talked about a theory of man as a basis for synthesis, leave the historian without any aid.[16]

Because history, as traditionally defined by the profession, concerns man's past and not all of past reality, it would seem that theories of human behavior would be the most useful on all levels of history writing. To modify our previous diagram to take account of the behavioral aspect of history, we find we must add the necessity of theory to the right-hand side, as in Figure 1–2.

Since neither the first step of obtaining facts nor the second step of producing a synthesis can be accomplished without theory, and since all the steps are interrelated through the mediation of theoretical schema, the arrows point in both directions to show the necessary reciprocity. To those historians who would object that the proposed

[16] Compare *ibid.*, Part 3, with Book 3 in Charles V. Langlois and Charles Seignobos, *Introduction to the Study of History*, G. G. Berry, trans. (London, 1903).

A BEHAVIORAL APPROACH
TO HISTORICAL ANALYSIS

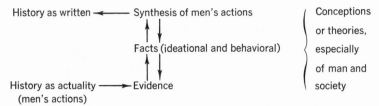

History as written ◄———— Synthesis of men's actions

Facts (ideational and behavioral)

History as actuality ————► Evidence
(men's actions)

Conceptions
or theories,
especially
of man and
society

Figure 1–2

23

process is a violation of scientific history, I would answer
that I only make explicit what needs be done implicitly
otherwise. I agree wholeheartedly with Carl Becker, who
argued that those who espoused the old ideal of scientific
history were

hoping to find something without looking for it, expecting to
obtain final answers to life's riddles by absolutely refusing to ask
questions—it was surely the most romantic species of realism
yet invented, the oddest attempt ever made to get something for
nothing.[17]

It was the ultimate fallacy of Baconian inductionism.

Historians do not recapture or reconstruct the past
when they analyze history; they interpret it according to
surviving evidence and conceptual frameworks. All of past
reality can never be known to them because not all evidence
remains. Furthermore, historians do not choose to deal
even with all the facts derivable from the available evidence.
They confine their interest to man's past, but not even all
of that concerns them, for they further select from these
data those parts that can be organized according to some
interpretation or theory. Thus an historical synthesis is a
highly selective account of a postulated past reality. Theory
in the most general sense is crucial to every phase of historiography, and behavioral theory is particularly neces-

[17] Quoted in Maurice Powicke, *Modern Historians and the Study of
History* (London, 1955), 236.

THE DIFFICULTY
OF STUDYING MAN
IN PAST TIME

sary to every step in the process of producing the sets of propositions about past human activity that we call *history*.

It should now be evident why history must be and is rewritten constantly in terms of the historians' own times. Every step of producing history presumes theoretical models of man and society, which in turn seem to change in terms of the shifting conceptions of man and society occurring in the historian's own society. Sometimes the changing judgment is only a superficial moral judgment; other times it may be a fundamental alteration in the conception of human nature and society. These changes account for the many interpretations over time of familiar figures. Andrew Jackson, for example, has been viewed as the representative of Western farmers, of the Eastern urban proletariat, of expectant capitalists, and of the American citizenry's fear of change in an age of rapid transition. The historians who produced these interpretations believed respectively in frontier democracy, urban liberalism, in a United States wedded to middle class entrepreneurship, and an America worried about losing an idyllic rustic past.[18] The first two interpretations seemed based upon societal assumptions of class conflict and moral judgments upon rural-urban liberalism. The latter two interpretations appear to rest upon societal assumptions of cultural consensus with the added fillip of social psychology in the last one. In fact, the great current debate among American historians about the conflict or consensus interpretation of their country's past depends upon the assumptions made about the basic nature of society.[19] European

[18] Sellers, *loc. cit.*
[19] The attention of the profession was called to the problem by John Higham, "Beyond Consensus: The Historian as Moral Critic," *American Historical Review*, LXVII (1962), 609–25. The results of the differing interpretations as applied to the whole of American history may now be found in a college readings book compiled by Allen F.

historians can see the same problems in the interpretations of Napoleon and the French Revolution.[20]

As shown in Figure 1-3, our diagram can be modified on the right-hand side to take this sociological factor of the historian's knowledge into consideration.

| Conceptions or theories, especially of man and society | Why the historian thinks as he does | Historian's society's model of man and society |

Figure 1-3

Thus the limits of the historian's objectivity, like those of the social scientist, are the theoretical conceptions prevalent in his own society. That both historians and social scientists depend upon intersubjective agreement about truth places them in no worse a position than that of the natural scientists, who also must base their disciplines upon similar intersubjective agreement about experimental results and theory. It only reminds us that the social determinants of knowledge apply to theorists today just as they applied to thinkers of yesterday.[21]

Because historians select their facts according to their conceptual framework does not imply that historians are not objective or scientific, as so many of them seem to think. Natural scientists approach their subject matter with

---

Davis and Harold D. Woodman, eds., *Conflict and Consensus in American History* (Englewood Cliffs, N.J., 1966). For clarification of the dispute, see Chap. 9 of this book.

[20] Some indication of this possibility is suggested in Paul Farmer, *France Reviews Its Revolutionary Origins: Social Politics and Historical Opinion in the Third Republic* (New York, 1944); Stanley Mellon, *The Political Uses of History: A Study of Historians in the French Restoration* (Stanford, 1958); and Peter Geyl, *Napoleon: For and Against,* Oliver Renier, trans. (New Haven, Conn., 1949).

[21] Both Carr, *op. cit.,* and Henri-Irénée Marrou, *The Meaning of History,* Robert J. Olsen, trans. (Baltimore, Md., 1966) stress the interaction between the historian and his data in the production of written history.

THE DIFFICULTY
OF STUDYING MAN
IN PAST TIME

a preconceived intellectual structure also. In fact, no scientist could ever make an observation without some such framework to gauge what he is doing and discovering. No man can ever discover something without some interpretation to guide him about how it relates to the rest of his understanding. If scientists had followed Bacon's precepts they would never have developed their knowledge to the point it is today.[22]

What makes theoretical structures or interpretations scientific and objective is whether or not they can be confirmed or disproven by test of evidence, not whether they should exist or not. Historians can and should formulate questions according to their interpretations to ask of evidence surviving from the past just as scientists frame experiments to test their theories about the material universe. So long as historians explicitly phrase questions as precisely as possible to test their interpretations against surviving evidence, then they are scientific. That they must employ a theoretical framework in order to derive this data as well as to interpret it places them in no special category apart from the scientist in either general method or objectivity. History, therefore, like physics or chemistry is a network of propositions and data about its subject matter based upon available evidence and tested theory.[23]

In the end, then, our theory of truth and science is as much based upon a theory of man and society as was our discussion of the nature of history. Since such theory is inescapable no matter where we turn, the problem becomes one of selecting an appropriate theoretical schema for the writing of history. To this task we turn in the succeeding chapters.

[22] This seems to be one of the main points of Thomas S. Kuhn, *The Structure of Scientific Revolutions* (Chicago, 1962).
[23] Danto, *op. cit.*, 88–111, is particularly persuasive in his refutation of the Beardian relativism so rampant in the profession today.

The first requirement for a behavioral approach to historical analysis is some basic theory or at least a general orientation to, human behavior. Such an orientation must incorporate, if not resolve, the problem of the relation between man's internal state and his external behavior, and must therefore also deal with

the concomitant dilemma of the actor-observer gap. Since these problems lie at the very foundation of any interpretation of human behavior, we cannot achieve, or even expect, agreement upon any one basic orientation at this stage of development in the behavioral sciences. Rather, we can only select from the competing views proposed by social theorists one that seems to fit the historian's needs particularly well and that accords with modern behavioral knowledge.

If the analysis of human behavior, whether in the past or the present, demands attention to the inner state of man, no matter how complex or seemingly impossible that task is, then the analyst must make some provision for the existence of the human organism as an entity mediating between external stimuli and the presumably resultant behavioral manifestations. For this reason the old symbolic designation of a pure stimulus producing a pure response, *S-R*, has given way to new representations, which I shall designate for the sake of convenience, *S-O-R*.[1] Today, in other words, the organism is seen as more complex than the

[1] This is my attempt to summarize the more complex S-R formulae of today. The specific designation was first proposed by Robert S. Woodworth in his *Psychology: A Study of Mental Life* (New York, 1921). A convenient history of the S-R school is in John W. Atkinson, *An Introduction to Motivation* (Princeton, 1964), 107–201.

older conception of it as a mere neural connection between stimulus and response.

Hence the great unknown was reintroduced into the study of human behavior. The presence of the organism in the S-O-R formula meant that the empirically unobservable, or the black box as some called it, was resorted to again as an explanation for man's actions. The behaviorism of the famous psychologist John Watson had discarded this unknown mystery deliberately in an attempt to be scientific. Modern psychologists reintroduced it in order to account for the empirical evidence produced by their efforts to be scientific according to Watson's cannon, for they had achieved results that could be explained in no other way but by the entities they had sought to abandon. The new behavioral approach to man is therefore quite unlike the old behavioralism of Watson and his followers.[2] This more complex model of man fulfills much better the historian's desire to understand past behavior.

More formally the black box is called an intervening variable in psychology. According to a recent definition of the term by its inventor, Edward C. Tolman, the theoretical orientation of his profession

distributes all descriptive and explanatory constructs into: (1) independent variables; (2) the dependent variable of behavior or action; (3) postulated intervening variables; and (4) postulated causal connections between these three types of variables.[3]

[2] Atkinson, *op. cit.*, is again valuable as is Charles Osgood, "Behavior Theory and the Social Sciences" in Roland Young, ed., *Approaches to the Study of Politics* (Evanston, Ill., 1958), 217–43. The black-box idea is briefly discussed in Eugene J. Meehan, *The Theory and Method of Political Analysis* (Homewood, Ill., 1965), 199–206. A more formal explication of the search for hidden factors is Paul F. Lazarsfeld, "Latent Structure Analysis," in Sigmund Koch, ed., *Psychology: A Study of a Science*, vol. 3, *Formulations of the Person and the Social Context* (New York, 1959), 476–543.

[3] Edward C. Tolman in Talcott Parsons and Edward Shils, eds., *Toward*

This scheme seems straightforward and easily applied to man's behavior until one considers it more carefully. The dependent variable, or the action or behavior to be explained, seems to offer the fewest problems. It is observable and, to a large degree, capable of being isolated from other observable phenomena without undue resort to abstraction or a theoretical system. But can one say the same of the other three categories? Are they not all connected and all dependent upon one another?

Let us look at what Tolman says the independent variables are. He lists the stimulus situation, the state of psychological "drive-arousal" or "drive-satiation," and such individual variables as age, heredity, and sex. Yet can the psychologist actually determine with certainty the stimulus he thinks he administers to a rat, let alone determine what perception a human being receives of a stimulus in even a seemingly uncomplicated experimental situation in the laboratory? Can a psychologist actually differentiate physiological drives from secondarily induced cultural expectations inside the human skin? It would seem such differentiations are heavily dependent upon the black box of intervening variables that both connect everything else and frequently act as the explanation themselves. What looks like a simple scheme for ascertaining empirically the internal component of man's actions dissolves under examination into just another postulation of entities inside the black box of the human skin.[4]

---

a General Theory of Action (Cambridge, Mass., 1951), 279. The original definition was Edward C. Tolman, "Operational Behaviorism and Current Trends in Psychology," *Proceedings of the 25th Anniversary of the Inauguration of Graduate Studies* (Los Angeles, 1936), 89–103.
[4] See Tolman's whole discussion in Parsons and Shils, eds. *op. cit.*, 279–84, and the model that follows. His original article and other articles relevant to this discussion are reprinted in Melvin H. Marx, ed., *Psychological Theory: Contemporary Readings* (New York, 1951), 68–129. See also the summary by Sigmund Koch in *op. cit.*, 729–88.

The postulated intervening variable or variables, whether as elaborate hypothetical constructs or simple assumed causal connection among manipulated experimental variables,[5] are crucial to modern behavior theory, just as they were in reality to earlier theory that had supposedly eliminated their need. No matter how theorists try to escape it, they must hypothesize a model of how man works in order to account for their data regardless of how "scientific" some of them attempt to be in the sense of eliminating such empirically unobservable entities from their experiments and their analysis. Whether it be modern behaviorism, psychoanalytic theory, field theory, neurophysiological theory, or cultural or sociological theories, or even an invention of his own, the theorist must create a model of man to explain human behavior.[6]

Years ago such a model was called human nature, and usually it was a single factor presumed overwhelming in its influence on man, whether it was sin, sex, or economic acquisitiveness. On the whole it was believed innate and universal to all men.[7] Social scientists have long since abandoned such a model, but many historians still base their analyses upon such a simple foundation. What historians obviously need is a more complex model of man based upon recent research. Yet the behavioral scientists do not agree upon any one model and, given the nature of their fields, probably cannot, for what are seen as independent

[5] This important distinction was pointed out by Kenneth MacCorquodale and Paul E. Meehl, "On a Distinction Between Hypothetical Constructs and Intervening Variables," *Psychological Review*, LV (1948), 95–107.

[6] Surveys of theoretical schemes are Gardner Lindzey, in Lindzey, ed., *Handbook of Social Psychology* (Cambridge, Mass., 1954), vol. 1, 3–258, and Calvin Hall and Gardner Lindzey, *Theories of Personality* (New York, 1957).

[7] A popular account of changing conceptions of human nature is M. F. Ashley Montagu, *The Biosocial Nature of Man* (New York, 1956).

and dependent variables and what are postulated as intervening variables depend as much upon what is to be explained from the viewpoint of the analyst as upon what
model he proposes to test. One psychologist, for example,
might wish to explore perception in terms of physiology,
whereas another might examine it in terms of cultural
experience. A social psychologist might concern himself
with aspects of motivation in a social structure, whereas a
sociologist might well assume the motivation in order to
research social structure. Lastly, by way of example, the
model of man assumed by most economists for their work
is open to grave question by other social scientists.

In such a situation, it would be useless even to summarize all the models, for their utility depends upon their
complexity, and the historian is better referred to the
original literature. Rather, some overall orientation is likely
to prove most useful to the historian in his everyday chores.
Given the peculiar demands of history as a discipline, such
an orientation should meet at least the following criteria:

1. It should be one in which psychological explanation has its place, but it should also provide for the social
variables involved in historical analysis. Too often historians
tend to stress the individualistic explanations of psychology
or psychoanalysis to the neglect of cultural or group factors involved in human behavior. The orientation should,
in other words, take account of the interpersonal as well
as the intrapersonal.

2. The orientation must be one of dynamic interpretation, because historians are concerned with time and
change in time.

3. It should allow men free will and rationality as well
as emotions and irrationality. Free will means merely that

men possess a choice of options without coercion, not that their predilection to choice is undetermined.[8]

4. It should permit complexity so as to mirror the reality the historian finds in his studies.

5. It should be an orientation widely used in the behavioral sciences so that it will constitute a guide to their various uses and yet at the same time act as a guide to their limitations.

6. Lastly, it should explain why the theorists think as they do today. It ought always be a reminder of the social determinants of behavioral knowledge.

In my opinion the most satisfactory orientation to human behavior in the light of these criteria is the one called the situational approach. This approach begins with the proposition that human behavior occurs in situations. The unit of analysis is the situation that combines the human organism and its environment into one analytical scheme. Neither the organism nor the environment can be considered separately, for as one psychologist says,

We cannot define the situation operationally except in reference to the specific organism which is involved; we cannot define the organism operationally, in such a way as to obtain predictive power for behavior, except in reference to the situation.[9]

The situation is the stimulus to which the organism reacts but the resultant action is a part of the new situation. Thus

[8] On free will and determinism in history, see Morton White, *Foundations of Historical Knowledge* (New York, 1965), 271–91; Arthur C. Danto, *Analytical Philosophy of History* (Cambridge, Eng., 1965), 183–200; Ernest Nagel, *The Structure of Science: Problems in the Logic of Scientific Explanation* (New York, 1961), 592–606; and May Brodbeck, ed., *Readings in the Philosophy of the Social Sciences* (New York, 1968), 669–736.
[9] Gardner Murphy, *Personality: A Biosocial Approach to Origins and Structure* (New York, 1947), 891.

A BEHAVIORAL APPROACH
TO HISTORICAL ANALYSIS

the scheme is a dynamic one of studying process, not objects as such.

The human organism responds to the situation in terms of how it defines or interprets the situation. This situational definition or interpretation includes, among other elements, the attitudes people possess about how to act toward one another; how to utilize their physical environment; how they should judge the good, the true, and the beautiful; how their group activities should be organized; who should rule and what crime is; who should possess the symbols of wealth; and many other attitudes and beliefs about themselves and others. Situational analysis studies the behavior of the whole human being in reaction to the totality of the situation as interpreted by the organism. At the same time, the observer can attempt to account for these behavioral manifestations in terms of aims, motives, drives, physical environment, and the societal arrangements that made for such an assessment of interpretation by the organism. In this sense, situational analysis combines all the factors that enter into human behavioral activity into one order of analysis, whether these be idiosyncratic, rational, cultural, social, psychological, or biological or physical environmental, and places them in relation to the concrete actions of individuals as perceiving, thinking, feeling, acting, and reacting organisms. The relationships in this approach may be shown by a simple diagram, as in Figure 2–1.[10]

Furthermore, it is concrete actions that are studied in relation to the situation. In this sense, the approach stresses the behavior of men, or what people do, as the focus of

[10] Adapted from Muzafer Sherif, "Social Psychology: Problems and Trends in Interdisciplinary Relationships" in Sigmund Koch, ed., *op. cit.*, vol. 6, *Investigations of Man as Socius: Their Place in Psychology and the Social Sciences* (New York, 1963), 69.

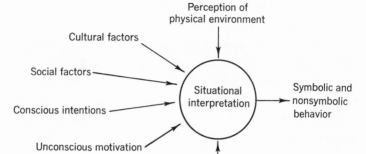

Figure 2–1

study. By focusing on the behavioral, situational analysis examines the complete set of responses in a situation rather than certain aspects selected in accordance with predetermined definitions. The basic data of the study are the behavioral activities in a situation; hence the approach is frequently spoken of as the "action frame of reference" as well as situational analysis.[11]

[11] On the behavioral situation as such, see Edmund H. Volkart, ed., *Social Behavior and Personality: Contributions of W. I. Thomas to Theory and Social Research* (New York, 1951) [Thomas coined the term *definition of the situation*]; Paul Meadows, "The Dialectic of the Situation: Some Notes on Situational Psychology," *Philosophy and Phenomenological Research*, V (1944), 354–64; and Arthur F. Bentley, *Inquiry into Inquiries: Essays in Social Theory* (Boston, 1954), 140–74. In addition to Atkinson, the Koch volumes, Murphy, Parsons and Shils, and the *Handbook of Social Psychology*, further reading in the basic orientation proposed here may be done in the following: Talcott Parsons, *The Structure of Social Action* (2d ed., New York, 1948); John Gillin et al., *For a Science of Social Man* (New York, 1954); Roy R. Grinker, ed., *Toward a Unified Theory of Human Behavior* (New York, 1956); Arnold Rose, ed., *Human Behavior and Social Processes: An Interactionist Approach* (Boston, 1962), especially 3–19; William P. McEwen, *The Problem of Social-Scientific Knowledge* (Totowa, N.J., 1963), especially 91–183; Ernest R. Hilgard and Daniel Lerner, "The Person: Subject and Object of Science and Policy," in Daniel Lerner and Harold Lasswell, eds., *The Policy Sciences: Recent Developments in Scope and Method* (Stanford, 1951), 16–43; and J. Milton Yinger,

From the observation of the concrete behavior or action, theorists have invented many different hypothetical constructs as intervening variables. Three general ones that have formed the foci of study in the basic behavioral sciences are personality, society, and culture. Frequently, the proponents of each concept argue that its concept has priority over the others, but situational analysis makes such bickering less worthwhile than attempts to explain just what accounts for given concrete actions. In the same way, the old general argument about nature versus nurture or heredity versus environment has lost its salience to human behavioral studies. In short, the search for a unicausal agent is abandoned for a study of interrelated independent and intervening variables. Today the analyst increasingly studies the whole person in terms of analytical constructs that take account of the totality of behavior as influenced by intrapersonal processes as well as by the physical and social environment in a situation. He searches for the configuration of factors conditioning the observable behavior.[12]

The situational analysis of human behavior can proceed on at least two different levels. On one level it can study the actor's conscious process involved in the interpretation of the situation that supposedly results in the action. On another level it can attempt to account for the nature of the actor's situational interpretation in terms of some of the biological, psychological, social, and cultural factors that produced a given interpretation and the resultant action. This means that analysis can proceed to explore the situational interpretation and action without necessarily accounting for the deeper processes at work. Such an ex-

---

Toward a Field Theory of Behavior: Personality and Social Structure (New York, 1965).
[12] McEwen, *op. cit.*, 194.

ploration, however, must not be mistaken for an account of the total reasons behind the action or the situation.

Situational interpretation or definition by the actor is a conscious process. The theorist Robert MacIver has described it well in what he calls the *dynamic assessment.*

1. A preliminary to conscious activity is a decision between alternatives—to do this or to do that, to do or not to do. In the process of decision-making the individual assesses a situation in the light of these alternatives. A choice between values congenial to the larger value-system of the individual is somehow reached.

2. The decision once taken, the other purposes or valuations of the individual are accommodated to it. Preparatory actions follow. In this orientation certain external factors are selectively reorganized and given subjective significance. They are construed as means, obstacles, conditions, and limitations, with reference to the attainment of the dominant desire or value. The dynamic assessment brings the external world selectively into the subjective realm, conferring on it subjective significance for the ends of action.

3. The dynamic assessment involves a type of causal judgment that differs from the *post factum* attribution of causality characteristic of the social sciences, in that it is doubly speculative. It rests always on a predictive judgment of the form: if this is done, this consequence will (is likely to) follow *and* if this is not done or if this other thing is done, this consequence will (is likely to) follow. We may observe in passing that even the most simple-seeming choice may conceal a subtle and unfathomed subjective process.

4. The selectivity of the dynamic assessment, as it reviews the situation prior to decision and as it formulates the alternatives of action, makes it subject to several kinds of contingency and practical hazard. First, the dominant objective registered in the decision to act may not persist throughout the process leading to its attainment. Second, the means-end nexus envisaged in the decision to act may be misapprehended. Third, the physical order assumed to be under control as the means and conditions of action may "erupt" into the situation in unanticipated ways. All

conscious behaving is an implicit reckoning of probabil-
ities, which may or may not be justified by the event.[13]

To many, MacIver's description will seem too rationally
calculative of means to ends and even, perhaps, of ends
themselves, but such calculativeness is not meant. The
causes of the values, the proclivities, the intellectual ability,
the intentions, and the perception and conception of the
physical and social environment involved in the process
are assumed for the purposes of the description. That they
are not mentioned does not mean they do not operate.

Just because MacIver, in this excerpt, does not explicitly state the causes of the situational interpretation and
the resultant action should not preclude any analyst from
searching for them. Rather, it should be remembered that
they constitute another level of explanation in the model
under consideration. One of the chief merits of the model
is the clear-cut division between the consciousness of the
situational interpretation and the consequent behavior and
the "deeper" elements involved in the process. The behavior resulting from unconscious biological or psychological intrapersonal processes is separated from the consciousness of the situational interpretation and the action that
takes place in accordance with it. Similarly, social and
cultural behavior produced by unconscious interpersonal
processes should be distinguished from the conscious situational interpretation and resultant manifestations. Of
course, such neatly separated levels may not exist in reality,
but they prove useful in the current state of behavioral
analysis. At the same time, the analytical separation of
levels necessitates the specification of causal connections
among them as well as within them.

[13] Robert M. MacIver, *Social Causation* (Harper ed., New York, 1964),
296–97. Copyright 1942 by Ginn and Company. Reprinted by permission
of Harper & Row, Publishers, Inc.

A BASIC ORIENTATION
TO HUMAN BEHAVIOR

The situational interpretation of human behavior postulates a connection between the conscious definition or interpretation of a situation and the action in that situation. The action is presumed to be partly, if not wholly, caused by the situational interpretations. The situation is thus a complex combination of objective and subjective reality. The objective reality of the actor's environment is perceived subjectively by him. His action results from his assessment of the situation as he defines it. In other words, the actor brings attitudes and beliefs to the situation that structure his perception of the situation and even define it. Furthermore, his reality is seen as his definition of the situation. In the oft-quoted words of William I. Thomas, "If men define situations as real, they are real in their consequences."[14] Since all situations are defined by the actor from his point of view, all his actions have a meaning to the actor in terms of that viewpoint. The point of view is the result of both intra- and interpersonal processes. Even if no one else is around, the definition of a situation and the action in it will be influenced by social factors as well as individual judgment. Lastly, the situational interpretation of human behavior is dynamic; it sees the interpreting of situations as an on-going process, for the actor is constantly evaluating "how things were, how they are, and how they may be."[15] Thus the evaluation of the elements in a situation involves the cumulative as well as the immediate experience of an individual in a society. Each individual therefore will have some image of his society's history as part of that cumulative experience.[16]

[14] William I. Thomas, *The Child in America* (New York, 1928), 572.
[15] Kenneth Burke, *Permanence and Change: An Anatomy of Purpose* (rev. ed., Los Altos, Calif., 1954), 14.
[16] The best brief analysis of the situational interpretation is in Paul Meadows, *op. cit.*

Another merit of the orientation is the gathering of all components that bear on human behavior into one configuration. In this way, it is related to the "image" as expounded by Kenneth Boulding in his book of the same name. In the words of the book jacket, the image is "the sum of what we think we know and [thus] what makes us act the way we do."[17] Boulding covered all levels from the physiological to the societal and the historical in an attempt to be complete in his catalog of factors creating and composing the image, but a catalog is no substitute for a detailed specification of the specific connections among these various levels.

This orientation thus poses as many questions as it precludes by its selection. How do we study man, given this model? In order to incorporate free will and decision-making into our model, we selected one that presupposes that the analyst can obtain data about the internal or subjective processes of situational interpretation. We also assume that we can as observers distinguish the actor's situational interpretation from the other internal processes responsible for the production of that interpretation, or, in other words, that we can separate conscious and unconscious causation of the behavior observed. We presume, too, that we can determine the elements of the environmental situation that are perceived and integrated with the already existing subjective component to produce the new definition and interpretation of a situation perceived as changing by the actor.

Ideally the actor's frame of reference for the defini-

[17] Kenneth Boulding, *The Image: Knowledge in Life and Society* (paper ed., Ann Arbor, Mich., 1961). Compare the more rigorous analysis of Peter L. Berger and Thomas Luckman, *The Social Construction of Reality: A Treatise in the Sociology of Knowledge* (Garden City, N.Y., 1966).

A BASIC ORIENTATION
TO HUMAN BEHAVIOR

tion of the situation would be the observed environmental situation itself, and this could (and would) correspond to the observer's observation of the concrete situation. As Paul Meadows reminds us, situational analysis "is an endeavor to construct the pattern of social action by means of analytical schema whose categories constitute at the same time the empirical structure of events."[18] To this extent the assumption of the method is phenomenological or existential, that is, the actor's flow of experience or *Lebenswelt* is accepted as the actual explanation for his behavior. Certainly the environment of physical objects and social relations may be determined by the analyst, and this is one of the advantages of the method; the perception of these, if they are perceived at all, and the interpretation of them by the actor is not so surely determined. The exact amount of overlap between the actor's and the observer's conception of the situation can never be known. That there is overlap seems hopeful in the eyes of those advocating this orientation and hopelessly small according to those opposing it.

The lack of certainty in pinpointing the exact overlap of the actor's and observer's definition in a given observable situation means that the analyst must use other means to determine the actor's subjective state. The major means lies in studying the behavior produced by the situational interpretation for clues to that interpretation. To some critics of this method, such a procedure looks like a vicious circle of reasoning. On one hand, the behavior is assumed to result from the actor's interpretation of the situation. On the other hand, the situational interpretation is hypothesized from the behavior. Yet there need be nothing vicious about such reasoning. To reconstruct the definition and the inter-

[18] Paul Meadows, *op. cit.*, 354.

pretation that produced them, one could read different kinds of behavior in a situation. The combination of behaviors, in this view, indicates the configuration that was the actor's situational analysis.

Proponents of the possibility of discovering the actor's subjective state frequency advocate *Verstehen* as a method for accomplishing this end. *Verstehen* can range in meaning from understanding the actor's view in some degree to a complete intuitive grasp of the actor's entire situational interpretation through emotional identification with him. Regardless of its meaning, *Verstehen* as an operation seems to involve three steps as pointed out by Theodore Abel.

1. The internalization of the stimulus by imagination.
2. The internalization of the response by imagination.
3. The application of behavior maxims from the observer's experience to connect the stimulus and response.

In a simple instance, you see a man hammering a nail with determination one moment, and the next moment he is sucking his finger. From your experience, you conclude immediately he hit his finger by error although you did not see this happen. In more complicated circumstances, the same process occurs with perhaps a longer and more imaginative search for the explanation connecting the stimulus and response. *Verstehen* defined in this way possesses two distinct disadvantages. The imaginative reconstruction of stimulus and response and the assumed connection are limited by the experience of the observer. The farther apart in culture the actor and observer are, the less the observer would seem able to bridge the gap through empathetic understanding. Second, and far more important, *Verstehen* does not provide a way of verifying the truth of the behavioral sequence and the aegis of it. The method can provide at best hypotheses about the "reason" behind the observed actions, but the validity of those hypotheses must be verified by other means.[19]

One of these other means must be analysis of the symbolic behavior of man. Man can be asked about reasons for his own actions, and certainly interviews and other evidence gathered from verbal behavior can help determine situational interpretations. For historians, documents provide clues to the situational interpretations of historical actors. Symbolic communication conceived broadly is a map to subjective states. Whether used in the training of the young in the ways of a family, in the linguistic categories used by a society to conceptualize its physical and social environment, or in the very personal communication of an artist or writer pouring out his inner feelings, symbolic behavior is intended by the actors involved to be indicative of their situational interpretations individually or collectively. Such a goal on the part of the actors presents real opportunities for an observer to gain insights into the actors' subjective states.[20] The historian surely has no other guide for past mental states or even actual behavior.

Yet symbolic behavior cannot be assumed to be a complete guide to the inner state of the actors. It is only

[19] Theodore I. Abel, "The Operation Called 'Verstehen,'" *American Journal of Sociology*, LIV (1948), 211–18, reprinted in Herbert Feigl and May Brodbeck, eds., *Readings in the Philosophy of Science* (New York, 1953), 677–87. Compare Max Weber, *The Theory of Social and Economic Organization*, A. M. Henderson and T. Parsons, trans. (New York, 1947), 87n., 96–98; Talcott Parsons, *op. cit.*, 583–91, 634–37; Carl Hempel, "The Function of General Laws in History," reprinted in Patrick Gardiner, ed., *Theories of History* (New York, 1959), 352–53; Richard S. Rudner, *Philosophy of Social Science* (Englewood Cliffs, N.J., 1966), 71–73; and McEwen, *op. cit.*, 467–75.
[20] Hugh D. Duncan, *Communication and Social Order* (New York, 1962) and Dell Hymes, ed., *Language, Culture, and Society: A Reader in Linguistics and Anthropology* (New York, 1964).

A BEHAVIORAL APPROACH
TO HISTORICAL ANALYSIS

part of man's behavior in the first place. Does a man really know why he acted as he did? Verbal and written espousal of aims and ideals must be checked whenever possible against other actual behavior to see whether the actor practiced what he preached. The actor's interpretation, no matter how sincerely he may think what he does, may not be the real reason for his actions. Behavior may be caused other than consciously. For all these reasons, the observer must seek to explain human action by recourse to all the levels of causation postulated in the model.

The actor's subjective state can and must be studied through behavioral manifestations, symbolic and nonsymbolic. That such a task is difficult and even tricky, I do not deny. That it must be studied if men's actions are to be fully explained, I accept. I do not claim, however, that the actor's situational interpretation explains a man's total behavior. Man must be studied on all the levels, conscious and unconscious, intra- and interpersonal. The situational approach to human behavior concentrates only on the conscious flow of experience as perceived and reacted to by the actor. The connection between the actor's situational interpretation and his action is assumed, but not all is explained by this nexus. The subjective state of the actor is postulated through the objective observation of behavior by the observer. Although empathy may produce "understanding," and hence hypotheses about the situational interpretation, this method of generating hypotheses must be checked against observable behavior and by rigorous analysis. The observer must refer to concrete behavioral evidence to prove his point about the nature of the situational interpretation he ascribes to the actor.

Behavior is to be understood, then, both in terms of the actor's situational interpretation and the observer's theory about those actions. Human action therefore has meaning both in relation to the actor's frame of reference and to the observer's theories about the actor as a conscious interpreter of situations and also as an unconscious being. To the observer, the causation of human behavior is not only in terms of the conscious situational perceptions and interpretations by the actor but also in terms of unconscious personal, social, and physical environmental processes.

In this way, all approaches to human behavior may be served by a situational orientation. Both those who advocate only the empirical observation of human behavior and those who argue for acceptance of hypothetical constructs in the explanation of man's actions must be listened to in order to avoid premature closure in the behavioral sciences. Both modern behaviorism and the phenomenological approaches, to give names to the two sides, have something to offer in my opinion. Thus I would side with those who espouse a toleration of method and theory in the hopes of gaining additional knowledge. In the current state of the behavioral sciences, any other position would seem to frustrate intellectual advancement in these disciplines.[21]

Historians must particularly practice such toleration because of the nature of their evidence and the goals of their profession. They must reconstruct all of the various kinds of past human behavior almost entirely from only one kind of source—symbolic behavior. They then usually examine that behavior as if they were objective observers,

[21] Such toleration is urged by Michael Scriven, "Views of Human Nature," in T. W. Wann, ed., *Behaviorism and Phenomenology: Contrasting Bases for Modern Psychology* (2d ed., Chicago, 1965), 163–83; Leon J. Goldstein, "The Phenomenological and Naturalistic Approaches to the Social," reprinted in Maurice Natanson, ed., *Philosophy of the Social Sciences* (New York, 1963), 186–301; and Abraham Kaplan, *The Conduct of Inquiry: Methodology for Behavioral Science* (San Francisco, 1964), *passim*.

A BEHAVIORAL APPROACH
TO HISTORICAL ANALYSIS

although they never witnessed it in the first place. Historic human action should and must be studied from the viewpoints of both the actors and the observer. The accomplishment of such a tricky task demands far greater attention to the complexities of human activity pointed out by behavioral scientists and philosophers than historians have previously given. Only a sophisticated set of categories derived from the current orientation to human behavior will enable historians to achieve their traditional aim of a complex interpretation of the human past.

CHAPTER 3

BEHAVIORAL CATEGORIES OF HISTORICAL ANALYSIS

The past postulated by today's historians should incorporate a modern approach to human behavior. Such a commitment suggests some fundamental categories for historical analysis and even a procedure for pursuing historical research. Certainly, any historiography faithful to the complexities of past human actions must distinguish, at the least, between the ideational and the behavioral, between inter- and intrapersonal processes, and between actors and observers. Combination of these distinctions provides at once a set of levels and basic categories and, ordered in the proper sequence, a set of rules by which to organize historical data.

The starting place for analysis is the basic orientation to understanding human behavior outlined in the last chapter. Human behavior occurs in situations in which the response or responses to the situational stimuli happen in terms of the definition or interpretation of the situation by the actor or actors. Behavior is not a direct reaction to the stimuli but a response made in accordance with ideational mediation. As shown in Figure 3–1, a simple diagram can summarize the relationships assumed in this approach.

Actor(s) ——→ Interpretation of situation ——→ Action

Figure 3–1

The first task of the historian, accordingly, is to study the actor, his interpretation, and his actions.

The accomplishment of this task entails several levels

of analysis. First, the observer must derive the situational interpretation and the resultant actions. In other words, he must answer the question, What are they? From this, he can proceed to explore the connections between the two. This is the question, How do they fit together? Then, he can try to account for the cause of both the situational interpretation and the action, or the question, Why was it that situational interpretation? and, Why that action? Here, then, we have at least three levels of analysis, as a result of using our basic model. The consideration of one question entails answers to the others.

Since this is an essay on methodology rather than methods, we shall not set forth an elaborate procedure for determining the situational interpretation. Rather, we shall examine the intellectual difficulties involved in such a process. Such a procedure would seem similar to what Karl Popper calls the logic of the situation.[1] According to one of his disciples, situational logic is an effort "to envisage the situation as it is faced by the individual [in it], and attempts to reconstruct those factors in the situation, including his own beliefs and proclivities, which led him to act in the way he did."[2] Neither Popper nor his disciple tell the reader how to go about this task.[3] Their approach resembles R. G. Collingwood's conception of "history as the re-enactment of past experience."[4] The method for

[1] Karl R. Popper, *The Poverty of Historicism* (Harper ed., New York, 1964), 147–52, and *The Open Society and Its Enemies* (Harper ed., New York, 1963), vol. 2, 97–98.

[2] Ian C. Jarvie in Don Martindale, ed., *Functionalism in the Social Sciences*, monograph No. 5 of American Academy of Political and Social Sciences (Philadelphia, Feb., 1965), 32.

[3] For an attempt to apply the scheme to an actual case, see Ian C. Jarvie, *The Revolution in Anthropology* (London, 1964). Also see Alan Donogan, "Historical Explanation: The Popper-Hempel Theory Reconsidered," *History and Theory*, IV (1964), 17–23.

[4] R. G. Collingwood, *The Idea of History* (Oxford, 1964), 282–302.

accomplishing this involves the imaginative reconstruction of past thought and experience in the historian's own mind. According to Collingwood, the historian can and *must* know the thoughts of past men in order to know what happened in history and why it happened. How to proceed upon this task is again unmentioned.[5]

Many historians profess little more methodology than such a leap of identification. For this reason, they believe one must be sympathetic to the subject of a biography or even be of the same social, economic, or racial background as a people in the past in order to understand them.[6] For these historians, "common sense" is an adequate guide to exploring past human behavior. A mind unclouded by sophisticated knowledge of modern social science or philosophy, these people argue, is better for historical research because it does not prejudice the reading of the documents. What seems to such practitioners the *tabula rasa* theory of "scientific history" is in reality the *tabula plena* of prejudice.

Situational logic, imaginative reenactment, and sympathetic understanding essentially depend upon analyzing the documentary evidence in such a way that the behavioral manifestations derived by the historical method can be accounted for by imagining the actor's viewpoint. The document or object studied is assumed to reveal both the interpretation and the action through intuition or empathy. In this way, these approaches resemble *Verste-*

[5] Consult also Alan Donogan, *The Later Philosophy of R. G. Collingwood* (Oxford, 1962), 182–96, 200–236. Compare William Dray, "Historical Understanding as Re-Thinking," *University of Toronto Quarterly*, XXVII (1958), 200–215, and Warren H. Walsh, *An Introduction to the Philosophy of History* (London, 1958), 48–71.

[6] A good example of such an attitude is the presidential address before the American Historical Association by Carl Bridenbaugh, "The Great Mutation," *American Historical Review*, XVIII (1963), 315–31.

A BEHAVIORAL APPROACH TO HISTORICAL ANALYSIS

hen as a process in both its strengths and its weaknesses. While such techniques may generate hypotheses for further study, they do not provide a valid test about the hypothetically asserted connections between cause and action. The peculiar nature of historical evidence complicates the usual problems of *Verstehen*. In live, present reality, the researcher can check his hypothesis derived through empathetic identification with the subject against the subject's own statements about his actions, untrustworthy as such statements may be. Yet in the case of dead, unseen actors, the historian frequently has only the evidence to prove his hypothesis from which he drew it by imagination in the first place. The nature of historical evidence obscures even the relations between behavior, ideation, and situation, let alone the testing of relationships among them and deeper processes. The stimulus and response that the *Verstehende* social scientist can observe to generate his imagined processes is forever hidden as such from the historian. The remaining evidence may only be the situational interpretation that intervened between the stimulus and the response, and can that even be accepted for what it seems to be?

Yet here again in a dispute over method we shall practice toleration in order to extract all possible benefits for the practice of history writing. Surely immersion in the sources to gain a "feeling" for the period is useful, if this means an attempt to find all possible clues to the thoughts and actions of past men so as to be able to consider them as normal to men of that period.[7] The value of "common sense" and "pure intuition" in this process is

---

[7] The desirability and necessity of *Verstehen* analysis in analytical historical studies are convincingly argued by Samuel H. Beer, "Causal Explanation and Imaginative Reenactment," *History and Theory*, III (1963), 6–29.

BEHAVIORAL CATEGORIES
OF HISTORICAL ANALYSIS

doubtful, however, given the social and cultural variability of past mankind, assumed by the very argument advanced by historians for immersing themselves in the sources in the first place. Rather, historians should bring to the task explicit theory about the nature of the entities assumed in the actor's internal state and external action, so they can analyze their evidence with greater rigor and frame their questions with more complexity. They will also know better the gaps in their evidence and present their syntheses with greater honesty and, perhaps, even more sophistication.

That the reading of historical evidence can reveal anything about the real situation, the situational interpretation, and the actual behavior depends upon the fundamental assumptions made in our basic model of human action about the nature of the connections among them. Such an assumption does not specify the exact nature of those connections, so we must examine them in detail. Consideration of seemingly overprecise behavioral distinctions is fundamental to both steps of history writing. The derivation of facts from evidence and the synthesis of these facts into interpretations or narrative require constant and conscious awareness of possible connections. Only precision in making careful distinctions will enable the historian to produce written history that even faintly approaches the historian's goal of understanding the actual complexity of past human behavior.

What at first seems a simple connection between the actor's situational definition and action has been shown by modern philosophers to be a network of many assumptions requiring much precise delineation if the analyst would avoid fallacious explanations. A whole philosophical literature has grown up about such terms as intention, reason, disposition, and motivation as well as the general conception of causality involved in understanding conscious and unconscious behavior. This extensive literature poses two fundamental questions for our basic orientation: Whether it does explain and how does it seek to explain human behavior? Leaving the first question for a later chapter on explanation, let us examine the second so that we may set up some criteria for what the historical analyst must prove in order to use a behavioral approach in analyzing the actor in the past. The historian must seek answers to two basic questions.

1. What connections must he assert existed in the actor's internal state to account for actions in a situation?
2. What can he say was the cause of these connections?[8]

Frequently historians imply or even declare that conscious intentions lie behind the actions of their subjects. For example, they maintain that a political leader or a general decided to do such an action in order to achieve a certain goal in parliament or on the battlefield. To show that behavior was intentional, the analyst must prove at least the following features, according to one philosopher:

(1) the agent must have known what his goal (or aim or purpose) was; (2) the agent must have believed in a connection between his goal and some action he took to be a means of arriving at it. The agent must have known or believed these things in a sense that he could display his knowledge or beliefs, either verbally or by other behavior. (3) In satisfying the first

[8] Good introductions to this literature are Robert Brown, *Explanation in Social Science* (Chicago, 1963), 58–108, and Quentin Gibson, *The Logic of Social Enquiry* (London, 1960), 27–46, 158–78. Other interesting works are Charles Taylor, *The Explanation of Behavior* (London, 1964); D. S. Shwayder, *Stratification of Behavior: A System of Definitions Propounded and Defended* (London, 1965); and A. R. Louch, *Explanation and Human Action* (Berkeley and Los Angeles, 1966).

condition, a person must also have believed that he would try to achieve his purposes when possible.[9]

Though the demands for establishing purposes and goals as the basis for behavior are high, it is not impossible for a historian to find evidence in the documents to satisfy them. The evidence must show knowledge of the conscious goal, knowledge of the connection between the end and the means, and the belief by the agent that he would attempt to achieve the end whenever possible. Shakespeare portrays Brutus as going through these steps in order to turn upon Caesar in the name of the Republic. The task of establishing such a linkage may be easier for the dramatist than for the historian to demonstrate, since the fact that either the action took place in reality or the intellectual process occurred is not sufficient alone to establish the action as one intended. Evidence of both act and ideation is necessary, and given the nature of historical data, some proof of either aspect may be missing.

Goal-seeking behavior may be constructed in terms of models either of rational man or of social and cultural man. Intention and conscious choice are most explicit in the rational-man models prevalent in several disciplines today. The best example of this model is the classic economic man who still survives beneath the sets of equations that constitute his garb today.[10] Similarly, game or de-

[9] Brown, *op. cit.*, 65. A lengthy analysis of the concept of intention is the monograph by G. E. M. Anscombe, *Intention* (2d ed., Ithaca, N.Y., 1963).
[10] See, for example, G. L. S. Shackle, *Decision, Order and Time in Human Affairs* (Cambridge, Eng., 1961); Paul Diesing, *Reason in Society: Five Types of Decisions and Their Social Conditions* (Urbana, Ill., 1962), 14–64; and Talcott Parsons and Neil J. Smelser, *Economy and Society* (New York, 1956). Compare, however, Lionel C. Robbins, *An Essay on the Nature and Significance of Economic Science* (2d ed., rev. and enlarged, London, 1952).

cision theory in political and military science also employs this model. The very terms of this approach—strategy, pay-off, information, rules, and coalition—suggest the conflict games that produced them. That formalized games still use the basic rational-man model can be seen in a summary of the theoretical assumptions of the approach as given by Anatol Rapoport.

It does say how people would behave (1) if they were guided entirely by unambiguous interests (that is, they would always decide in each situation involving both alternative outcomes and risks which outcome they would prefer at which risk); and (2) if they were able to utilize all the information available to them and calculate the outcome in determinate situations and expected outcomes in situations involving risks; and (3) if the rules governing the sequence and range of permissible acts were explicit and fixed.[11]

In short, he gives the necessary assumptions of the rational-man model as such.

Intentionality as conscious goal-seeking behavior can also be phrased in terms of social and cultural models of man. Talcott Parsons found the essence of modern social theory in just such a model. According to him, the basic unit of action possesses at a minimum,

[11] Anatol Rapoport, "Uses and Limitations of Mathematical Models in Social Science," in Llewellyn Gross, ed., *Symposium on Sociological Theory* (New York, 1959), 369. Compare Herbert Simon, *Models of Man; Social and Rational: Mathematical Essays on Rational Human Behavior in a Social Setting* (New York, 1957). Brief introductions to game theory are Richard Snyder, "Game Theory and the Analysis of Political Behavior," in S. Sidney Ulmer, ed., *Introductory Readings in Political Behavior* (Chicago, 1961), 271-76; Karl Deutsch, *Nerves of Government: Models of Political Communication and Control* (New York, 1963), 51-72; and T. C. Schelling, "What is Game Theory?" and Martin Shubik, "The Uses of Game Theory," in James C. Charlesworth, ed., *Contemporary Political Analysis* (New York, 1967), 212-72.

(1) an end, (2) a situation, analyzable in turn into (a) means and (b) conditions, and (3) at least one selective standard in terms of which the end is related to the situation.[12]

This selective standard may be cultural rules and societal conventions as well as idiosyncratic judgment. In social and cultural models of man, the goals and even the means may be prescribed by custom in the society, but that does not deny either purposefulness or intentionality. Interpersonal processes, then, may also fulfill the criteria for the intentional explanation of human action.[13]

The main problem with documentary evidences of announced intentions is whether or not the analyst can accept them at face value. Documents often mention goals, purposes, desires, wishes, programs, and other explicitly declared intentions, but how much significance should the historian ascribe to them in explaining his subject's behavior? Are they the real intentions of the actor or merely ones professed to hide the real intentions? Furthermore, even if they are the real intentions of the actor as consciously held by him, can the historian accept them as the real causes behind the behavior? The historian must differentiate, therefore, the professed intention from the actual intention, and the actual intention as understood by the actor from the real causes for his action. In some cases, they might be one and the same; then again, in other cases, they might not.

This problem led historians to differentiate between the real reason behind the action and the rationale or rationalization for the action. This is an important distinction to be looked for always, but does the historian possess the evidence to back up his conclusion every time he draws the

---

[12] Talcott Parsons, *The Structure of Social Action* (2d ed., New York, 1948), 77, but see entire book.
[13] Social and cultural models of explanation will be analyzed at greater length in the next three chapters.

A BEHAVIORAL APPROACH
TO HISTORICAL ANALYSIS

distinction between what his actors say in documents and what he says these documents really prove? Can he ever get such evidence, given the nature of historical documentation? More often than not, the only evidence cited for such a conclusion is the very document that he maintains is the rationale offered by the actor. To ascribe the real reason for the behavior to be explained, the historian must depend in most cases upon a general theory for which he has no concrete evidence other than his own strong belief in the validity of his system—a system that is often implicit, unsystematized, and referred to as "common sense." In such a circumstance, common sense often means an explanation based upon a theory of unconscious motivation as an intrapersonal process.

The concept of motivation as used by many historians depends upon an ambiguity of meaning that seems almost deliberate in its practice. On one hand, historians use the word "motives" to insinuate that the real reason for the behavior is morally bad and that, furthermore, it is hidden in the unconscious. In this case, motivation is moral assessment as well as an explanation by a factor presumed more real than the mouthed rationalization. On the other hand, historians assume motivation is a scientific psychological concept that accounts for behavior by combining the goal to be explained with some explanatory cause such as internal drive. Motivation is thus presumed to be a blanket explanation for many different types of behavior, often to the confusion of both what is to be explained and what explains it. By merging the two meanings in his practice, an historian can both judge the morality of an action and offer a seemingly scientific explanation of the behavior he condemns.[14]

Motivational assessments according to some over-

[14] A good discussion of this confusion is R. S. Peters, *The Concept of Motivation* (London, 1958). Compare Hans Gerth and C. Wright Mills,

simplified psychology, whether Freudian or otherwise, have long plagued the historical profession. More often than not, such an assessment substitutes an individualistic explanation without proof for one of a social nature, for which proof exists. The tendency to denote intrapersonal drives rather than interpersonal processes as the cause of historical human behavior rests upon the assumption by many "common sense" historians that mankind has always possessed universal biological and psychological equipment, and that most of human behavior can be subsumed under such a view of human nature, despite the proven social and cultural variability of men. It may also be a denial of conscious motivation in favor of unconscious motivation.

Historians advocating the economic interpretation of history frequently commit these errors in the ardour of their argument. Acquisitiveness is presumed common to all men regardless of time or place, and this greed is assumed more basic than any other possible motivation in man. If a man says that he acted for another reason, the economic interpreter discards this profession in favor of the powerful hidden motive he "knows" existed. It is for this reason that Charles Beard searched beneath the political polemics in the period of the Constitution for the "true" reason behind the founding fathers' actions. In the

---

"Sociology of Motivation" in *Character and Social Structure: The Psychology of Social Institutions* (New York, 1953), 112–29, and Robert M. MacIver, "Cause as Incentive" in *Social Causation* (rev. ed., New York, 1964), 195–223. Traditional usage by a historian is illustrated by H. Stuart Hughes, *History as Art and Science: Twin Vistas on the Past* (New York, 1964), 42–67. No historian should miss Kenneth Burke's *Grammar of Motives* (New York, 1945), and *Rhetoric of Motives* (New York, 1950), for a comprehensive analysis of ways of viewing and talking about motives by a man writing in a tradition quite different from that of this writer but wrestling with the same basic problems.

A BEHAVIORAL APPROACH
TO HISTORICAL ANALYSIS

Preface to his *An Economic Interpretation of the Constitution*, he urges other scholars similarly "to turn away from barren 'political' history to a study of the real economic forces which condition great movements in politics."[15] The fallacy of such monocausal interpretations of human behavior becomes even more evident when applied cross-culturally.

Thus one historian has decided that the cause of the seventeenth-century Iroquois wars was solely the desire of that American Indian tribe to become economic middlemen between the white traders at Albany and the tribes to the west of them.[16] This conclusion is odd in light of the century of ethnological literature available to the author that demonstrated many other cultural reasons for Iroquois warfare.

Perhaps the best chance for attributing the real reasons behind human behavior would be in terms of dispositions or tendencies to do certain acts.[17] A dispositional statement is an explanation based upon the likelihood or probability of a repetition of similar behavior already manifested in the past. For confirmation, the historian would seem to need only evidence of recurrence. Ideally, this proof would be statistical, but a few instances in the life of an individual might suffice at times, depending upon the

---

[15] Charles Beard, *An Economic Interpretation of the Constitution* (New York, 1913) v. For a detailed critique of this book, see Robert Brown, *Charles Beard and the Constitution: A Critical Analysis of "An Economic Interpretation of the Constitution"* (Princeton, N.J., 1956).

[16] George T. Hunt, *The Wars of the Iroquois: A Study in Intertribal Trade Relations* (Madison, Wisc., 1940). Criticism of his evidence and thesis is in Allen Trelease, "The Iroquois and Western Fur Trade: Problem in Interpretation," *Mississippi Valley Historical Review*, XLIX (1962), 32–51. A modern anthropological analysis of Iroquois warfare, which contrasts sharply with Hunt's, is in George Snyderman, "Behind the Tree of Peace: A Sociological Study of Iroquois Warfare," *Pennsylvania Archaeologist*, XVIII (1948), nos. 3–4.

[17] I follow Robert Brown, *op. cit.*, 75–98, but compare Gilbert Ryle, *The Concept of Mind* (London, 1949), 116–35.

specific disposition to be demonstrated and the number of actors involved. Dispositions may be expressed as conscious or unconscious behavior, as habits, instincts, neuroses, or social conventions, but again can the historian accept this form of explanation without resort to some theory of motivation as cause?

Thus the historian must always depend upon general theories of behavior in order even to infer the real reason behind the actions he seeks to explain. The choice of such theories should be in accordance with the latest research and theorizing upon the subject so that he may present an explanation acceptable to sophisticated modern theorists instead of an outmoded scheme denied by years of research and thinking in other disciplines. The success of such an approach by a modern psychoanalyst is attested to by the popularity of Erik H. Erikson's *Young Man Luther* among historians.[18]

The concept of motivation is, of course, culture-bound like all our ideas. We can use only those theories that seem best in the light of today's appraisal. According to a psychologist currently researching the problem of motivation, any adequate study of it must include

(a) consideration of the conscious experience of desire, or want; (b) analysis of a person's behavior which is directed towards things he apparently likes or wants and away from things he apparently dislikes or wants to avoid; (c) considera-

[18] Erik H. Erikson, *Young Man Luther: A Study in Psychoanalysis and History* (New York, 1958). An anthology on this subject, with bibliography, is Bruce Mazlish, ed., *Psychoanalysis and History* (Englewood Cliffs, N.J., 1963). On method, consult Frederick Wyatt and W. B. Willcox, "Sir Henry Clinton: A Psychological Exploration in History," *William and Mary Quarterly*, 3d ser., XVI (1959), 3–26, reprinted in Edward Saveth, ed., *American History and the Social Sciences* (New York, 1964), 134–54; see also Richard L. Bushman, "On the Uses of Psychology: Conflict and Conciliation in Benjamin Franklin," *History and Theory*, V (1966), 225–40.

tion of those factors, both internal and external, that influence the strength of desire and subsequently the behavior of a person with respect to the liked or disliked object; (*d*) the fact that individuals seem to differ in the strength of their desire and their tendency to seek certain things and avoid others.[19]

This psychologist suggests that all current theories of motivation can be summarized by two basic formulae. One school advocates "expectancy $\times$ value," which means "that the tendency to act in a certain way depends upon the strength of the expectancy that the act will be followed by a given consequence (or goal) and the value of that consequence (or goal) to the individual."[20] Such a formulation stresses purposive behavior on a nonphysiological level. It is close to our model of situational interpretation. The other school studies "drive $\times$ habit," which is based upon physiological drive and previously learned habit. Both of these variables emphasize the unconscious element in man's behavior, even though goal seeking may be involved in the actions. Motivational theory today, then, attempts to account for both personal and social behavior whether consciously or unconsciously caused. The historian can use either theory just so long as he has the evidence to back up his choice.

That a choice between these two general theories of motivation produces quite different interpretations of men and events can be seen in the current controversy over the personalities of ante-bellum abolitionists. One part of the debate revolves not so much about the thoughts and acts of these people as about the reasons for these thoughts

[19] John W. Atkinson, *An Introduction to Motivation* (Princeton, N.J., 1964), 6.
[20] *Ibid.*, 274. This book presents motivational theory from a historical perspective, which makes it an excellent introduction to the subject for the historian. A recent survey of theories is Charles Cofer and M. H. Appley, *Motivation: Theory and Research* (New York, 1964).

BEHAVIORAL CATEGORIES
OF HISTORICAL ANALYSIS

and actions, since the records of ideational and actual behavior are relatively voluminous in comparison with most historical movements. The debate does not center primarily upon who were and therefore how many were abolitionists. Although the number is variously assessed according to different definitions of abolitionism, all sides agree that abolitionists were a minority in the population of the North before the Civil War. The debate focuses instead on whether these people were reformers or fanatics, to use the subtitle of one recent anthology on the subject.[21] Were the abolitionists a lunatic fringe in the grip of neuroses and martyr complexes and perhaps in need of psychiatric aid, like John Brown, for example, or were they, including Brown, superbly mature people who "understood the constructive role of violence and suffering for the individual and for his society," to borrow one analyst's phrase?[22] Essentially, then, this argument hinges upon the attribution of motivation and the judgment as to the normality of a set of motives in a given population at a given time.

Not only do the recent participants in this rather old debate realize explicitly that some theory of motivation is involved, but they also know that the espousal of a par-

---

[21] Richard O. Curry, ed., *The Abolitionists: Reformers or Fanatics?* (New York, 1965). This anthology contains a good introduction and bibliography on abolitionism historiography, as does Charles Crowe, ed., *The Age of Civil War and Reconstruction, 1830–1900: A Book of Interpretative Essays* (Homewood, Ill., 1966), 199–237.

[22] As used in the subtitle of the article by Silvan Tomkins, "The Psychology of Commitment: The Constructive Role of Violence and Suffering for the Individual and for His Society," in Martin Duberman, ed., *The Antislavery Vanguard: New Essays on the Abolitionists* (Princeton, N.J. 1965), 270–98. For a discussion of John Brown's mental condition, see Louis Ruchame's Introduction to his *A John Brown Reader: The Story of John Brown in His Own Words, in the Words of Those Who Knew Him, and in the Poetry and Prose of the Literary Heritage* (New York, 1959).

---

ticular set of motives is tied closely to the analysts' judgment upon the desirability of radical reform in a society then and now.[23] The modern civil rights agitation may have sparked the recent reassessment of the earlier movement, and a modern recommitment to Negro equality may have fostered a new *Verstehen* of abolitionist thinking, but as I argued earlier, such a genesis of new hypotheses about the connections between the actor's behavior and internal processes neither proves nor disproves the asserted hypotheses. Only an examination of the foundations of each side's theories of motivation can clarify why they differ so radically in judging personality traits and action, and such an examination will reveal why there can be no easy resolution of the argument.

61

Those historians who believe the abolitionists to be constructive reformers accept the ideals professed in their literature as their real reasons for acting, while their opponents see the ideational evidence as a mere subterfuge or rationalization for deep personality disturbances. At its simplest, the latter interpretation by a past generation of historians was in terms of fanaticism; today this view is more likely phrased in such psychoanalytically oriented terms as egoism, emotional impotence, latent homosexuality, and escapism, as David Donald did in his biography of Charles Sumner.[24] No matter what words are used, the behavioral foundations of this viewpoint lie in an attribution of an unconscious motivation of deeper internal processes

[23] Martin Duberman recognizes explicitly that a theory of motivation is tied to current concerns in both his Introduction to *The Antislavery Vanguard*, vii-x, and "The Abolitionists and Psychology," *Journal of Negro History*, XLVII (1962), 183–91, republished slightly revised and without footnotes in Crowe, ed., *op. cit.*, 204–209. So do several of the other authors in Duberman's anthology.
[24] David Donald, *Charles Sumner and the Coming of the Civil War* (New York, 1960).

BEHAVIORAL CATEGORIES
OF HISTORICAL ANALYSIS

far beneath the explicit situational interpretations espoused by the actors. The opponents of this view of the abolitionists as demented likewise use a theory of motivation, but this theory accepts the situational interpretation of the actors at face value as part of it. Thus Martin Duberman, one of the so-called "neo-abolitionists," depicts James Russell Lowell, who was previously seen as a lukewarm abolitionist at best, as a normal, happy individual who was sincerely dedicated to the antislavery cause.[25] Both Donald and Duberman therefore employ a theoretical framework about motivation both to explain the ideational and behavioral data derived from the evidence and to read the documentary remains themselves. Duberman explicitly rejects the Donald approach by arguing that private pathology does not explain public commitment.[26] Donald, for his part, cannot accept the profession of ideals as sufficient evidence of the true reason for the behavior. Thus the resolution of this phase of the controversy is not so much a matter of finding evidence, especially about the actors' thoughts and actions, although both men and both sides could be more careful and conscious about the nature of the evidence needed to prove their cases. Rather, the settlement of this argument must await greater general agreement among historians as to the relations between ideation, action, and the true causes of behavior. Better theory, not better evidence, alone can quench the fires of this conflict.

The nature of historical evidence has definite implications for the selection of a general theory of motivation. First of all, conscious motives are far easier to study than unconscious motives. Then, too, dealing so frequently with the records of individuals, historians have a tendency to

[25] Martin Duberman, *James Russell Lowell* (Boston, 1966).
[26] Duberman, "The Abolitionists and Psychology."

A BEHAVIORAL APPROACH
TO HISTORICAL ANALYSIS

utilize psychological or presumed psychological theory for the explanation of human actions rather than social or cultural theory. Yet given the scantiness of historical data, there are usually far too few documents in even the most voluminous manuscript collections to serve as evidence for a psychological appraisal of personality. On the other hand, just a few scraps of paper here and there in various individual's collections can serve to establish the nature of and conformity to the social conventions and cultural attitudes of a populace, for each additional piece of evidence testifying to a practice serves to prove that it is common to the members of a given society. Dispositions to obey societal custom are therefore far easier to prove than dispositions to individualistic psychological attributes. Accordingly, historians should direct their efforts far more than they do to seeking social and cultural interpretations of their subjects rather than the oversimplified psychology so often urged upon them. I do not believe that this effort should never be made to prove the psychology of a past man; I only say it is a far harder task than others an historian could choose.[27]

Explanation in terms of dispositions to follow the practice common to a society does not preclude individual variation. We presume that in a society the tendency is to conform to the beliefs of that society as to what is ideal, allowable, and forbidden behavior in group-defined cir-

[27] See for example the discrepancy between aim and practice in the widely cited article by William L. Langer, "The Next Assignment," *American Historical Review*, LXIII (1958), 283–304, reprinted in Mazlish, ed., *op. cit.*, 87–107. The problem of sources for psychological interpretations is briefly discussed in Frederick Wyatt, "Psychoanalytic Biography," *Contemporary Psychology*, I (1956), 105–07. Compare my argument here with that of Charles Tilly in "The Analysis of a Counter-Revolution," *History and Theory*, III (1963), 30–58; he provides a splendid example of the difference between explaining by motive and ideology and explaining by social factors.

cumstances. An actor expects certain behavior in certain situations upon the part of others in his society and in turn meets the expectations of others in these same situations. Mutual expectations and reciprocal behavior lead to a social organization of interlocking roles, which is frequently taken as the whole of society by modern theorists. The major problem in using such a model of social behavior as explanation is to account for less than complete obedience to the group rules by all the members of a society. Since social tendencies need to be motivated just as much as idiosyncratic ones, individuals may be committed in varying degrees to the shared attitudes and actions of their society. Through this loophole, psychological interpretation enters social phenomena to offer an intrapersonal explanation for seemingly interpersonal processes. In fact, the antisocial behavior of great men is of particular interest to the historian in his attempt to understand the past. Innovators in past societies cannot be explained by social and cultural factors alone, although the acceptance of their ideas can be.[28]

Again the controversy over abolitionism provides a good example of the confusion between intrapersonal and interpersonal processes in the study of the actors. This side of the dispute also requires the use of the distinction between the actors' interpretation and the observer's view of the situation, and so offers an opportunity to apply all the distinctions made so far in this chapter. Unlike the side

[28] For two quite different approaches to social change in these terms, compare Homer Barnett, *Innovation: The Basis of Cultural Change* (New York, 1953), with Neil J. Smelser, *Theory of Collective Behavior* (New York, 1963). An interesting debate about psychological versus social factors in change that illustrates the problems mentioned in this paragraph occurred among Robert J. Lifton, Frederick Wyatt, and Kenneth Keniston, in *Comparative Studies in Society and History*, VI (1964), 369–83, and VII (1965), 117–32.

A BEHAVIORAL APPROACH TO HISTORICAL ANALYSIS

of the argument analyzed previously, this phase of the debate very much involves the matter of evidence, but the neglect of these important distinctions has concealed even the types of evidence needed.

David Donald initiated this aspect of the debate over abolitionism in his essay, "Toward a Reconsideration of Abolitionists."[29] In this influential article, Donald attempted a social interpretation of the rise of a new kind of antislavery movement in the 1830s. By comparing the biographical profiles of one hundred six abolitionist leaders, he decided that these men were primarily from old families that had once comprised the New England elite but were now displaced in power and prestige by the newly risen industrialists. They joined the antislavery movement to reassert traditional values against the bustling business world that eclipsed them. Thus he sees their protest against slavery as a mere rationale for the true reason of anxiety about declining status.

In adopting the status-anxiety hypothesis of explaining group motivation, first propounded by Richard Hofstadter, Donald falls heir to several demands of proof. Historians employing this method of explaining a group's behavior must prove at the least, as one analyst points out, "that (1) persons of certain statuses (2) engaged in a specified type of activity because (3) those persons were anxious about status as a result of (4) shifts in power and prestige in the overall community."[30] Donald, needless to

65

[29] David Donald, *Lincoln Reconsidered: Essays on the Civil War Era* (New York, 1956), 19–36.

[30] Robert W. Doherty, "Status Anxiety and American Reform: Some Alternatives," *American Quarterly*, XIX (1967), supplement, 331. This whole article is worth reading. A less sweeping but specific critique of Donald's essay is Robert Skotheim, "A Note on Historical Method: David Donald's 'Toward a Reconsideration of Abolitionists,'" *Journal of Southern History*, XXV (1959), 356–65.

BEHAVIORAL CATEGORIES
OF HISTORICAL ANALYSIS

say, does not examine any one of these factors explicitly and therefore proves none of his argument, but this is not the point I am trying to make. If Donald had tried to prove each factor, what would be the nature of the evidence needed to do such a task?

Each factor's significance depends as much upon the perception of it by the actor as it does upon its objective establishment by the observer, but items three and four need to be particularly explained in terms of the actor's interpretation of the situation. It matters little whether or not the status of the persons becoming abolitionists diminished in reality from the observer's construction of the situation, and it matters just as little whether social and political organization of the situation really changed as a result of industrialism. What does matter in this argument is whether the actors saw their situation in that context. Only if they did, does status anxiety perhaps constitute an explanation of abolitionist behavior. Because Donald does not differentiate carefully between the situation as seen by the actors and as seen by himself, he fails to adduce all the kinds of evidence he needs to support his case. In fact, he seems unaware that he even needs to consider the actors' viewpoint apart from his own in stating his case. Ideally he needs to produce evidence about how interpersonal aspects of the situation as reconstructed by the historian were interpreted in the same manner by the actors. Then he must further show this to be the real reason for their behavior rather than some other intrapersonal factor. Only careful attention to the difference between the actor's and observer's viewpoints, between intra- and interpersonal processes allow the researching of the documents to derive the evidence necessary, let alone sufficient, to prove an hypothesis as elaborate as that about status anxiety. For lack of a theoretical framework, evidence was not looked for, and for lack of evidence, the argument was lost, even though Donald did not realize it.

In summary, then, the first task of historical analysis is the study of the actor's situation, his interpretation of the situation, and his actions in the situation, difficult as this study may be in the light of the nature of historical evidence. To accomplish this task fully, the historian must separate what the interpretation of the situation was and what the behavior was from the situation as such, and then establish the connections among the three. In turn, the establishment of such connections as may have existed among the three must be differentiated from the full explanation of the behavior, if the historian includes unconscious motivation in his purview of history. Only such precise delineation will allow the historian to explore and reconstruct the complexity he sees in past eras. Given the nature of historical evidence, furthermore, the historian can prove conscious motives and use interpersonal models of society as explanation with far more certainty than he can establish unconscious motives and intrapersonal models of explanation.

Now we must turn to the second major task of historical analysis: the observer's view of the actor, his actions, and his situation. The linkage between the observer and the actor is achieved through a comparison of the consequences of the actor's behavior as seen by the actor or actors and by the analyst. To see why this should be the case, we must elaborate our basic model of human behavior.

Up to this time, we have represented the actor's viewpoint in an essentially static manner. It is, however, dynamic. The situation of the actor may change because of the actions of the actor or other actors, the combination of perceived elements in the situation, or even from a reevaluation of the situation by the actor. Regardless of the reasons, the actor is constantly reassessing the situation in terms of feedback to him. To indicate this dynamic reassessment, if we may paraphrase MacIver's term, we must change Figure 3–1 to look like Figure 3–2. This feedback,

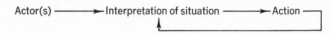

Actor(s) ——————▶ Interpretation of situation ——————▶ Action ┐

Figure 3–2

from the actor's viewpoint, discloses whether his actions produced the expected and intended results or unexpected and unintended consequences. Such consequences can only be understood by the actor in terms of his perception of their benefits or disadvantages gauged by his values. They may be considered desirable or undesirable; they may be seen as crucially important or relatively insignificant; they may be viewed as changing or maintaining the status quo; or they may not be recognized at all. Unanticipated consequences can only be perceived and measured by the actor according to his viewpoint. Furthermore, the actor can and often does misconstrue completely the causes of the consequences he does see.

Thus the consequences of the actor's actions must be analyzed also from the viewpoint of the observer. The observer may regard the consequences in the same way as the actor, or he may judge them to be quite different. The results of many actions may be quite unlike what the actor thinks, if he sees any consequences at all.

For this reason, no matter how accurately and how completely the historian presents the actor's viewpoint, he accomplishes only half the job of historical analysis. The actor's view must be combined with the observer's viewpoint to produce an analysis approximating historical reality. The combination of the distinctions between ideation and behavior and between the observer and the actor produces two basic levels of analysis of three categories each. We must examine historical reality for both the actor and the observer in terms of the situation, the behavior, and the consequences. For the actor, this means his situational interpretation, his action in the situation, and the perceived feedback then and later as he connects it with the action and the situation. The observer must differentiate between the actor's interpretation and the real situation as he understands it, the actor's behavior as it is observed (or reconstructed by the historian), and the consequences, both intended and unintended, of the behavior. The levels and categories are clearly discerned in Figure 3–3. It is obvious

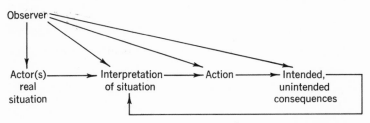

Figure 3–3

that the success of such an analysis depends upon the historian's ability to distinguish

1. The "real" situation from the actor's interpretation of the situation.
2. The aims of the actor or actors from the actions in the situation.
3. The "real" consequences of the actions from the feedback to the actor or actors.
4. All the ramifications, both short- and long-term, of the actor's or actors' behavior in the situation.

That attention to all these distinctions, difficult as they

may be to make in history, produces quite different results from traditional historiography may be seen in a comparison of two famous writers on the American farmers' movements in the late nineteenth century. John D. Hicks in his *Populist Revolt*[31] accepts the actors' version of their situation as reality. Hence, he sees railroads, grain elevators, mortgages, and inelastic currency as the cause of the farmers' troubles and their cooperatives and attempts at forming new political parties as realistic ways to deal with their plight. Richard Hofstadter in his widely-read volume, *The Age of Reform*,[32] questions this whole interpretation by separating the actors' and observer's levels of analysis. He argues that the farmers' interpretation of their situation was quite inaccurate in light of the real situation he thinks existed. The farmers adhered to a myth of themselves as self-subsisting yeomen, whereas in reality they operated commercial ventures in an impersonal, international market. Hence their activities in the Grange, Alliances, and People's Party were futile, even utopian. His chapters are organized and even titled in line with his fundamental categories of analysis. The first chapter, "The Agrarian Myth and Commercial Realities," contrasts his idea of their reality as commercial agriculturalists faced with market problems in a society rapidly industrializing with the farmers' myth of themselves as independent frontier yeomen. As a result of this incongruence between their perceptions and reality, he shows in a chapter entitled "The Folklore of Populism" that the farmers evolved a conspiratorial interpretation of their situation. Attempts to co-operate or inflate the currency were doomed to failure

70

[31] John D. Hicks, *The Populist Revolt: A History of the Farmer's Alliance and the People's Party* (Minneapolis, Minn., 1931). Compare Solon Buck, *The Agrarian Crusade* (New Haven, Conn., 1920).
[32] Richard Hofstadter, *The Age of Reform: From Bryan to F.D.R.* (New York, 1955).

given Hofstadter's acceptance of the inevitability of industrialism in the United States. He believes the farmers succeeded eventually in helping themselves only through pressure lobbies, which he takes as indicators of their acceptance of the inevitability of an industrialized nation. He indicates the story behind their adoption of a new situational interpretation in the third chapter title, "From Pathos to Parity."

Certainly, this dramatically different interpretation illustrates the desirability of considering both the observer's and actors' level of historical analysis, but even Hofstadter's case falls short of the ideal procedure outlined in this chapter. Although he, unlike Hicks, attempts to separate the actors' situational interpretation from the observer's reconstruction of the "real" situation, he fails to make this distinction consistently throughout his argument. Thus although he sets up in the first chapter the discrepancy between the farmers' perception of their situation and the situation he sees them really facing, he does not carry this dual view through to the end of his case. In Chapter 3 he only asserts rather than proves that the actors' view of the situation, which he dealt with impressionistically in Chapter 2, does not fit the reality he sees. He shows neither that the reality is as he says it is nor by elaborating an observer's view of the economy at the time, that their proposed panaceas of cooperation, inflation, or nationalization would not work in the situation. Merely to point out a contradiction between his and their outlook is no substitute for a more systematic examination of the aimed-for consequences in the actual situation by some such method as a counterfactual model. He does not even demonstrate that the farmers actually did change their situational interpretation to bring it in line with his presumed reality. He devotes a whole chapter to the ideology of Populism but only a few sentences to the ideology of parity. So on both the levels of the actors and the observer, he fails to produce all the evidence needed to clinch his argument.

The failure to establish a reality independent of his reconstruction of the actors' view is again manifest in his discussion of the Progressives in the same book. Their attitudes, he argues, were moralistic, hence their actions were unrealistic. However, he does not prove this point by explicit comparison of their ends and their means with an "objective" analysis of the situational context of their ideas and actions. Again only a study of the full effects of the proposed reforms he mentions and their subsequent failure to produce the aimed-for ends, plus evidence that this failure was due to the "real" situation as he conceives it, could prove his basic thesis. All in all, Hofstadter's book, provocative and influential as it has been, illustrates the "soft side" rather than the "hard side" of historical analysis, to use his own terms about the farmers' movements.

This critique of Hofstadter is not meant to give comfort to his many critics, for they have been equally deficient in clearly differentiating between the actors' and observer's level of analysis. They often controvert him on only one or the other level, either the situational interpretation of the actors or the observer's view of the actual situation.[33] Not one but all levels and categories of analysis are needed. Only attention to both situation *and* situational interpretation, both inter- *and* intrapersonal, both ideational *and* actual behavior, both actors' view *and* observer's

---

[33] In many ways, Hofstadter's critics fail to distinguish between the actors' and observer's levels and combine them more than he does. The most notorious example is Norman Pollack, *The Populist Response to Industrial America: Midwestern Populist Thought* (Cambridge, Mass., 1962), and "Fear of Man: Populism, Authoritarianism, and the Historian," in *Agricultural History*, XLIX, 1965), 59–67. The best guide to the current status of the debate with bibliographical references is the set of articles by Oscar Handlin, Irwin Unger, and J. Rogers Hollingsworth in *ibid.*, 68–85.

A BEHAVIORAL APPROACH
TO HISTORICAL ANALYSIS

viewpoint will produce the complex approach to evidence about the Populists and Progressives that will resolve the current controversies. In like manner, the debates in the profession today about the causes of the American Revolution, the ratification of the Constitution, the coming of the War of 1812 and the Civil War, the reasons for Reconstruction, and a multitude of other historiographical impasses can be decided only by a more conscious and rigorous attention to the behavioral categories discussed in this chapter.

At long last we are ready to summarize the basic procedure for historical analysis according to the distinctions drawn in this chapter. At the risk of oversimplifying the previous argument, I shall cast the distinctions into a brief set of rules for easy remembrance:

1. Determine the actor('s') interpretation(s) of the situation.

2. Discover the actor('s') behavior in the situation.

3. Detect the feedback to the actor(s). Did it agree, i.e., was it the expected and intended result, or did it disagree with his or their aims?

4. Define the "real" situation of the actor(s) as seen by the observer.

5. Trace the full consequences of the actions both anticipated and unanticipated by the actor(s).

6. Compare steps four and five with one, two, and three.

7. Attribute connections, according to various theories, now that the different behavioral levels and categories are differentiated.

Historical study, then, in my view, is the combination of the actors' and observer's levels of analysis into a unified representation of past reality. Written history is an attempt to see a complex human past through the many-sided prism of the behavioral approach to man. Anything less distorts and confuses the representation of the past.

The now complete basic procedure for historical analysis demands the use of the social sciences to make the many distinctions it assumes at the same time as it facilitates their use by providing a guide to that usage. What behavioral concept the historian can best use will depend upon what level or distinction he is trying to make. The clear-cut analytical differentiation of levels and categories in this approach enables the historian to see quickly the utility and validity of various theories and concepts for his purposes.

To provide such aid, the behavioral sciences must be divided according to their basic conceptual orientations to human action. Such a task is too great in its requirements to be done in a number of volumes, let alone in this brief essay. Again we are forced to choose some very fundamental orientations that will help the historian in his everyday chores. We have already discussed in this and the preceding chapter such an orientation to individual behavior; in the next chapter we shall discuss a fundamental approach to group behavior. By studying these two types of analysis, we shall round out a broad behavioral approach to men as individuals and as groups.

Our argument up to this point has only assumed a plurality of actors, either by including them as elements in situations and therefore in situational definitions, or by suggesting that groups of men possessed collective as well as individual interpretations of situations. Now we must turn more specifically to group behavior if we are to aid historians in their at-

tempt to classify the consequences of behavioral activity, for chief among the historian's concerns is the effect of individual and group actions upon the whole life of past societies. Once again, we need a basic orientation, and once again, we must choose an approach useful to the needs of the historian.

An elementary but valuable scheme of classifying group behavior emerges from a comparison of whether the individuals in a situation viewed the consequences of their actions as fulfilling their aims or not and whether they acted as a self-conscious group or only as individuals. This scheme builds upon the analytical procedure advo-cated in the last chapter, which hinged upon a comparison of the actor's goals and the consequences of his intended acts with the observer's examination of the same thing to see if they corresponded. An investigation of the possibili-ties in this classificatory scheme will develop the basic categories of group behavior according to our orientation. This examination will quickly lead us into the problem of analyzing the conceptions of culture and society, which are the major orientations used by social scientists in the study of group behavior.

In one type of group behavior, various individuals possess a relatively similar interpretation of a situation and as a result take concerted, though not necessarily similar, action as a group. The individual actors need not act similarly because different people do different tasks, but the totality of the behavior leads to unified, collective action. Such group phenomena as demands for legislation, organized social movements, political revolutions, and even much of the organization of a society itself are examples of what we shall call, following Robert MacIver, collective phenomena.[1]

Another type of group phenomena results from the convergence of separate activities of a like nature by various individuals. These are not consciously group planned, but merely the total result of separate individuals' acts. Yet they add up to such statistical categories as birth and crime rates or to such phenomena as styles and fads. We shall speak of such phenomena as aggregative, because individually planned actions result in aggregations or statistical distributions as observed by the analyst.[2] Such phenomena are the grouping together of behavior not seen as collective by the actors.

The third type of group behavior can be termed conjunctive, because it arises "from variant assessments and activities of interdependent individuals and groups, as they issue in unpurposed resultants."[3] Such phenomena are the

[1] This category and the two that follow are developed by Robert M. MacIver, *Social Causation* (Harper ed., New York, 1964), 300–21. Compare, for another scheme, Donald T. Campbell, "Common Fate, Similarity, and Other Indices of the Status of Aggregate of Persons as Social Entities," *Behavioral Science*, III (1958), 14–25.

[2] I use my own term here in preference to MacIver's "distributive." For another view of such phenomena, see Neil J. Smelser, *Theory of Collective Behavior* (New York, 1963).

[3] MacIver, *op. cit.*, 305. He uses the term "conjunctural."

mere conjunction of individual or group intended actions that affect a society in part or in entirety by the aggregate of their unintended consequences. Business cycles, so-called "social disorganization," and a large part of the overall social organization are examples of conjunctive phenomena. Analysis of group behavior of this sort must be a combination of the actors' and observer's viewpoints.

Complex social processes may involve more than one type of group phenomena, and one type of phenomena may turn into another. If, for example, the birth and death statistics bother enough people, they may organize collective action to change the situation. Or, for another example, the conjunctive phenomenon of a depression causes much collective behavior in today's highly industrialized societies. Aimed-for collective action may also have the unintended consequences of producing new conjunctive phenomena.

While it may be difficult to separate the three types of group phenomena in practice or even remember their names, it is important to have the categories in order to clarify historical analysis. Essentially the distinctions among them revolve about whether the actors' aims are individual or group planned, and whether the observer sees the total consequence of the group's actions in the same light as aimed for by the actors so grouped. As presented in Table 4–1, a chart may prove helpful in remembering these distinctions. Such an elementary classification of group behavior enables an analyst to clarify plural behavior immediately, even if it does not help him to account for it.

From this classification of group behavior follows immediately the classification of the actors the historian studies. He may view them as individuals or as groups. The latter may be divided into whether they were conscious of each other as being in the same group or whether

Table 4-1

Group Consequences / Who planned?	Observer sees total consequences as aimed-for by the actors	Observer sees total consequences differently than aimed-for by the actors
Individually planned actions	AGGREGATIVE	CONJUNCTIVE
Group planned actions	COLLECTIVE	CONJUNCTIVE

historians have merely grouped them together according to some criterion of the observer. Groups are therefore collective or aggregative—to extend our previous terms to groups as well as group behavior—according to whether they are related in the eyes of the actors or merely categorized by the observer in line with some standard of his own judgment.[4] In a collective group the participants consciously desired their social relationships. They acted collectively in knowing concert. An aggregative group is the juxtaposition of members manifesting similar behavior in the eyes of the observer but unknown to each other as such in real life. They are only a group in the eyes of the observer.

The utility of this elementary classification of groups can be demonstrated by applying the distinctions to the current controversy about the nature of the Progressive movement. When did it begin? Was Populism a forerunner or not? Who were Progressives? Should the group include businessmen historians usually list as conservative

[4] Compare the conceptions of *relational* and *categorical groups* as used by Conrad M. Arensberg and Solon T. Kimball, *Culture and Community* (New York, 1963), 136. This distinction is not to be confused with *Gemeinschaft* and *Gesellschaft* or *Status* and *Contract,* both of which are of quite a different order.

but who advocated legislation usually considered Progressive? The answers to these questions and others depend upon whether historians believe that the reformers knew of each other and consciously acted together, or whether they merely advocated certain ideas and actions in a certain period of American history called Progressive by historians. In other words, was it a truly collective movement or just an historian's aggregation of acts by separate groups? If it was a collective group or a movement composed of people acting in conscious concert, then it started later and the Populists were not a precursor according to present historical data. Furthermore, such a definition would probably exclude the businessmen. But if Progressivism is a mere observer's classification of certain ideas and actions, then there not only is no movement but it is difficult to distinguish it from Populism and industrial reform in general. Then it started as early as the historian likes and comprises businessmen and others as well. Until analysts agree upon the criteria of membership, these questions cannot even be researched in a fruitful fashion.[5]

Whether membership in a group is only aggregative or really collective poses several knotty problems in current and historical sociology. Is the index to social class the collective conscious awareness of the members of a social stratum of their similar position and style of life, or is it only that their style of life and economic resources place

[5] The sides in the controversy may be seen in Richard Hofstadter, *The Age of Reform: From Bryan to F.D.R.* (New York, 1955), 131–299; George Mowry, *The Era of Theodore Roosevelt, 1900–1912* (New York, 1958), especially 85–105; Samuel Hays, *The Response to Industrialism, 1885–1914* (Chicago, 1957); Robert H. Weibe, *Businessmen and Reform: A Study of the Progressive Movement* (Cambridge, Mass., 1962); and Arthur Mann, "The Progressive Tradition," in John Higham, ed., *The Reconstruction of American History* (New York, 1962), 157–79.

A BASIC ORIENTATION
TO GROUP BEHAVIOR

them in conjunction upon the same social level?[6] Does this index, hence class, vary throughout history? Is a change in the definition of class again signaled today by the increasing use of the phrase social status in place of economic class?[7] Surely every historian must document his conception of class because of the ambiguity of definition. The importance he attaches to class as an explanatory factor, or even whether he thinks it significant at all, will depend upon the definition of class he uses. The basic problem of aggregative versus collective membership again arises in the analysis of the city as a sociological entity. Does urban history exist in the sense that the city is a special way of life as perceived by its citizens, or is urban history merely an artificial classification of any behavior that occurs in places called cities? Arthur M. Schlesinger, Sr., argued that urban history may prove as useful a causal factor for interpreting American history as the frontier had.[8] If this is true, must not the city be viewed as a special entity different from all other possible human aggregations? How else could such influence be ascribed to it? Even if it pos-

[6] The standard anthology on the subject is Richard Bendix and Seymour Lipset, eds., *Class, Status and Power: A Reader in Social Stratification* (New York, 1953). A recent volume with historical examples is Bernard Barber, *Social Stratification* (New York, 1957). An analysis of the evolving conception of class by American sociologists is Milton M. Gordon, *Social Class in American Sociology* (Durham, N.C., 1958). Some interesting recent works by historians who attempt to portray the dimensions of class are Stephan Thernstrom, *Poverty and Progress: Social Mobility in a Nineteenth Century City* (Cambridge, Mass., 1964); Jackson T. Main, *The Social Structure of Revolutionary America* (Princeton, N.J., 1965); and Bernard and Elinor Barber, eds., *European Social Class: Stability and Change* (New York, 1965).

[7] So suggest Arthur J. Vidich and Joseph Bensman, *Small Town in Mass Society: Class, Power and Religion in a Rural Community* (Anchor ed., Garden City, N.Y., 1960), 78–79n.

[8] Arthur M. Schlesinger, Sr., "The City in American History," *Mississippi Valley Historical Review*, XXVII (1940), 43–66, reprinted in Schlesinger, *Paths to the Present* (New York, 1949), 210–33.

*A BEHAVIORAL APPROACH
TO HISTORICAL ANALYSIS*

sesses such influence, is it due to an organizational form in which the participants have a commonly shared culture, or is it merely an aggregation in which the members merely live in close proximity with one another? The answers to these questions determine the nature of urban history, or whether urban history should even exist.[9]

Even the overall analysis of the organization of a society centers upon the distinctions between collective and aggregative composition and the three types of group phenomena. A social structure, as was said earlier, may be seen as composed of interlocking roles performed by individuals with reciprocal expectations and resulting in mutually adjusted behavior. Such a view of social organization implies that individuals in it possess a relatively similar interpretation of their statuses and roles and perform them according to their own and others' expectations. This is a model of society collective in membership engaged in aimed-for concerted action. Other theorists believe that the total social structure contains, in addition to the above, conjunctive phenomena of unaimed-for consequences.

[9] See especially William Diamond, "On the Dangers of an Urban Interpretation of History," in Eric Goldman, ed., *Historiography and Urbanization: Essays in American History in Honor of W. Stull Holt* (Baltimore, 1941), 67–108; and three articles by Eric E. Lampard: "American Historians and the Study of Urbanization," *American Historical Review*, LXVII (1961), 49–61, "Urbanization and Social Change: On Broadening the Scope and Relevance of Urban History," in Oscar Handlin and John Burchard, eds., *The Historian and the City* (Cambridge, Mass., 1963); and "Historical Aspects of Urbanization," in Philip Hauser and Leo F. Schnore, eds., *The Study of Urbanization* (New York, 1965), 519–54. Two anthologies on urban sociology are Paul K. Hatt and Albert J. Reiss, Jr., eds., *Cities and Society: The Revised Reader in Urban Society* (2d ed., New York, 1957), and Ernest Burgess and Donald J. Bogue, eds., *Contributions to Urban Sociology* (Chicago, 1964). Historians would do well to start their study of urban sociology with Leonard Reissman, *The Urban Process: Cities in Industrial Societies* (New York, 1964) and the Hauser and Schnore volume cited earlier in this note. No one needs to be reminded of the pioneering works by Lewis Mumford on the city.

A BASIC ORIENTATION
TO GROUP BEHAVIOR

Such a model means that the observer's view of the total social organization is one that the members who comprise it never see themselves.[10]

Historians use both models of society and often in seeming paradox. In order to understand what was once seen as the disorder of medieval history, today's historians have employed the concepts of feudalism and manorialism, which are based upon an implicit and highly ordered model of collective membership and consciously aimed-for action. On the other hand, historians trace the impact of the rationalization of industrial production on modern society, which in theory should produce order, in terms of conjunctive phenomena resulting in a social organization of aggregative relationships. Whether the models are truly paradoxical must be left to a longer discussion elsewhere, but surely the selection of any model ought to be done consciously. In my opinion, as I hope to develop in the following chapters, the historian can only neglect one or the other view to the detriment of his goal of understanding past complexity, but the question of when to use which model as well as what model to use must be based upon recent behavioral theory.

Whenever the historian discusses group behavior, whether seen in small or large groups, cities, or even whole societies, he must therefore classify it as collective, aggregative, or conjunctive if he would understand it. The necessity for categorizing group behavior and groups in this fashion rests upon the assumptions of modern social theory. According to current analysts, a great gulf exists between human behavior in general and that termed social

[10] An analysis of the development of the concept is sketched by Florian Znaniecki, "Social Organization and Institutions," in Georges Gurvitch and Wilbert E. Moore, eds., *Twentieth Century Sociology* (New York, 1945), 172–217, but see the rest of this chapter for further analysis.

behavior. Social behavior is interaction in which complementary adjustment occurs among human beings from the viewpoint of the observer. Further, this behavioral reciprocity is presumed by many analysts to be based upon similar internalized orientations in the actors. The validity of the second assumption and the justification of the first is dependent upon the conceptions of culture and society prevalent today.

From comparison among peoples, social theorists derived the concept of culture and the role of culture in men's lives. Activities previously assumed biological in origin were seen to shade subtly, but nevertheless definitely, into socially variable practices. Man's body needs food and sleep but the number of meals, the diet, and times of sleeping vary greatly among peoples. Sexual intercourse has a physiological basis, but its practice differs around the world. Much of what Westerners had associated with maleness and femaleness was shown to be cultural in character. Even behavior formerly presumed determined by geography was discovered to be shaped in most cases by cultural interpretation of the inhabitants. Similar climates and similar terrains do not produce similar ways of life. Time and reason had seemed universal, but our calendar and our logic are confined to our world.[11]

If all the preceding phenomena are influenced by men's cultures, then it is obvious that such things as religion, economics, and social relationships must also have cultural bases. Much of what had seemed rooted in the very nature of man and even the notion of human nature

[11] Good examples of studies of cultural behavior for the layman are contained in Edward T. Hall, *The Silent Language* (2d ed., New York, 1963), and the relevant portions of Clyde Kluckhohn, *Mirror for Man: A Survey of Human Behavior and Social Attitudes* (2d ed., New York, 1957).

came to be seen as culturally variable among peoples. For all these reasons, social theorists believe that most of what groups of men say they think and believe, how they relate socially, and what they do with their material environment—or what are sometimes called *mentifacts, sociofacts, and artifacts*—are all manifestations of culture, for these behaviors are socially learned and socially transmitted. All these thoughts were part of the first scientific definition of culture formulated by E. B. Tyler in 1871.

84

Culture . . . is that complex whole which includes knowledge, belief, art, morals, law, custom, and many other capabilities and habits acquired by man as a member of society.[12]

Cultural behavior conceived in accord with our basic orientation to human action would stress both internal states and external manifestations. Culture in the strictest sense would seem to be the name applied to the *socially derived* variables intervening between the stimuli and the responses in men's behavior. Much of human activity occurs in physical and social situations learned by the actors through living together. More precisely, then, these group-

[12] Edward B. Tyler, *Primitive Culture* (Boston, 1871). A history and exhaustive survey of the term's many meanings until the date of its publication is Alfred Kroeber and Clyde Kluckhohn, *Culture: A Critical Review of Concepts and Definitions, Papers of the Peabody Museum of American Archaeology and Ethnology,* Harvard University, XLVII, no. 1, (1952). Two useful introductions to the concept for the historian are Philip Bagby, *Culture and History: Prolegomena to the Comparative Study of Civilizations* (Berkeley and Los Angeles, 1958) and David Bidney, *Theoretical Anthropology* (New York, 1953). Anything by Clyde Kluckhohn is valuable in my opinion; among many papers are "The Study of Culture" in Daniel Lerner and Harold D. Lasswell, eds., *The Policy Sciences, Recent Developments in Scope and Method* (Stanford, 1951), 86–102; "Culture and Behavior," in Gardner Lindzey, ed., *Handbook of Social Psychology* (Reading, Mass., 1954), vol. 2, 921–76; "Parts and Wholes in Cultural Analysis," in Daniel Lerner, ed., *Parts and Wholes* (New York, 1963), 111–33; and with W. H. Kelly, "The Concept of Culture," in Ralph Linton, ed., *The Science of Man in the World Crisis* (New York, 1945), 78–107.

A BEHAVIORAL APPROACH
TO HISTORICAL ANALYSIS

learned definitions and interpretations constitute the culture of that group. Culture as such, in this view, is not the behavior manifested, but the resultant behavior is a manifestation of the cultural definitions and interpretations of the situations.

By adopting a definition of culture in accord with our basic orientation to human behavior, we eliminate many controversies over the concept, but we are still left with the greatest problem of all. To define culture as group-derived ideation within an actor or actors does not really say whether the learned situational definitions and interpretations are the same or not for everyone said to be sharing the culture. The concept of culture or more particularly of *a* culture implies a dimension of sharedness among the actors hitherto assumed by our analysis but not examined very carefully. This element of group sharing provides the great riddle in social and cultural analysis today, for it raises new problems about the actor-observer and ideational-behavioral distinctions not previously considered in this book and not analyzed rigorously until recently by anthropologists or sociologists. Although it raises many problems, the emphasis on group sharing is the concept's chief merit as a key to understanding human group behavior.

The difficulty arises from the consideration of culture in its specific sense. Culture in the abstract is common to all mankind who are said to constitute society in general as Tyler's definition stated. Culture in reality is only manifested in specific, unique cultures, such as Zuni, Eskimo, or French. *A* culture is the distinctive manner of life of a group of human beings in a specific place at a specific time. In like manner, the term society is applied to all mankind, but in actuality it is only manifested as societies of men. The conception of *a* culture implies certain notions of culture wholeness and fit between the given culture and a group of people in behavioral interaction, or *a* society. Theorists do assume that a total culture has a certain relationship to the total society said to possess it. This relationship in the broadest sense is the relationship between culture and society both considered as wholes, and this holism causes the trouble in determining the relationship between the two concepts in theory and in practice.

For some theorists, no problem exists at all, because they conceive of *a* culture as coterminous with a group of people and their collective behavior, or *a* society. According to these analysts, a *society* refers to the people possessing a common culture, and a *culture* refers to the meanings and outlook upon their social and physical environment shared by the members of that society. All the people of a society would know what to expect of each other because of their shared views, and they would do as expected since each person would be fully *socialized* into the society or *enculturated* into the culture. The *modal*, or typical, *personality* would be the only personality and the *basic personality* or *national character* at the same time. The *social integration* of the society would be complete, for all the social relationships would neatly mesh into *roles, organizations,* and *institutions,* which in turn would compose the *social structure,* or *social system.* The *cultural* and *social integration* would be apparent, for all the goals, rules, and beliefs of all the people would be consistent with each other and would be manifested in behavior. The goals, rules, and beliefs would be organized into an overall hierarchical pattern or *cultural configuration.* Thus the *style* of the culture would also be evident.[13]

[13] The best guide to the current usage of these terms is Julius Gould and William L. Kolb, eds., *A Dictionary of the Social Sciences* (New York, 1964). A vigorous protest against the assumptions underlying these

These are classic usages of *culture, society,* and related terms. Underlying all the terms is an assumption of ideational and behavioral conformity by all members of a group. In social and cultural analysis of this sort, the more localized, homogeneous, and stable the society, the easier it is to call it a culture. In fact, anthropologists probably developed these definitions as a result of their dealings with small, exotic, isolated populations presumed static because no written histories existed. The less a society resembles this model, the more difficult it is to describe or to delimit its culture. Do the peoples of the United States or Canada or Russia possess a culture or cultures? Are Americans and Frenchmen part of Western culture, or do they have separate cultures?

Sociologists always dealt with complex societies called civilizations, and so they did not see a culture as totally coincident with a society. Their solution to the problem took the form of differentiating subculture from culture. The differentiation probably arose from concern over ethnic, racial, and religious minorities and from attempts to cope with occupational, class, and regional variations in attitudes and practices in modern societies. A subculture is the culture of a group smaller than the society whose culture is the reference point. To determine the existence of a subculture, the researcher examines among other things the time it persisted, the number of persons involved, and its origin and migration. The concept was an obvious attempt to explain variability within a society rather than among societies. A subculture might also arise from an emerging approach to life that resulted from frustration with the society's prevalent culture or from plain conflict with that

---

usages was made by Dennis H. Wrong, "The Oversocialized Conception of Man in Modern Sociology," *American Sociological Review,* XXIV (1961), 183–93.

culture. Perhaps such a subculture might better be called a *contraculture,* to use one sociologists term.[14]

All the attempts to define subcultures are not entirely satisfactory because they do not lay down adequate guidelines for determining when and how behavior should be classified as cultural, subcultural, contracultural, or even supercultural,[15] to conceive of another possibility. The proponents of these cultural divisions still presume that the subcultural groups in a society share identical ideation and behavior and that the population at large still possesses enough common situational definitions and interpretations to call them a culture. Even though these theorists no longer suppose that culture as ideation and society as behavioral interaction of a group are completely coterminous, still they believe sufficient overlap exists to justify retaining the basic idea of sociocultural fusion. To them the locus of culture is in the actors, and culture is shared outlook as well as similar or complementary behavior.

All who adopt the coterminous, or overlap, view of culture and society support their hypothesis by pointing out how actors in a group appear oriented to each other in such a way that their behavior is similar to or mutually adjusted to each other's expectations. Accordingly, the Hobbesian problem of accounting for social order within a population is solved through reciprocal interaction based upon the rules of the game, which they say are the shared identical definitions and interpretations of the social and physical environment possessed in common by all the mem-

[14] J. Milton Yinger proposes the term in his general discussion of subculture in his article, "Contraculture and Subculture," *American Sociological Review,* XXV (1960), 625–35. Also see Milton M. Gordon, "The Concept of Subculture and Its Application," *Social Forces,* XXVI (1947), 40–42.
[15] The term is adopted from Bagby, *op. cit.,* 105.

bers of a group or society. As a result of these shared, identical situational definitions and interpretations, the actors can predict their group behavior, that is, know what to expect of each other in situations defined as similar by the group. To these theorists, culture in its sharedness is the "glue" of society in that it integrates that society and keeps it at peace with itself. This view emphasizes that culture not only derives from men living together in groups but also that as a result of social life, culture is shared in identical forms by all those living within the group.

Other theorists question whether similar or complementary behavior over time that seems mutually adjusting upon the part of individuals in a group or society really does indicate identical shared internal goals, attitudes, and rules for living among that group. They are even more confirmed in this opinion when it is discovered that many of the participants in a culture seem to lack any explicit or conscious knowledge of many of the so-called cultural "rules" of the game they are said to play. The anthropologist Anthony F. C. Wallace phrased the fundamental query in this manner: "Is it necessary that all participants in a stable socio-cultural system have the same 'map' of the system in order that they may select the correct overt behavior under the relevant circumstances?"[16] After an elaborate argument in logic, he answers that neither cognitive nor motivational sharing is required for stable social interaction. Nothing need be shared except the idea of behavioral activity involved in the interaction. The reasons for doing the actions, the meanings attached to those actions, and the feelings surrounding the actions could all

[16] Anthony F. C. Wallace, *Culture and Personality* (New York, 1961), 31. His whole discussion of this problem is good, pp. 29–41, as is his article, "The Psychic Unity of Human Groups," in Bert Kaplan, ed., *Studying Personality Cross-Culturally* (Evanston, Ill., 1961), 129–63.

be different for all the participants in a group or society.

In other words, no man need have the same "culture" as another man in that society, and yet he could and would participate fully in that society's interactions. In fact, Wallace argues that such nonsharing by the participants is requisite for the erection of complex institutional arrangements, for otherwise all the structure and all the ideas of a society would have to be known similarly and completely to all the members of a society—to him (and to us) a manifest impossibility. Wallace does not doubt that some actors in a society do share some ideas as well as some actions in common, but he questions the total equivalence of cultural and social wholes. His scepticism forces a fundamental reconsideration of the relationship between *a* culture and *a* society.

In light of his critique, a society may still refer to a group of people in behavioral interaction or interdependence. Society comprehends indirect relations among individuals mediated by others as well as direct face-to-face contact. Supposedly the boundaries of a society would be determined by the limits of this intermediary "groupishness." The boundary would be the point where the indirect relationships of the people were self-contained and independent of contact with others, or at least the number of such contacts would be far fewer than those relations among the members of the society. Such a society would have structured behavior but no necessarily shared ideational content behind the behavioral relations.[17]

To define a society as the behavioral interactions of its members only without any shared cultural content behind

[17] Current practice is to differentiate culture and society and to define society in this manner. The difficulty and the necessity are both demonstrated by James W. Vander Zanden, *Sociology: A Systematic Approach* (New York, 1965), which uses the two concepts very explicitly as its organizational framework.

those social relationships is as false to observable reality as was the total equivalence of a society and a culture. Men group themselves together on the basis of ideation as well as mere behavioral interaction. What a group of men delimit as their society is quite important in terms of their actual behavior. In modern times, for example, some businessmen or members of the so-called "international set" may have more relationships with people across national boundaries than with the citizens of their own countries, but come a war and all this would be expected to and frequently has changed over night. A society cannot, then, be defined without implying some aspect of shared cultural ideation, even if it is only the definition of that society by the people within it. The greater question is whether the concept of *a* culture bears a larger relationship to *a* society than the shared definition of that society's boundaries by its members.

The problem of connecting the conception of a culture to that of a society in terms of the individuals said to manifest them comes to focus in the notion of social role. *Role*, a term obviously borrowed from the vocabulary of the theater, attempts to link the individual with the rest of a group or society both ideationally and behaviorally at the same time. Therefore, it has the problem of reconciling culture as identical group ideation with a group of individuals in stable behavioral interaction. For that reason, it falls heir to all the conceptual difficulties of social science terminology and cannot have a single, simple meaning. The concept must comprehend at once (1) the idea of position (sometimes called status) in the organization of a group or society in meshed behavior, (2) the group ideational definition of that position, and (3) how the individual actually sees and behaves in that position. Role is therefore in the realm of the sociological, the cultural, and the psychological at the same time, and it can be and has been explored in terms of society, culture, and personality. Role must be considered cultural insofar as the individual does understand that he is or should be guided in his actions in a certain position by the definition of others as to how a person acts in that position; he realizes that he is expected to perform according to his and their group definition. The concept is sociological insofar as a study of role is a study of social relationships involved in a set of structured behavioral interactions. To the extent that an individual may recognize the rights and demands of a role and yet refuse to meet group expectations for an incumbent in that position, role is a matter of personality, dependent on psychological factors.[18]

Thus the theory of role embraces all the problems we have encountered so far. Theorists for a long time had presumed consensus between what the individual and what each member of the group or society expected of a person in a given role and also between what the individual did and the other members wanted done in that role. Even though roles may be defined precisely or vaguely, by a small group (often termed a defining or prescribing or sometimes a reference group) or by a whole society, these theorists presumed precise correlation of all persons' conceptions of the position, role activities, and the actual performance of that role. Empirical analysis has not supported this assumption. Just as the historian would expect from his studies, individuals do not have the same definitions of the role or its place in the overall organization of a society.

[18] The classic definition of role and status was given by Ralph Linton, *The Study of Man: An Introduction* (New York, 1936), 113–14. A brief history of the concepts is given by William R. Catton, Jr., "The Development of Sociological Thought," in R. L. Faris, *Handbook of Modern Sociology* (Chicago, 1964), 936–43. Michael Banton, *Roles: An Introduction to the Study of Social Relations* (London, 1965), is an introductory treatment of the subject.

This means that the analyst who would use the theory of role must explore just what consensus on the position and the rights and obligations of the role existed within a society and between the group and the actual incumbent of a position.[19]

The most extensive use of the concept by an historian probed just these problems. Thomas Cochran examined the letters of sixty-one United States railroad executives during the period between 1845 and 1890 to determine their conception of their position and role, their reference group, and the individual variation in the actual performance of the role.[20] Although he did find some personal variety among the executives in concept and action, he discovered on the whole a remarkable similarity in their conception of their position and the "proper" way to conduct business over the forty-five-year period. As time changed, the reference group for the executives became increasingly the small number of Eastern financiers who controlled the stock, although Cochran maintains that they always remained sensitive to the limits on earnings and activities imposed by what they felt were the attitudes of the general society. As a result of his study, Cochran strongly urges

[19] The starting place for those who would deny consensus and seek the relationships by empirical research is Neal Gross, Ward S. Mason, and Alexander McEachern, *Explorations in Role Analysis: Studies of the School Superintendency Role* (New York, 1958). Other works of interest, which contain good bibliographical footnotes, are Daniel J. Levinson, "Role, Personality, and Social Structure in the Organizational Setting," *Journal of Abnormal and Social Psychology*, LVIII (1959), 170–80; J. Milton Yinger, *Toward a Field Theory of Behavior: Personality and Social Structure* (New York, 1965), 98–138; and Ward Goodenough, "Rethinking 'Status' and 'Role': Toward a General Model of the Cultural Organization of Social Relationships," in Max Gluckman and Fred Eggan, eds., *The Relevance of Models for Social Anthropology*, A.S.A. monograph no. 1 (London and New York, 1965), 1–24.
[20] Thomas C. Cochran, *Railroad Leaders, 1845–1890* (Cambridge, Mass., 1953).

the extension of role analysis to other groups and times by historians.[21]

Historians do have frequent recourse to the notion of role and its problems of application even though they may not acknowledge the concept explicitly. How often do historians judge the abilities of a president, or a king, or a capitalist by what they presume are the attributes of the role as ascribed by the society or group they study? Nowhere do we see the advantages and the problems of role theory more than in the field of medieval European history with its emphasis on the feudal organization of society at that time. The whole exposition of feudalism resembles a sociological table of role theory. Though medievalists are interested in proving the consensus upon the pattern in concept and action, they are equally concerned to show the problems of an individual occupying a role or set of roles or the conflict between an individual's and a group's definition of a role. For example, King John, according to one historian, had quite a different interpretation of his position as king of England than did his barons. As a result, the latter felt it necessary to define the role carefully through an explicit contract, the Magna Charta.[22] At another time an historian might examine the conflict among the different roles an individual must play as a result of occupying several positions that demand contradictory actions because of differing expectations about the duties of an incumbent of those statuses. The martyrdom of Thomas Beckett or Thomas More illustrates historically the problem of consistency in what is called the role-set

[21] Thomas C. Cochran, "The Historian's Use of Social Role," in Louis Gottschalk, ed., *Generalization in the Writing of History* (Chicago, 1963), 103–10, and *The Inner Revolution: Essays on the Social Sciences in History* (New York, 1964), 114–56.

[22] C. Warren Hollister, "King John and the Historians," *Journal of British Studies*, I (1961), 1–19.

of an individual. From these common examples, we can see that the notion of role is used often by historians, particularly medievalists, and we also see that they are well aware of the problems of lack of consensus among position, role, and personality.

This brief examination of role theory exemplifies the problem of reconciling the concepts of a culture and a society upon even the elemental level of a social position held by an individual. At the same time, role studies as well as others show that many individuals in a society share an outlook on how to behave as well as manifest similar or complementary behavior.[23] Although an analyst cannot presume identical total cultural ideation for all members of a group in behavioral interaction, neither should he leap to the conclusion that nothing is shared beyond their behavioral interdependence and the idea that they are a society. Rather, the analyst must determine empirically just what is shared or not shared by whom. He must first research what ideation is shared, and in what manner it is shared, and then he must ascertain to what extent the various aspects of shared ideation are possessed by the same people. Much must be shared by most of the same people in behavioral interaction in order for the concept of culture to be applicable to a society or, for that matter, for the concept to be of any use in behavioral analysis at all.

Viewed in the manner developed here, the concepts of a culture and a society have great advantages, for little is

[23] Perhaps the most extended study of this kind is the Harvard Values Project, some of the results of which may be found most conveniently in Evon Z. Vogt and Ethel Albert, eds., *People of Rimrock: A Study of Values in Five Cultures* (Cambridge, Mass., 1966). Relevant to our purposes here is Florence R. Kluckhohn, Fred L. Strodtbeck et al., *Variations in Value Orientations* (Evanston, Ill., 1961). Quite another tack is taken by Theodore M. Newcomb, "The Study of Consensus," in Robert K. Merton, Leonard Broom, and Leonard S. Cottrell, Jr., eds., *Sociology Today: Problems and Prospects* (New York, 1959), 277–92.

presumed in a purely definitional sense alone. The criteria for establishing the referents for the two terms in any given instance are relatively clear. To call a group's total common ideation a culture or their total behavioral interdependence a society would seem to require that the analyst seek to answer how many share how much (behavior or ideation) how similarly (identically or not)? All three parts of the question must be answered because the concepts of culture and society as used traditionally imply that more than one or two people possess or do more than one or two things in a way common to them. Only an empirical study can tell an analyst whether a number of people possess a culture or if they constitute a society. By avoiding the definitional equivalence of the two terms, an analyst can do research on just how a culture, if it is shown to exist, is related to a society, if it is demonstrated to exist, in any given situation. Neither complete overlap nor complete separation need be assumed *a priori* between group behavior labeled a culture and a society, and so the degree of congruence between a total culture and a total society can be studied just as much as the existence of either one of them.[24]

Conceiving of culture and society in such problematical senses aids the historian in clarifying some of the greatest problems in his profession. Not only does this view enable the historical analyst to understand the group behavioral categories and relevant problems expounded in the beginning of this chapter, but it also makes possible new ways of operationalizing or constructing empirical test criteria for some traditional "forces" in history. Surely the study

[24] My whole approach in differentiating culture and society in the manner I have done is in line with the trends in the behavioral sciences. The attempt to specify the separate realms of culture and society found notable expression in the manifesto issued by Alfred Kroeber and Talcott Parsons, "The Concepts of Culture and of Social System," *American Sociological Review*, XXIII (1958), 582–83.

of nationalism, sectionalism, and regionalism can only benefit from the rudimentary distinctions observed here about
culture and society. For example, does not the study of the
causes of the American Civil War need the fresh perspective provided by redefining regionalism as a subculture of
American life and sectionalism as a contraculture? Furthermore, do not these concepts require empirical research in
terms of how many shared how much how similarly? In
short, have not historians assumed a relationship between
a society and a culture that was not proven in this case?[25]
These same comments apply to peoples in other times and
places involved in revolutions, consolidation of nationality,
and even social and cultural change. By separating culture
and society analytically, the historian has added another
way of examining how peoples change their ways of life.
Rather than assuming culture-lag theories or external impetus, the historian can research the dynamics of internal
change by showing the varying relationship between social
changes and cultural changes. Rather than assuming that
one or the other always occurs first, as for example Marxian
theory does, the historical analyst can study the time point
at which changed social practices led to new cultural ideation or vice versa.

Even if we grant all these advantages of our problematical conceptions of culture and society, we still have a
great problem: Just how does the historian go about the
task of establishing the existence of a culture and a society
and the relationship between the two in any given population? Can an historian utilize such an approach to culture
when his subjects are no longer alive and can no longer be
studied at first hand?

[25] A stimulating critique of historians' assumptions about nationalism
has been written by David Potter, "The Historian's Idea of Nationalism
and Vice Versa," *American Historical Review*, LXVII (1962), 924–50.

THE HISTORICAL INVESTIGATION OF SOCIETY AND CULTURE

A problematical approach to the concepts of culture and society presumes that the analyst can investigate the ideation and behavior of the actors so as to determine empirically the specific references for each term in a given case. Is the historian able to explore past men's lives in such a way that he can meaningfully employ culture and society defined this way to aid in historical analysis? Or does the nature of historical evidence preclude the use of these conceptions defined problematically and researched empirically? Is there and must there be a difference between the analyst who investigates a living society and culture and the historian who studies a past society and culture?

The student of a living people goes into the field to explore the answers to his questions about a culture and a society. There he examines human behavior, as manifested by individuals in many forms, for regularities of commission and omission. The late Clyde Kluckhohn describes the process and the hoped-for results of such a search for a culture alone, but I think the passage is equally applicable to the exploration of a society as discussed in this essay.

Behavior is observed for its sequences, tempo, and periodicities; for its incidences and distributions by age, sex, and other roles. Style (emphasis, intensity, and the like) is noted. Behavioral products are analyzed with reference to observed behavior and as sources of information on technologies and motor habits; discriminative choices of materials, as evidencing degree of knowledge of the natural world and attitudes toward nature; and stylistic and aesthetic bents. The recurrent "choices" manifested in behavior and in the products of behavior, are taken as evidence as to which values are most pervasive and what is their rank order. Verbal behavior is studied as is any other behavior sequence but, in addition, as bases of models for: (a) what people say they do; (b) what they say they ought to do. The anthropologist aims at eventual construction of the modalities:

1. Of actual behavior and behavioral products.
2. Of the images individuals have of themselves and others as behaving in the context of this culture.
3. Of conceptions of ideal or desirable behavior in existent or hypothetical situations.

In other words, one needs to deal with regularities on three dimensions: in actuality, in expectation on the part of participants, and in the optative mode.[1]

With behavioral regularities sorted into these three modalities, or dimensions, an analyst could establish step by step just what was a culture, a society, and the connection between the two in any given case.

In theory, if not in practice, a team of social scientists could list all the things that a number of people did in common, said they expected to do in common, and said they ought to do in common because all behavior would be available to the researchers in life. But even in theory the historian's data restrict him to only partial aspects of cultural and social behavior, so he must reconstruct the other aspects from those he possesses. In order to do this, he must utilize the theoretical relationships just to derive what other social analysts have in raw data and from which these other analysts developed the theoretical connections in the first place. Only after deriving as well as he can the behavioral aspects of a culture and a society, can the historian even talk about the relationship between an actual whole culture and whole society. But he presumes the

[1] Clyde Kluckhohn, "Parts and Wholes in Cultural Analysis," in Daniel Lerner, ed., *Parts and Wholes* (New York, 1963), 115.

HISTORICAL INVESTIGATION
OF SOCIETY AND CULTURE

whole culture and whole society in theory initially just so he can interpret his fragmented data and reach this second step. For this reason, the historian should know how social and cultural behaviors connect into societies and cultures so that he can assess his evidence. In other words, he must

understand how actual, expected, and ideal group behaviors might relate to each other in cultural and social theory.

Kluckhohn's tripartite division of all behavioral regularities into the actual, the expected, and the ideal is an attempt, and a successful one I believe, to cut the Gordian knot of confusion surrounding the dichotomy usually denominated the normative and the normal, or more simply the ideal and the real. Few question what the normal means, but it is otherwise with the normative. The normative in social analysis refers to the cultural ideation shared by a group as to what they ought to do and is usually divided into values and norms. Both values and norms are used variously, even interchangeably at times, by social theorists. The dispute over terminology, as it is so often in these cases, is more than mere semantics. In one case, the issue is whether the two terms should refer to the ideally desirable or preferable or the really desired and preferred.[2] On the other hand, a dispute rages over which term should be the more general and comprehensive in referring to the normative regardless of the preceding controversy.[3] In both cases the confusion and profusion of terminology result from the discrepancy between what is said to be social—

[2] For example, Franz Adler, "The Value Concept in Sociology," *American Journal of Sociology*, LXII (1956), 272–79, and Judith Blake and Kingsley Davis, "Norms, Values, and Sanctions," in R. L. Faris, ed., *Handbook of Modern Sociology* (Chicago, 1964), 457–64.

[3] Abraham Edel, "The Concept of Levels in Social Theory," in Llewellyn Gross, ed., *Symposium on Sociological Theory* (New York, 1959), 189–92. In both this debate and the one over ideal versus real, I have made choices of terminology that I believe consistent with the trends in the behavioral sciences.

as opposed to cultural—behavior, and therefore the debates are worth examining from our perspective.

Philosophers usually define values as ends,[4] but sociologists follow John Dewey in stressing the evaluative side of values. Thus to them a value implies a process of evaluation or valuation, and cultural values as opposed to individual values are the standards by which objects and objectives are judged according to an interpersonal process of ranking. The judgment may be explicit as in conscious choice among carefully considered alternatives according to consciously voiced standards or implicit as a predisposition to value those things usually selected or preferred in the society of which the valuator is a member. Evaluation in a cultural sense is then the selection of alternative ends in the ideational process according to a group's standards of the desirable, the worthwhile, the preferable. A cultural value, like any value, is not the object or objective itself; it is the standard by which those are judged. Values are not found in a one-to-one correspondence with a specific object or objective but rather in the pattern of choices. A value is revealed not by one act but by a series of acts. Classically, values have been divided into the good, the true, and the beautiful, but now are termed in some social scientists' jargon, the "directive," the "cognitive," and the "cathectic" orientations.[5]

[4] Two cooperative symposia on the subject edited by Ray Lepley are *Value: A Cooperative Inquiry* (New York, 1949) and *The Language of Value* (New York, 1957). A recent attempt by a philosopher to clarify the concept is George H. von Wright, *The Varieties of Goodness* (London, 1963).

[5] The standard reference is Clyde Kluckhohn, "Values and Value-Orientations in the Theory of Action: An Exploration in Definition and Classification," in Talcott Parsons and Edward A. Shils, eds., *Toward a General Theory of Action* (Cambridge, Mass., 1951), 388–433. Also see F. Kluckhohn, Strodtbeck, et. al., *Variations in Value Orientations* (Evanston, Ill., 1961) and Otto Von Mering, *A Grammar of Human Values*

Regardless of terminology, historians have long used the notion of cultural values as developed by social theorists. Whether historians talk about the pursuit of profit or the traditional middle class virtues of industry, thrift, and sobriety, they are referring to the idea of cultural values pervading a whole series of acts by many people with a similar ideational orientation. The degree to which values are explicit or implicit and the implications of this problem for historical analysis are best left to the next chapter.

Evaluation of ends frequently involves the judgment of means also. Some theorists include the desirable means for accomplishing the desirable ends in their definition of value, but in another sense means constitute another level. The socially preferred or required means for accomplishing cultural ends are called normative rules, or cultural norms for short. Laws, customs, folkways, mores, taboos, conventions, and even etiquette all come under the rubric of cultural norms. Those theorists who argue for the separate use of the term say that it is particularly important to designate this aspect of group ideation for the sake of analyzing social organization. Human populations, they maintain, form social institutions and even a whole society as a result of the group's adherence to cultural norms. According to these theorists, norms define roles, and roles organize into associations, which in turn constitute institutions, and the institutions of a group form a society. In this view, the normative, and particularly norms, represent a blueprint for social interaction.[6]

(Pittsburgh, Pa., 1961). The history of the concept is William L. Kolb, "The Changing Prominence of Values in Modern Sociological Theory," in Howard Becker and Alvin Boskoff, eds., *Modern Sociological Theory: In Continuity and Change* (New York, 1957), 93–132.

[6] A valuable discussion of norms but in a sense broader than I use is Robert Bierstedt, *The Social Order* (2d ed., New York, 1963), 162–67,

The old saying, "a rule is a rule," expresses the conventional wisdom that a rule has many meanings because of variability in its application. So, too, theorists defining norms concern themselves about the degree of conformity required and the diversity of application. William Graham Sumner approached this problem as early as 1906, when he coined the words "folkways" and "mores."[7] Now the terminology is more diverse to take into account more factors, but it still tries to cope with the same basic problems. Kluckhohn alone has employed three different sets of terms: dominant, variant, and deviant; prescriptions, permissions, and prohibitions; and compulsory, preferred, typical, alternative, and restricted.[8] Kluckhohn's, Sumner's, and others' schemes attempt to specify among other things the number of people in a society covered by a given norm, the degree of explicit or implicit recognition of it, the number of situations referred to by the norm, and the nature and severity of the sanction prescribed for its violation by an individual in the society. In other words, distribution, enforcement, and conformity are the chief topics analysts must consider in talking about the cultural norms of a present or a past population.[9]

220–56. Another textbook treatment is James Vander Zanden, *Sociology: A Systematic Approach* (New York, 1965), 38–62. A philosopher's analysis is George H. von Wright, *Norm and Action: A Logical Enquiry* (London, 1963).

[7] He has a whole book devoted to the topics, *Folkways: A Study of the Sociological Importance of Usages, Manners, Customs, Mores, and Morals* (Boston, 1906), especially chaps. 1 and 2.

[8] Compare his own and his use of Linton's terms in "Study of Culture," in Daniel Lerner and Harold D. Lasswell, eds., *The Policy Sciences, Recent Developments in Scope and Method* (Stanford, 1951), 88–9, 95, with those in "Values and Value-Orientations," in Parsons and Shils, eds., *op. cit.*, 415.

[9] See the typologies in Blake and Davis, *op. cit.*, 464–65; Robin C. Williams, *American Society: A Sociological Interpretation* (2d ed., New York, 1961), 26–27; and Richard T. Morris, "A Typology of Norms," *American Sociological Review*, VII (1956), 611–12.

It is this element of sanction, whether ridicule or coercion or even murder, that distinguishes a norm from a value. Social theorists point out that cultural norms have sanctions to ensure conformity to the group's standards; values do not. Values in this sense are only goals or principles in terms of which specific norms are claimed to be desirable. Not everything valued has a specific norm, for example, participation in a national sport, and not all norms have values attached as such, for instance, stopping at a traffic light. The worth of these two concepts for the historian is not to differentiate between them but to look for them beneath group behavior.

"A rule is a rule" for other reasons, the reader thinks, and he is correct. Thus far our analysis has concerned only the "theoretical" side of rule making and rule following. What about the actual practices of individuals in a population? Does their behavior individually and collectively conform more or less to the supposedly prescribed rules? Here we encounter another definition of norm that means normal. Norm, in this sense, may indicate the average, the typical, the modal, but it is essentially a statistical term for conceptualizing the most recurrent in a range. Applied to human behavior, this norm means what most people actually do or did.

In the realm of social theory, the norm as normative and the norm as normal should coincide, for after all the normative was supposedly derived from the normal of behavioral regularities. In the language of diagram, the two norms should appear ideally identical as shown in Figure 5–1. Or at least the majority of people's practices should cluster close to the ideal standard, as shown in Figure 5–2. Far too frequently, however, the graph of actual behavior, as shown in Figure 5–3, departs greatly from the norm of supposedly ideal behavior.

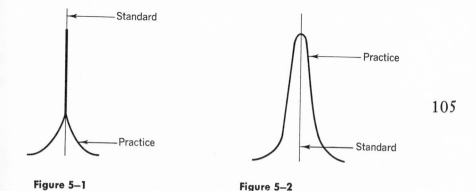

Figure 5–1   Figure 5–2

That the two do not always or even frequently coincide results partly from the discrepancy between culture as group ideation and society as behavioral interdependence. Partly, however, the discrepancy arises because people do not always act according to their professed values or norms. What they assert as desirable is not what they do desire. In both cases, there are those theorists who would confine the conception of value and norm to whatever is really desired and done as shown by deed rather than by word. Should the terms value and norm refer only to the real realms of behavior?[10]

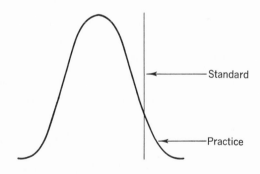

Figure 5–3

[10] As argued by the authors cited in note 2 of this chapter.

HISTORICAL INVESTIGATION
OF SOCIETY AND CULTURE

If there is an ideational side to behavior, then this dispute is not merely a distinction between professed ideals and real practices as so frequently alleged. Given our basic orientation to human action, what people actually do is as much a result of ideation as what they say they ought to do. Rather the difference between "ideal" and "real" must be conceived of as different values and norms discovered through different types of behavior. Ideals are usually derived from symbolic expressions, or what people state they ought to do, whereas so-called "real" values and norms are deduced from observed choices of artifact and activity, or from what people do do. Both ideal and real are forms of behavior then, and both are based upon ideational sources. Only an invidious comparison of one type of behavior as more "real" than another type of behavior could produce the confused division between actuality and the normative so often propounded in the texts, which imply that the normative is ideational alone and that "actual" behavior is based somehow on a more "basic" source.

An analyst may choose to say that the normative only refers to ideal values and norms rather than operational values and norms, but this distinction seems arbitrary if real actions are also ideational in source. For this reason, many theorists would use "normative" as the overall designation for both ideal and real behavior, and then use "values" to designate the ideational ideals and "norms" to refer to the ideation behind real behavior. Others, however, would reverse these meanings to confuse further the problem of definition.[11]

At this point Kluckhohn's tripartite division demon-

---

[11] A brief but good statement of the problem is Arnold Rose, "A Systematic Summary of Symbolic Interaction Theory," in Rose, ed., *Human Behavior and Social Processes: An Interactionist Approach* (Boston, 1962), 6n. Also see Edel, *op. cit.*

strates its superiority by both clarifying the controversy and eliminating the jargon in favor of more usual language. The normative includes both the ideal and the expected in his terms, and the normal comprehends both the expected and the actual. From the actor's standpoint, the normative may be both the ideal and the actual behavior he anticipates. From his view, he may profess one ideal but expect to do something quite different, and he anticipates the same in others. In both cases, however, the resulting behavior is expected, hence predictable to him. For this reason the normative should be divided into the ideal values and norms and the operative values and norms. The objective behavior seen by an observer may be ideal, expected, or actual. If it is ideal and/or expected, then we have normative behavior. If it is neither ideal nor expected, then it is nonnormative. Yet if all three modes of behavior are based upon regularity of observed repetition, then it means that the nonnormative behavior is not individualistic but social in origin and must be the result of recurring unanticipated consequences of aimed-for behavior. It is noncultural social behavior, which means it must be studied from the observer's viewpoint alone. On the other hand, values and norms, whether ideal or operative, are ends and means in group-held ideational interpretations. As such they can be and must be studied from the actor's viewpoint.

In this view, discrepancy between rhetoric and reality, profession and practice is as natural as the correlation between the two, and the social analyst should expect both to occur in his study of group behavior. For this reason the analyst must pay attention to both symbolic and nonsymbolic behaviors. He must not study just verbal statements of what they ought to do or want to do or even what they ought to want to do. Neither should he examine artifact and activity alone and feel he has the whole picture. Like any social analyst, the historian too is obliged to study both word and deed in order to avoid a fallacious contrast between the ideal and real, or worse, confuse the one with the other.

Given the nature of his evidence, it is far harder for the historian to distinguish between the ideal and the expected, let alone between the expected and actual group behavior, than for the observer who can witness his data in the living present. Only a constant awareness of the distinctions developed here can serve the historian in his search in his sources for the truth about past group behavior. He must constantly ask, Does the evidence really show what it purports to about the "ideal" and "real" in group behavior? In any given instance, there would seem to exist nine possibilities as indicated in Table 5–4.

Table 5–4

EVIDENCE PURPORTS TO SHOW	EVIDENCE REALLY SHOWS		
	Ideal	Expected	Actual
Ideal	1	4	7
Expected	2	5	8
Actual	3	6	9

While an historian may presume that historical sources can give insight into both behavior and ideation, any given set of documents may be biased in favor of one aspect of the ideal, expected, or actual more than another aspect. In fact, given the ideational source of documents, it is likely that historical evidence would particularly reveal the ideal and the expected far more than actual behavior. Therefore, historians would be particularly prone to commit the fallacy of asserting that people actually did what they only maintained they ought to do or expected to do. On the other hand, the historian might well maintain erroneously that people really desired to do what he believes they actually did according to his evidence.

Perhaps the most blatant example of an historian committing these two fallacies is that of Frederick Jackson Turner. Because Turner accepted the rhetoric of newspaper, diary, and travel accounts at face value, he assumed that the American trans-Appalachian West was settled by self-subsisting yeoman farmers who practiced a high degree of economic, social, and political democracy and who as a result produced a classless society. Such a conclusion disregarded the plantations of the Old Southwest with their slave pioneers and the huge speculative land holdings and large estates populated by tenants in the Old Northwest. Turner erred in his analysis of the frontier because he accepted the nineteenth-century American ideology of equalitarianism and individualism as an adequate description of real behavior. His substitution of a professed ideal value system for the operative values (and norms) resulted in a particularly mistaken description of the actual social and economic behavior of most nineteenth-century frontiersmen. As a further consequence of his confusion, he wrongly attributed the cause of his mythical reality to the westward expansion of American society, which he then maintained promoted the very ideology that he accepted as his proof of all this in the first place.[12]

In a second error, Turner presumed documents purporting to show actual behavior indicated operative and ideal values likewise. Because many pioneering farmers

[12] For both an analysis of Turner's assumptions and an alternative approach to the frontier, see Robert F. Berkhofer, Jr., "Space, Time, Culture and the New Frontier," *Agricultural History*, XXVIII (1964), 21–30.

built log cabins and tilled small self-subsisting plots of ground in a newly settled frontier area did not mean that they preferred crude accommodations and nonprofit to the joys of commodious frame houses and large commercial farms worked by hired men or slaves. Documents reporting how men lived at a given moment on the frontier, then, do not reveal necessarily what these men really desired in the long run nor even the aims sought by moving to the frontier. Turner simply presumed that pioneers wanted to do and liked to do what they did—a clearly unwarranted assumption in light of Kluckhohn's three categories of the ideal, the expected, and the actual in group behavior.[13]

110

The lesson to be learned from these two examples is the obvious one learned long ago by the historian: Never accept a document at face value. What the distinctions between ideal and operative values and norms and between expected and actual group behavior add is a more sophisticated checklist to the process of the derivation and synthesis of facts. The categories reinforce and expand the elementary distinction between the ideational and the behavioral as applied to group activities. They also remind the historian that his evidence for group behavior is the result of an actor's or actors' interpretation of a situation, and that frequently the culturally normative enters into such an interpretation so as to conceal the actual behavior and perhaps even cloud the difference between the ideal and the expected as well.

An application of these categories to the debate over colonial American democracy mentioned in the first chapter makes a positive contribution. Dividing group behavior into the ideal, the expected, and the actual immediately

[13] Rodney C. Loehr, "Self-Sufficiency on the Farm," *Agricultural History*, XXVI (1952), 37–45.

shows that the polarization of the controversy into two sides oversimplifies the possibilities. Those historians who prove the existence of democracy by statistics of actual voting neglect the ideal and the expected.[14] Their opponents who deny colonial democracy by reference to ideal values espoused in literary sources and to ideal norms as codified in laws omit the expected and the actual.[15] Both sides need an agenda for further research in the evidence based upon the categories of the ideal, expected, and actual developed in this chapter. Such an agenda must contain the following queries at a minimum:

1. Who could vote according to the laws of the various colonies? The answers to this question would provide the ideal norms as codified by law.

2. Who were allowed to vote but did not meet the legal standards? This question elicits the operative norms, for apparently men voted who did not possess the legally specified privilege.

3. Who did vote in the elections? Many men did not bother to vote although they could legally or extralegally do so. Thus this answer would specify actual behavior.

4. For whom did the voters vote? This query produces the actual, expected, and ideal values represented by the candidates. Studies suggest that the electorate voted generally for the "better sort," as they would have phrased it, and this fact indicates an identity of the ideal and operative values underlying representation.

[14] The leading representative of this school is Robert E. Brown, *Middle-Class Democracy and the Revolution in Massachusetts, 1691–1780* (Ithaca, N.Y., 1955) and, with B. Katherine Brown, *Virginia, 1705–1786: Democracy or Aristocracy?* (East Lansing, Mich., 1964).

[15] There is no clear representative of this school today, but see the complex analysis of Charles S. Sydnor, *Gentlemen Freeholders* (Chapel Hill, N.C., 1952).

5. Whom did the officials once elected think they represented? Did the officials believe they were of, by, and for the people? If not, as several studies indicate, then the officials did not conceive of democracy as the system of values and norms we mean today.

6. How was the term *democracy* used at that time? Most historians would maintain that the term as then employed possessed a deprecative connotation unlike today's usage. Thus this question probes the ideal and expected values surrounding the concept as used then.

By just posing this brief agenda of queries we see how oversimplified much of the debate has been and the irrelevancy of some of the research based upon those over-simplifications.

The utility of Kluckhohn's distinctions is seen again in analyzing the seeming hypocrisy of Jacksonian Americans, who professed one set of ideals and yet operated in quite another way. The period that Turner erroneously saw as the fruition of the frontier heritage was indeed one in which many Americans professed a belief in the ideal values of equality and individualism whether they were expected to be manifested in small yeoman farms, minimal laissez-faire government, or universal white manhood suffrage. In other words, Americans said they hoped and expected to create an atomistic, equalitarian society of small entrepreneurs. Yet at the same time they professed these values, most Negroes were enslaved, large plantations and farms did exist, and perhaps most incongruous of all, industrialism was in the take-off phase, to borrow a fashionable phrase. Industrialism was to introduce the hierarchical organization of men into a tightly knit society of economic and social interdependence that made a complete mockery of the earlier ideals. How can an historian explain this bundle of seeming paradoxes?

Resort to our analytical system clarifies the problems at issue so that they may be explained and even partially explains them at the same time. The contradictions concern the inconsistencies between ideal and operative values and norms in some cases and between the expected and the actual in other cases. The paradoxes may be resolved in several ways. Men in a society may not realize the long-range implications of the values and norms they believed compatible at one time. Surely, many of the long-term effects of industrialism were seen by very few Americans before the Civil War, and even they were still fascinated by its promise of plenty and its mechanical index of the nation's progress.[16] Then, too, men may never have seen that certain of their basic values were incompatible with each other. Even today most Americans believe that equality and achievement, for example, are compatible, but achievement introduces inequality in some way, and equality would change to some degree the results of achievement. Yet Americans seem not at all bothered by this contradiction.[17] In still another way, some avowed ideals may be subordinated in the system of values to ideals deemed higher in the hierarchy of evaluation, because these higher values demand at times action denying those lower in the hierarchy. Was the pursuit of profit a higher value in the ante-bellum South than the equality of all individuals?

113

[16] The ambivalence of Americans toward industrialism can be seen in Leo Marx, *The Machine in the Garden: Technology and the Pastoral Ideal in America* (New York, 1964).

[17] The conflict between the values of achievement and equality in the history of the American people is the theme of Seymour M. Lipset, *The First New Nation: The United States in Historical Perspective* (New York, 1963). Although Lipset implies the conflict began in 1776, his evidence would indicate that the incongruity can be traced back no farther than the time of Jackson.

Were Negroes then more merchandise than men?[18] When encountering such a conflict of values and the subordination of one value to another as shown by contradictory actions, the analyst must determine whether this subordination is common to the whole population or only to part of it. If it is true of the whole population, then we have discovered a portion of their value rankings. If it occurs in only a portion of the population, then we have perhaps uncovered a subgroup or a subculture.

Once again we have returned to the basic problem of relating a culture to a society and its implications for defining subculture, contraculture, regionalism, sectionalism, nationalism, and a host of other terms assuming degrees of sociocultural integration. This time, however, we have refined our analysis by an additional set of categories. To the quantitative question of how many shared how much in what way (or how similarly), we have added the group behavioral categories of the ideal, the expected, and the actual. Sociocultural integration must be studied in terms of how many of a population espouse and/or practice how many ideals, expectations, and actual behaviors in how similar a way? The answer—or really answers, for it is such a compound question—will help establish to what extent a population is (1) a society, (2) a culture as well as a society, and (3) has subcultures within the culture. A society may be simply a group of people in behavioral interdependence in which neither ideals nor even expectations are held in common. Although such a case would be unusual, it is nevertheless possible theoretically. Surely few values and only some norms need be shared between a conqueror and a subjugated people, but they still form a society. To be said to constitute a culture many people

---

[18] A good analysis of values regarding bondage in Western civilization is David B. Davis, *The Problem of Slavery in Western Culture* (Ithaca, N.Y., 1966).

should share many ideals and expectations in common as well as practice similar behavior. Just as a society could be composed of several cultures, so a culture could contain several societies, as in the case of the living patterns of certain American Indian tribes in which the people interacted together in groups smaller than the culture shared by the tribe or even across tribes,[19] or of the relation, say, of French, German, and English societies to the culture of Western civilization. If many ideals, expectations, and/or actual behaviors are confined to a group smaller than those said to constitute the culture, then we have a subculture. A few ideas or a few acts do not establish a subculture, but a system of ideas and many acts practiced by a group in behavioral interdependence make a subculture.

Historians must view the problems of regionalism, sectionalism, and nationalism in terms of sociocultural integration, if they are to ask complex enough questions of their data. Only empirical analysis of agreement and disagreement upon ideal and operative values and norms, the amount of similarity in actual behavior, and the degree of behavioral interdependence will reveal the answers needed by historians to reconstruct the nature of sociocultural integration in a past population. Regionalism and sectionalism both involve subcultural phenomena but in the former case the ideals and expectations of the subgroup are permitted as variant behavior within the society, whereas in the latter case both the bearers of the major culture and the subculture see the variety as conflicting. A nation in theory may range from relatively close correlation between a society and a culture to an amalgam of subcultures and

[19] Although a controversial article, I believe this is one of the clear implications of Alfred L. Kroeber, "Nature of the Land-Holding Group," *Ethnohistory*, II (1965), 303–14. Also see Julian N. Steward, *Theory of Cultural Change: The Methodology of Multilinear Evolution* (Urbana, Ill., 1955), 43–63, and George P. Murdock, *Social Structure* (New York, 1949), 79–90.

even cultures with nothing binding together the population to allow it to be called a nation except the idea of nationhood. By posing the queries raised here, an analyst of nationalism could construct an index of possibilities ranging from complete sociocultural integration to nothing but a population possessing the idea of common boundaries. With such a scale he could compare one nation with another at the same time or even with itself at different times. The more a nation approaches relative sociocultural integration, the more national character and basic personality studies would be possible and the more revealing they would be. The more a nation departs from this integration, the less possible it would be to perform national character and basic personality studies, because both depend upon the assumption of equivalence between cultures and society. Their utility rapidly diminishes and soon disappears as that equivalence decreases.[20]

[20] Vast quantities of material exist on the notion of national character, but the historian should begin with David Potter, *People of Plenty: Economic Abundance and American Character* (Chicago, 1954), especially 3–72, and Walter P. Metzger, "Generalizations about National Character: An Analytical Essay," in Louis Gottschalk, ed., *Generalization in the Writing of History* (Chicago, 1963), 77–102. Commentaries on the behavioral sciences approach to national character are Alex Inkeles and Daniel J. Levinson, "National Character: the Study of Modal Personality and Sociocultural Systems," in Gardner Lindzey, ed., *Handbook of Social Psychology* (Reading, Mass., 1954), vol. 2, 977–1020, and Margaret Mead, "National Character," in Alfred L. Kroeber, ed., *Anthropology Today: An Encyclopedic Inventory* (Chicago, 1953), 642–67. Two good introductions to the field of culture and personality are two books with the same title: Victor Barnouw, *Culture and Personality* (Homewood, Ill., 1963), and John Honigman, *Culture and Personality* (New York, 1954). An annotated bibliography of studies of culture and personality, national character, and of American character specifically is compiled by Michael McGiffert, "Selected Writings on American National Character," *American Quarterly*, XV (1936), pt. 2, 271–88. Julian N. Steward, *op. cit.*, attempts to provide a scale of sociocultural integration. For a method of analyzing sociocultural integration as an index of nationalism, consult Karl W. Deutsch, *Nationalism and Social Communication: An Inquiry into the Foundations of Nationality* (Cambridge, Mass., and

Both culture and society are here viewed as concepts referring to human social behavior but in terms of different analytical aspects of that behavior. Culture is the shared ideation behind social behavior among groups, and society is the group of people in social behavioral interdependence. Although both concepts can refer to the same people doing the same things at a given time, it is not necessarily the case that both terms need refer to coterminous behavioral phenomena in a population. For this reason, it was felt necessary to set up quantitative criteria and categories of behavior to specify the criteria for determining what was *a* culture and *a* society and the possibilities of sociocultural integration in any given population. At the same time that the behavioral categories tell us what to look for in behavior, they also give us the possibilities of finding such data in historical evidence, given the sources of that evidence. The ideal and the expected are more likely to be the basis of historical evidence than the actual behavior that was neither ideal nor expected by a population. If this probability is a limiting factor on historical evidence, then it would seem that a culture would be more readily accessible to historical reconstruction than a society. It would also mean that the concept of culture is more important to the historian than the concept of society in terms of use. Although the historian must use one conception to check and balance the other in his research and his writing, still he will apply cultural concepts to his data more frequently than social concepts given the ideational source of his documentation. Thus even further refinement in the concept of culture would appear desirable, and this is the task of the next chapter.

New York, 1953). A political scientist's excursion into the historical domain to research this kind of topic is Richard L. Merritt, *Symbols of American Community, 1735-1775* (New Haven, Conn., and London, 1966).

HISTORICAL INVESTIGATION
OF SOCIETY AND CULTURE

CULTURE AND
THE STUDY OF
THE ACTORS'
VIEWPOINT

The essential task of the culture concept is to tell us something about the viewpoint of a group of actors. No matter how problematical or empirical a definition of culture advocated, the analyst's construction of a culture still purports to suggest why the actors do what they do in terms of how they collectively define and interpret situations. The attempt to understand collective situational definitions and interpretations as the actors who shared them understood them poses grave problems for translating the actors' view into observer's analysis. The problems revolve about the extent to which cultural ideation can be viewed by the historical or other analyst in the same manner as the actors who are said to possess the culture view it.

One problem of translation arises from the effort to specify the degree of consciousness with which the supposedly common definitions and interpretations are held. Social theorists agree that culture is a pervasive aspect of human life and a crucial, if not central, element in shaping men's activities, whether men are aware of it or not—just as a grammar pervades and shapes a language even though the speakers may be unaware of the rules. That the people said to bear the culture may be unaware of many of the shared rules, so to speak, raises this problem of translation. How can the analyst call these unformulated rules culture if the people do not see their ideation in that manner? This problem may appear less troublesome for the historian than other analysts because so much of his evidence is in the form of consciously articulated ideation. Further examination, however, will show that the problem is no less difficult for the historian than for other analysts of culture.

Another problem of translation results from the attempt to treat a culture as a whole. Even if an analyst listed all that a group of people did in common, said they expected to do in common, or said they ought to do in common, he still in the opinion of many theorists has not characterized a culture. They would maintain that he has merely provided a catalog, for an ethnographic enumeration, they argue, is to culture what a chronological list is to history. It is considered a beginning, but only a beginning, in the depiction of a culture, for it tells at best how much of what was shared by how many. Although it is important to answer these queries, the question of in what way the whole ideation was shared is left unanswered, and to the proponents of cultural holism this question is fundamental. In other words, they assert that the ideational parts composing a culture form a cultural whole that is a very particular configuration of those parts. Some theorists even argue that the whole of a culture is more than the sum of its parts.

At first glance, this second problem would seem to be resolved by a mere statement of the components of a culture and how they fit together, but our analysis of the concept in the preceding chapters precludes such an easy answer. Even if we admit that ideation may be shared to some extent by a group of people, we still are left with many problems concerning the actor-observer relationship in depicting the whole of a culture. Is the locus of a total culture in the individual actors as well as in the analyst observing them? Is a culture considered as a whole only a logical entity in the mind of the observer constructed from observed symbolic and nonsymbolic behavior; or is it also present in a similar manner in the minds of the population to whom it is attributed? Some theorists avoid the problem by urging that the depiction of a total culture is a construction of the observer alone. Like all concepts, the concept of a culture is, of course, a construction of the theorist, but is it more than that? More precisely, therefore, the question is, To what extent does and can the observer's construct of a whole culture have reference to some reality in the actors being studied?

In order to explore these problems of translation, we must divide culture into its components and then try to put them back together again. Traditionally, culture has been divided into mentifacts, sociofacts, and artifacts, or what men think, do, and have, but this scheme is confusing and superficial in light of current theory. It would seem to imply that how men relate socially and what they produce is of a different order from what they think. Such an implication is untenable from the viewpoint of the behavioral orientation adopted in Chapter 2. Sociofacts and artifacts are just as much products of ideation as the symbolic manifestations called mentifacts. Therefore, we must divide a culture according to categories of ideation, and this is what causes the dilemmas of research for the would-be analyst. The difficulty occurs not because the possible classifications might be infinite, as any good encyclopedia shows, and not because the ideational realm is difficult to explore, which it is, but because the observer can hardly understand the totality of one person's cultural ideation without translation difficulties, let alone understand all the ideation shared by a group denominated a culture. Nevertheless, we must resolve this translation problem of a total culture in the end if we are to utilize the culture concept in historical analysis.[1]

---

[1] The whole problem of translation of cultural ideational categories is the subject of many of the essays in F. S. C. Northrop and Helen H. Livingston, eds., *Cross-Cultural Understanding: Epistemology in Anthropology* (New York, 1964).

The analyst must reduce the chaos of infinite possible divisions of cultural ideation to an intellectually manageable number in order to talk about the problems of this phase of cultural analysis. By this very process, however, the analyst, like the historian who by the very selection of facts from the past distorts history in a sense, may distort the actors' culture he attempts to portray. Thus, in this very first step at clarification, we must try to arrive at categories that are both comprehensive and also true to the shared ideation of a specific culture. Essentially, we face the task of creating general categories for the delineation of cultural components that do not distort the culture bearers' specific methods of categorizing. Again we can thank Clyde Kluckhohn for his plan to reduce chaos to complexity and not simplicity. In his opinion a portrait of a whole culture must detail three basic divisions of ideation.

1. Salient Categories. Which categories are used most frequently to order experience? Do some categories have a kind of evident primacy, either in the sense that they are ultimate and not discussable or in the sense that many other categories can be shown to be merely group-specified subsets of a more embracing concept? The major categories may be named in the lexicon or they may be cryptocategories (that is, features of the implicit culture). If the culturally distinctive categories are named, they are likely to present peculiar difficulties in rendering the terms into another language.
2. Existential Premises. How is the world and experience in it conceived? What forms of relatedness are held to exist between events? What inexorable limits does nature, including human nature, put upon the satisfaction of human desires and aspirations?
3. Evaluative Premises. What are the final standards of the right and the good?[2]

From his distinctions we derive two basic categories of

2 Clyde Kluckhohn, "Parts and Wholes in Cultural Analysis," in Daniel Lerner, ed., *Parts and Wholes* (New York, 1963), 121.

group definitions and interpretations: the existential, or what a group believes is (knowledge) and believes to be (belief), and the normative, or what a group thinks and feels is desirable and preferable. Kluckhohn's first category would seem to be a combination of the other two and yet

122

more comprehensive than the mere sum of them.

Of all the categories the existential would seem easiest for the historian to portray accurately according to the views of the actors he studies without superimposing his ideas on theirs. Knowledge and belief shade into one another, for both are aspects of the situational definition and interpretation considered existentially true by the actors. Both gods and houses are asserted to exist, but only one has an empirical reference—according to *our* definition of the situation. The defining of what really is (knowledge) and what is only believed to be (belief) depends upon the culture under study. The historian's dual perspective upon the past requires him to be careful to label what is knowledge and what is belief both according to the thinking of the people he studies and according to the attitudes prevailing in his own society. To do otherwise would falsify past thinking, hence past action.

Historical evidence readily discloses beliefs and knowledge, but the problem is to differentiate between the two in the past. The further we recede in time from our culture, the more difficult it would appear to be to distinguish knowledge from belief. Hence, the more likely it is that what others in the past considered existential truth will be labeled myth or legend. Myth and legend in this sense connote the false or unreal as well as being neutral terms designating a viable, that is, a believed-in system of propositions about reality. In fact, most analysts who deal with the realms of myth take as their subject matter

the beliefs of primitive or ancient men, whom they assume
possess a prelogical, mythopoetic intellect inherent in the
early stages of man's social evolution as opposed to the
mature rationality of modern man.[3] Myth as understood
by these people is equated with superstition and is judged
to be that by comparison with current beliefs about presumably the same categories of experience. Although an
analyst may judge past men's thoughts in this manner,
such action upon the part of an historian is a denial of his
attempt to understand the past in the same manner as the
actors did who lived then.[4]

This unhistorical approach to myth and reality is not
confined to students of ancient man. Many of the authors
of the so-called "image" school of American Studies commit the scholarly sin of deliberately implying that what
the actors believed to be actuality was really only a myth.
Henry Nash Smith, who has already two generations of
imitators, shows this confusion in his very definition of
the terms myth and symbol. According to him, he uses
the two words "to designate larger or smaller units of the
same kind of thing, namely, an intellectual construction
that fuses concept and emotion into an image." He goes
on to say, "The myths and symbols with which I deal
have the further characteristic of being collective representations rather than the work of a single mind." Then he
continues in two confusing sentences: "I do not mean to

[3] Among many in this school, some of the more famous recent works
are Gilbert Murray, *Five Stages of Greek Religion* (London, 1943);
Ernst Cassirer, *Language and Myth*, Susanne K. Langer, trans. (New
York and London, 1946); Susanne K. Langer, *Philosophy in a New
Key: A Study in the Symbolism of Reason, Rite, and Art* (Cambridge,
Mass., 1942); Henri Frankfort, H. A. G. Frankfort, *et al.*, *The Intel-
lectual Adventure of Ancient Man* (Chicago, 1946).
[4] Good, brief introductions to the subject of myth are David Bidney,
Theoretical Anthropology (New York, 1953), 286–326, and Ben Hal-
pern, " 'Myth' and 'Ideology' in Modern Usage," *History and Theory*,
I (1961), 129–49.

CULTURE AND THE
STUDY OF THE
ACTOR'S VIEWPOINT

raise the question whether such products of the imagination accurately reflect empirical fact, they exist on a different plane. But as I have tried to show, they sometimes exert a decided influence on practical affairs."[5] How can myths and symbols as he defines them not exert influence upon practical affairs if they really are "collective representations"? If the actors thought their images were reality, why should the observer not accept this as the actors' view, if that is what he is trying to study? If the observer does want to separate actors' and observer's views, then he does question whether the images reflected empirical fact despite his disclaimers to the contrary. As a result of this confusion between the actors' and the observer's beliefs and knowledge, Smith becomes hopelessly entwined in separating what he calls "myth" from reality and contradicting his espoused aim. Why does he use the word "myth" at all in this case with its ambiguous meaning, unless he means to trade upon both meanings of the word?[6]

To determine what is myth as opposed to what is knowledge, the historian must produce explicit evidence that the actors of the past believed a certain story or certain proposition about reality to be false. He cannot use as his guide to the distinction between "myth" and "reality" the modern judgment upon the same categories of experience. The time when a population moves from considering some of its fundamental beliefs no longer true to reality but to be myth does mark a significant turning point in its cultural history. The evidence for such a transition must not be a theory, particularly one based on social evolution, but explicit behavioral indication by word or deed that what they

[5] Henry Nash Smith, *Virgin Land: The American West as Symbol and Myth* (Cambridge, Mass., 1950), v.
[6] Compare Barry Marks, "The Concept of Myth in *Virgin Land*," *American Quarterly*, V (1953), 71–76.

A BEHAVIORAL APPROACH
TO HISTORICAL ANALYSIS

once believed true is now seen as false by them. This is the
only proof that can be adduced to prove this important
transition, for any other method of judgment violates the
historian's attempt to reconstruct the past in terms of the
actors' definitions and interpretations of situations. Any
other position on this question is, in fact, a contradiction
of the fundamental premise of the culture concept, for if
nothing else, this concept urges the observer to attempt to
see the world as those under study saw it.

Although the normative must contain an existential
element, its chief characteristic is independent of that.
Values and norms must presume the natural conditions of
the universe as conceived by the actors bearing a culture,
but at the same time values and norms are not limited by
those conditions. What *is* determines what might be, but
what *ought to be* is not limited solely to what is. On the
other hand, what ought to be frequently does shade into
what is as believed by the actors. Thus the normative may
be separated analytically from the existential, although the
two realms interpenetrate to some extent.

The normative also shades into the emotional in the
sense that the definition of normative implies that values
and norms are more than mere mental notions. The normative implies that what ought to be elicits an emotional response of desire or repulsion. Feeling as well as thought
composes the realm of the normative, so that some motivation underlies what ought to be in order that the ought
should promote activity. The ought to be of the normative
implies that an interpersonal selection of the desirable has
an emotional commitment to it.[7]

[7] The best starting places for an introduction to the normative realm
are given in notes 5 and 6 of the last chapter plus the essays by Clyde
Kluckhohn and William L. Kolb in Donald N. Barrett, ed., *Values in
America* (Notre Dame, Ind., 1961), 17–54.

*CULTURE AND THE
STUDY OF THE
ACTOR'S VIEWPOINT*

This element of choice poses the problem we are considering in this chapter, for the normative is more than the merely desired; it is the standard by which the selection is made. Thus values and norms cannot be identified with specific ends or means but rather with the criteria by which the specific ends and means are chosen. The normative therefore has no specific referent but must be derived from a number of actions, verbal and nonverbal. As we said in the last chapter,

> A value is not the object or objective itself; it is the standard by which those are judged. Values [and norms] are not found in a one-to-one correspondence with a specific object or objective, but rather in the pattern of choices. It is not one act but the orientation of a series of acts.

Such a definition raises the question of just how well the actors understand the cultural values and norms attributed to them. Is the pattern observed and called a value or a norm by the analyst also known in the same manner to the actors? If values or norms were equated with specific ends or means, we would have no problem at all.

Again Jacksonian America affords a good example of the dilemma. John H. Ward discovers individualism manifested in actions as diverse as Andrew Jackson's justification for the expulsion of the Cherokees by force from Georgia, Ralph Waldo Emerson's essay *Politics*, and an anonymous author's article, "The Course of Civilization." In each case, he finds the value through an explicit espousal of individualism, and we have no trouble in seeing that the analyst and the actors see the value in the same way. But when Ward continues to find individualism manifested in general acts of incorporation, landscape gardening and architecture, and the religious doctrine of the perfect law of liberty for the righteous, we wonder whether the actors conceived these in the same manner as the pattern Ward traces. I do not question Ward's analysis for I believe it is correct, but can we say individualism in the second list of things is part of the American culture of the period in the same way that explicit individualism is in the first list? Did Jacksonian Americans even see individualism and equalitarianism, which they talked about a great deal as part of their way of life, in the same manner that, for example, de Tocqueville did?[8]

The problem outlined here is usually solved in terms of explicit and implicit culture, but is such a simple solution really satisfactory? The problem is more dramatically posed in the first of Kluckhohn's divisions of culture, salient categories.

In all the examples in this and the last chapter from Jacksonian America, it is obvious that it is difficult to separate specific values and norms from a larger complex of values and norms and even, in the case of the frontier, from belief and knowledge. If evaluation occurs, then the whole chain of ends, means, and conditions can be evaluated. It follows that knowledge, beliefs, values, and norms will and can be all combined in the actors' ideation. For example, what some men feel is desirable and ought to be desirable even influences their perceptions of existential reality as well as their behavior toward it. Thus the frontier seemed to nineteenth-century Americans and therefore to Turner to be an actual place of classlessness and rampant individualism because that was their ideal.[9] Evaluation as an

[8] In anticipation of his forthcoming book on the history of American individualism, we can only cite his speech before the American Historical Association at San Francisco on December 29, 1965, "Cultural Anthropology and History." For his techniques, see John W. Ward, *Andrew Jackson: Symbol for an Age* (New York, 1955).

[9] For the nineteenth-century background on Turner's thinking, consult Smith, *op. cit.* The confusion between ideology and actual practice in

overall process involves the selection of alternative orientations to the total perception, definition, and interpretation of the situation by a group of people.

Cultural ideation may then be examined in larger categories that embrace this notion of overall evaluation. Clyde Kluckhohn coined the term "value-orientation" to designate such "a set of linked propositions embracing both value and existential elements."[10] Specific values, norms, beliefs, and ideas cluster into a patterned whole called the orientation or, in his later terminology, the "salient category." When a social analyst employs the term "value," he frequently means this broader category of the orientation. Such an orientation again has no one manifestation, for the orientation is the thread running through the diverse actions. Many other terms have been invented to describe such a basic aspect of the cultural definition and interpretation of situations—culture theme, core or dominant values, cultural premises[11]—but all refer to the fundamental orientations of the culture bearers in their approach to the world as they think it is and ought to be. A value orientation is, to use Kluckhohn's words again, a "generalized and organized conception, influencing behavior, of nature, of

---

observations on Jacksonian America are easily found by the reader in an anthology by George E. Probst, ed., *The Happy Republic: A Reader in Tocqueville's America* (New York, 1962).

[10] Clyde Kluckhohn, "Values and Value-Orientations in the Theory of Action: An Exploration in Definition and Classification," in Talcott Parsons and Edward A. Shils, eds., *Toward a General Theory of Action* (Cambridge, Mass., 1951), 409.

[11] "Culture themes" and "postulates" are the terms of Morris E. Opler, "Themes as Dynamic Forces in Culture," *American Journal of Sociology*, LI (1945), 198–206. "Dominant values" probably arose from Florence Kluckhohn's work, "Dominant and Substitute Profiles of Cultural Orientations: Their Significance for the Analysis of Social Stratification," *Social Forces*, XXVIII (1950), 376–94, and "Dominant and Variant Value-Orientations" in Hugh Cabot and Joseph A. Kahl, eds., *Human Relations* (Cambridge, Mass., 1953), vol. 1, 88–98. "Core values" likewise seem an adaptation of Laura Thompson's idea of "core culture."

man's place in it, of man's relation to man, and of the desirable and nondesirable as they relate to man-environment and inter-human relations."[12] To many social scientists, the understanding of the core or dominant values affords the greatest insight into a group's behavior. Ranking values and deriving basic cultural premises therefore becomes a favorite sociological pastime.[13]

Arthur O. Lovejoy would make the search for value orientations, if I understand his term "unit-idea," the foundation of intellectual history. Lovejoy urged scholars in that field not to study formal philosophies or intellectual systems, for they are but compounds of unit-ideas. His advice for finding these ultimate unit-ideas also defines for us the nature of value orientations.

> [1.] There are, first, implicit or incompletely explicit *assumptions*, or more or less *unconscious mental habits*, operating in the thought of an individual or a generation. It is the beliefs which are so much a matter of course that they are rather tacitly presupposed than formally expressed and argued for, the ways of thinking which seem so natural and inevitable that they are not scrutinized with the eye of logical self-consciousness, that are often most decisive of the character of a philosopher's doctrine, and still oftener of the dominant intellectual tendencies of an age. . . .
> [2.] These endemic assumptions, these intellectual habits are often of so general and so vague a sort that it is possible for them to influence the course of men's reflections on almost any subject. . . .
> [3.] Another part of his [the intellectual historian's] busi-

[12] Clyde Kluckhohn, *op. cit.*, 411. Compare Florence Kluckhohn, Fred L. Strodtbeck, et al., *Variations in Value-Orientations* (Evanston, Ill., 1961), 1–48, 340–67, and Opler, *loc. cit.*
[13] Interesting examples of this pastime in relation to American society are Robin Williams, *American Society: A Sociological Interpretation* (2d ed., New York, 1961), 415–68; Cora Dubois, "The Dominant Value Profile of American Culture," *American Anthropologist*, LVII (1955), 1232–39; and Elting E. Morison, ed., *The American Style: Essays in Value and Performance* (New York, 1958), especially 145–217, 246–313.

CULTURE AND THE
STUDY OF THE
ACTOR'S VIEWPOINT

ness, if he means to take cognizance of the genuinely operative factors in the larger movements of thought, is an inquiry which may be called philosophical semantics— a study of the sacred words and phrases of a period or a movement, with a view to a clearing up of their ambiguities, a listing of their various shades of meaning, and an examination of the way in which confused associations of ideas arising from these ambiguities have influenced the development of doctrines, or accelerated the insensible transformation of one fashion of thought into another, perhaps its very opposite. . . .

[4.] . . . Any unit-idea which the historian thus isolates he next seeks to trace through more than one—ultimately, indeed, through all—of the provinces of history in which it figures in any important degree, whether those provinces are called philosophy, science, literature, art, religion, or politics. The postulate of such a study is that the working of a given conception, of an explicit or tacit presupposition, of a type of mental habit, or a specific thesis or argument, needs, if its nature and its historic rôle are to be fully understood, to be traced connectedly through all the phases of men's reflective life in which those workings manifest themselves, or through as many of them as the historian's resources permit. It is inspired by the belief that there *is* a great deal more that is common to more than one of these provinces than is usually recognized, that the same idea often appears, sometimes considerably disguised, in the most diverse regions of the intellectual world. . . .

[5.] Another characteristic of the study of the history of ideas, as I should define it, is that it is especially concerned with the manifestations of specific unit-ideas in the collective thought of large groups of persons, not merely in the doctrines or opinions of a small number of profound thinkers or eminent writers. . . .[14]

For Lovejoy such a basic unit-idea was the great chain of being, which according to him was "probably the

[14] Reprinted by permission of the publishers from Arthur O. Lovejoy, *The Great Chain of Being*, Cambridge, Mass: Harvard University Press, Copyright, 1936, by the President and Fellows of Harvard College; pp. 7, 10, 14, 15, 19 (author's italics), but see all of chap. 1.

A BEHAVIORAL APPROACH
TO HISTORICAL ANALYSIS

most general scheme of things, of the constitutive pattern of the universe [in Western civilization]."[15] Generated by notions of Plato and Aristotle and systematized by the Neo-Platonists, the idea came to include a scale ranking all entities existing in the universe from lowest to highest with each form continuing in attributes from the one lower to the next higher and with a form for every conceivable position on the scale.

The result was the conception of the plan and structure of the world which, through the Middle Ages and down to the late eighteenth century, many philosophers, most men of science, and, indeed, most educated men, were to accept without question—the conception of the universe as a "Great Chain of Being," composed of an immense, or—by the strict but seldom rigorously applied logic of the principle of continuity—of an infinite number of links ranging in hierarchical order from the meagerest kind of existents, which barely escape non-existence, through "every possible" grade up to the *ens perfectissimum*—or, in a somewhat more orthodox version, to the highest possible kind of creature, between which and the Absolute Being the disparity was assumed to be infinite— every one of them differing from that immediately above and that immediately below it by the "least possible" degree of difference.[16]

The doctrine received its widest dissemination and greatest popularization in eighteeenth-century literature, science, and social and political theory. Alexander Pope even put the idea into couplets.

> Vast chain of being! which from God began
> Natures aethereal, human, angel, man,
> Beast, bird, fish, insect, what no eye can see,
> No glass can reach; from Infinite to thee,
> From thee to nothing.—On superior pow'rs
> Were we to press, inferior might on ours;
> Or in the full creation leave a void,

[15] *Ibid.*, viii.
[16] *Ibid.*, 59.

Where, one step broken, the great scale's destroy'd;
From Nature's chain whatever link you strike,
Tenth, or ten thousandth, breaks the chain alike.[17]

The idea of progress only temporalized the chain over history, but evolution questioned its premises and romanticism denied its worth.

Certainly the chain was a salient category for Western man for many centuries. It was a value-orientation that combined the existential, in that it contained a conception of empirical reality, and the normative insofar as it involved moral judgments on that reality. The chain not only described the universe as it was supposed to be, but it also insisted that that was as it ought to be, and given God's perfection, had to be. The layman is probably most familiar with its descriptive and judgmental side through Shakespeare's plays with their excellent portrayal of the Elizabethan world picture, to use E. M. Tillyard's title.[18] The linking of is and ought, belief and value, is no better seen, according to the chain, than in the classification of angels in descending order from Seraphs, Cherubs, Thrones, Dominations, Virtues, Powers, to Principalities, Archangels, and Angels on the basis of inactive contemplation only, potential action, and manifest action. Beneath the lowest order of angels is man, who can contemplate somewhat like an angel but who is still more active and imperfect because of his lower position in the chain of being.

The problem of using such a comprehensive category of cultural ideation as value orientation is how to talk about it without violating the very notion of culture. Is the

[17] Quoted in *ibid.*, 60.
[18] E. M. W. Tillyard, *The Elizabethan World Picture* (New York, 1944).

A BEHAVIORAL APPROACH
TO HISTORICAL ANALYSIS

value orientation so abstract, that is, so fundamental, that the people said to possess it never understand it in the way that the analyst does? Are the people even aware of such salient categories in their experience? If the actors are not aware of such orientations as such, should an analyst designate such cultural premises or themes as part of their culture? Must all aspects of what is called a culture be consciously known to the actors said to possess the culture in the same manner that they are known to the analyst? We have approached these questions several times in this chapter, but we have not yet fully answered them.

Many social theorists solve this problem by asserting that the concept of a culture is a logical construct existing only in the mind of the observer and derived from the behavioral manifestations of the actors.[19] Such a simple solution is really begging the question by confusing semantic levels. The concept of a culture like all concepts as such is, of course, a construction in the mind of the analyst. The real question is more precisely stated, To what extent does the observer's construct correspond to the actors' cultural ideation said to be the source of the observed behavior? In answer to this question, theorists have developed the ideas of overt and covert culture, explicit and implicit patterns.[20] Essentially, overt culture designates explicit patterns that are presumably understood by the actor and the observer in the same conscious way. Covert culture

[19] This is the conclusion, for example, of Alfred Kroeber and Clyde Kluckhohn in their important monograph, *Culture: A Critical Review of Concepts and Definitions, Papers of the Peabody Museum of American Archaeology and Ethnology*, Harvard University, XLVII, no. 1 (1952), 182.

[20] The best background on these terms is obtained from Clyde Kluckhohn, "Covert or Implicit Culture," in Julius Gould and William L. Kolb, eds., *A Dictionary of the Social Sciences* (New York, 1960), 145–46.

CULTURE AND THE
STUDY OF THE
ACTOR'S VIEWPOINT

is composed of implicit patterns formulated by the observer to explain certain behavior he sees manifested but not explicitly recognized by the actors. Covert culture is derived from a group's activities as if the participants thought and acted according to the implicit pattern the observer postulates though they do not profess such a pattern explicitly.

At first glance, implicit patterns would seem to be purely an observer's construct. Yet at the same time, we know that just because the actors cannot verbalize an explanation for their behavior in certain situations does not mean they are not conscious of the appropriate behavior in the situation. How many times are people conscious of something incongruous in a social situation but just "can't quite put their finger on what's the matter"? Certainly such a reaction indicates something conscious behind the actors' behavior, although it is unformulated symbolically.

The distinction between consciousness and self-consciousness helps clarify the analysis at this point. The source of behavior may be conscious, but not necessarily conscious of its consciousness. On the other hand, acts could be conscious in source and recognized as such by the actor. Explicit patterns would seem in this view to be those aspects of cultural ideation in which the actors are conscious of their own ideation and can symbolize that fact by spoken or written words. Implicit patterns would be those that are conscious behavior but not self-conscious. The many aspects of a culture may then be ranged along a continuum from fully self-conscious, in that they are recognized and understood by the actors and the observer in the same manner, to the only conscious, in which the ideational source of the behavior is conceived in different terms by the actors and the observer. Perhaps at the very end would be unconscious implicit culture, unknown to the actor at all but always acted out identically by the group in the sense that the action is neither ideal nor expected but actual, and obviously learned. An example would be the arm's-length conversational distance of Americans today.[21]

Even the latter case, however, presupposes some sort of referent in the actor, but the riddle for the analyst is how much his explicit construction of the actor's implicit ideation conveys a true picture of that ideation. The concept of culture adopted in the last two chapters demands that the analyst represent the actors' group ideation as closely to the original as possible. It is the great problem of cultural translation. Complete success in such translation would make the analyst a member of the culture studied and incapable of conveying it to others. This is the ultimate solipsistic dilemma of cultural analysis. The historian need not solve the dilemma, but the idea of a continuum from explicit self-conscious culture through implicit conscious culture to unconscious implicit culture can aid him in more accurately reconstructing the culture of past men.[22]

The usual problem of defining the historical phenomena called mercantilism can be clarified if not partly resolved by the application of this continuum. Economic historians argue whether the hodge-podge of economic maxims and jumble of political devices between the end of the Middle Ages and the rise of laissez-faire can be said

[21] Compare my terms and conception with the idea of reflective and unreflective values of William P. McEwen, *The Problem of Social Scientific Knowledge* (Totowa, N.J., 1963), 34–35, and of objectivation and objectification of Peter Berger and Stanley Pullberg, "Reification and the Sociological Critique of Consciousness," *History and Theory*, IV (1965), 199–200.

[22] The problem is well posed in Northrop and Livingston, eds., *op. cit.* Anthropologists' attempts to solve the problem are seen in the rise of ethnographic semantics. A good review of this new field is B. N. Colby, "Ethnographic Semantics: A Preliminary Survey," *Current Anthropology*, VII (1966), 3–32.

CULTURE AND THE
STUDY OF THE
ACTOR'S VIEWPOINT

to constitute a system of economic and political policy to advance the power and wealth of the state. In other words, is the "ism" of mercantilism justified, or does it imply an entity that never really existed? In this debate, no one denies that some thoughts were expressed or some political-economic actions occurred. Rather, the point in dispute is whether these thoughts and actions formed one unified system or if either the thoughts or the actions, even separately considered, constituted a system that can be called mercantilism.

By applying the distinction between conscious and self-conscious ideation, we immediately see the clarification needed to resolve this debate. Ideas were consciously expressed and actions consciously occurred as both sides to the argument recognize. How self-conscious a system either these thoughts or these actions formed is quite questionable. Even more unlikely is the connection of these ideas and actions into a unified self-conscious system. The self-conscious systematization of these ideas and actions into an "ism" commenced with Adam Smith's castigation of them as a prelude to the laissez-faire system he advocated. Later in the 1880s Gustav Schmoller and William Cunningham continued this self-conscious systematization, which culminated in the great two-volume work of Eli Heckscher in 1931. Thus from scattered pamphlets, law codes, and other pieces of data was constructed the self-conscious system styled mercantilism. With that much clarified, the real question that must be investigated and debated is whether the observer's self-conscious system accurately describes a conscious, but not self-conscious, orientation in the actors of the period, and if such an orientation existed, did it produce the scattered laws and policies?[23]

[23] The present stage of the debate may be seen in a recent exchange: D. C. Coleman, "Eli Heckscher and the Idea of Mercantilism," *Scan-*

Historians have coped with the problems of conscious and self-conscious value orientations, implicitly at least it seems to me, in terms of myth and ideology. Myth and ideology possess many meanings, and it is not proposed that we examine all of them here.[24] Rather we shall point out what seems like a basic distinction between the two in terms of our framework and then examine some historical examples. Ideology would seem to refer to one or more value orientations that are self-consciously held by a group of people and seen by them as a system. Ideology is an explicit view of ends, means, and conditions (values, norms, beliefs, and knowledge) professed as such by the group. Ideology is codified by the people who profess it as evidenced by their symbolic representation of it. The actors see ideology in the same manner as the observer views it, and therefore ideology is easily found in historical documents.[25] Myth, on the other hand, refers to group value orientations that assume complete systematic codification as to their true meaning only in the observer's mind. Myths link the normative and the existential like ideology but not self-consciously to the participants in the way they do to the analyst. Myths, too, have symbolic

---

dinavian Economic History Review, V (1957), 1–25, and A. W. Coates, "In Defence of Heckscher and the Idea of Mercantilism," ibid., 173–87. Both articles' footnotes provide bibliographical references to study the problem. Another article of interest is Jacob Viner, "Power Versus Plenty as Objectives of Foreign Policy in the Seventeenth and Eighteenth Centuries," World Politics, I (1943), 1–29.

24 See Halpern, loc. cit.

25 This definition of ideology applies regardless of whether the codified system is ideological or utopian according to the scheme of Karl Mannheim, Ideology and Utopia: An Introduction to the Sociology of Knowledge, Louis Wirth and Edward Shils, trans. (New York, 1936). In addition to Mannheim on ideology, see Clifford Geertz, "Ideology as a Cultural System," in David Apter, ed., Ideology and Discontent (New York, 1964), 47–76; Norman Birnbaum, "The Sociological Study of Ideology (1940–1960)," Current Sociology, IX (1960), no. 2. Compare the interesting essay by Gustav Bergmann, "Ideology," Ethics, LXI (1951), 205–18.

representation, but the whole meaning of the myth is not formulated in the explicit way of ideology. Myth considered in this manner is not a false set of ideas and beliefs but a neutral term for implicit value orientations. When a myth becomes self-conscious, it can become an ideology or a myth, in the sense of false ideas and beliefs.[26]

The history of the idea of progress illustrates the utility of this view of myth and ideology at the same time as their application brings a precision to the delineation of the phases of that history heretofore lacking in the discussion of it. The controversy over the origins of the idea is resolved by specifying whether an analyst means to trace the beginnings of the specific idea of progress as a fully formulated and explicitly espoused ideology embodying a comprehensive conception of the past, present, and future of mankind as linear development toward an ideal condition; or whether the analyst means to study the unformulated general conception of the idea or even the antecedents of that in specific components of the general conception. In the first case, the analyst seeks to establish as the initial point the beginnings of the ideology; in the second case, the analyst chooses as the origin the myth or even the components of the myth before the actors see them as a cluster of ideas. Certainly, the idea of progress did move from the period of myth, whether in millennial and utopian imagery or in some other form, to a specific ideology as expounded by the philosophers of the Enlightenment. Today most social theorists would deny the validity of any idea of progress, and so once again the idea is mythical but

[26] Good beginning references on the conception of myth are the two works cited in note 4 of this chapter. On ideology the reader may start with George Lichtheim, "The Concept of Ideology," *History and Theory*, IV (1965), 164–95, and Harry M. Johnson, *Sociology: A Systematic Introduction* (New York, 1960), 587–624.

in the second sense of untrue. By employing the two meanings of myth and the idea of ideology as a guide to the consciousness and explicitness of formulation of the value orientation by the actors and whether they believe it true or false, the analyst of the idea of progress has specific guidelines to use when describing the evolution of this notion so important to the history of modern Western man.[27]

The history of the conception of the frontier, to once again recur to that important theme of American historiography, also illustrates the utility of this distinction between ideology and myth. Turner's presentation of the frontier thesis of American history was certainly an ideology because he formulated the doctrine very explicitly. It was also an ideology before him because the thinking that went into it was explicitly recognized prior to his famous paper, but how long before we do not know because of inadequate research. Until the time of Crevecoeur colonial Americans did not even remotely conceive of the frontier as Turner did. The Frenchman pictured the western movement of Anglo-American society in stages just as Turner did, but he made a less favorable judgment upon frontiers-

[27] The classic work is J. B. Bury, *The Idea of Progress: An Inquiry into Its Origin and Growth* (New York, 1932). Recent contributions to the discussion are Charles Frankel, *The Faith of Reason: The Idea of Progress in the French Enlightenment* (New York, 1948); Ernest L. Tuveson, *Millennium and Utopia: A Study in the Background of the Idea of Progress* (Berkeley and Los Angeles, 1949); R. V. Sampson, *Progress in the Ages of Reason: The Seventeenth Century to the Present Day* (London, 1956); and Norman Cohn, *The Pursuit of the Millennium* (Fair Lawn, N.J., 1957). W. Warren Wagar, "Modern Views of the Origins of the Idea of Progress," *Journal of the History of Ideas,* XXVIII (1967), 55–70, provides a summary of the argument to date in terms similar to mine. Failure to distinguish between progress as ideology and myth as used here accounts partially for the confusion in J. R. A. Bailey, *National Ambitions: Being a Critical Study of the European Desire for Progress* (Oxford, 1958).

CULTURE AND THE
STUDY OF THE
ACTOR'S VIEWPOINT

men than Turner did. Prior to Crevecoeur, people journeying westward merely saw "decent" whites and rude whites intermixed, but all part of civilization, and then they encountered savages. The frontier, if the term was used at all, seemed to indicate merely a dividing line between white civilization and red savagery. After Crevecoeur, travelers saw the stages of society spread out geographically as they had been lived once in the history of mankind. If this brief sketch is accurate, then the myth of the frontier rapidly became an ideology at the time of Crevecoeur. It is only recently that the ideology was seen to be a myth because American history never really happened that way. To call the myth an image does not alter the story. The frontier was an image because it was a myth and then an ideology during a certain period of time, and in both instances had real consequences for the settlement of land that Americans believed to exist in the way they viewed it.[28]

The real worth of the distinctions drawn between myth and ideology, between cultural ideation as conscious and self-conscious value orientations, is not in the specific terminology as such but in their use as a guide to the spectrum of cultural ideation and the aid of that guide in making an historical analysis of past cultural ideation. The historian should specify what a group in the past thought as such and what he maintains they meant by that thinking. Did the population under study possess the ideation in

[28] More work needs to be done upon the image of the frontier but the trend may be followed in Hector Crevecoeur, *Letters from an American Farmer* (London, 1782), especially Letter III; Rush Welter, "The Frontier West as Image of American Society: Conservative Attitudes Before the Civil War," *Mississippi Valley Historical Review*, XLVI (1960), 594–614; Smith, *op. cit.*; and John T. Juricek, "American Usage of the Word 'Frontier' from Colonial Times to Frederick Jackson Turner," *Proceedings of the American Philosophical Society*, CX (1966), 10–34.

exactly the same way that the historian attributes it to them? The historian is too prone to make unformulated conscious myth into explicit ideology because he must convey his interpretation of past ideation very systematically and very consciously to his readers. At the same time, documents are more likely to reveal ideology than myth because the person or persons who produced them had to formulate thoughts in order to produce the documents. This means that the historian is more likely to miss the previous stage of myth, if it existed. The likelihood of either case is good, and so the historical analyst must search his evidence with a range of possibilities in mind, neither extrapolating myth into ideology nor failing to look for a possible prior stage of myth.

Lastly, one wonders whether historians can discover value orientations very basic to a group, especially in their own civilization, until they become mythical in the sense of false value orientations. Are most value orientations so basic and therefore so unformulated by the participants in a culture that the observer too only sees them after they become articulated and are believed to be false? Certainly, the history of the idea of progress or of the frontier myth would seem to demonstrate this possibility. Maybe this is the true sense of historical perspective in intellectual history. Perhaps the cycle of myth to ideology to myth must be completed before a value orientation is perceived in its full ramifications. If this is so, then it means that cultural ideation in the most comprehensive category must always be a construct of the observer. Even so, the historical analyst is still under obligation to his craft to distinguish between the actors' actual ideational categories and his categorization of their ideation.

With the nature of value orientations examined, we

CULTURE AND THE
STUDY OF THE
ACTOR'S VIEWPOINT

are ready at long last to consider how the components of culture relate to the whole of a culture. Those analysts who carry the logic of evaluation to its ultimate conclusion hypothesize that no cataloged enumeration of parts is sufficient to represent the true sum total of a culture. Rather, a total culture in their view is a patterned whole resulting from a hierarchy of evaluations. Values and value orientations are ranked by the process of evaluation so that the whole culture is pictured as a specific configuration of components that is not necessarily more than the sum of its parts but is certainly a unique and specially organized combination of its components. Theoretically, according to this view, two cultures could have the same components and yet the overall configuration in each case could be so patterned that there existed two distinct cultures, just as two languages might employ the same sounds and yet be perfectly distinctive.[29]

Students of societies have long recognized this distinctive overall organization of customs, thoughts, and feelings that sets one people off from another. Such a characterization of a culture is known popularly through the works of the metahistorian Spengler or the anthropologist Ruth Benedict. Historians since Burckhardt's attempt to characterize Renaissance Italy as individualistic have followed the same procedure of delineating a cultural configuration by the dominant themes. The terms *genius of a civilization, spirit of an age, mental climate, zeitgeist,* or *ethos* all indicate this method of conceptualizing a culture. In most cases, historians use these terms to designate the underlying configuration of themes found in the formal

142

[29] A strong statement of the configurational unity and patterning of culture is Ruth Benedict, *Patterns of Culture* (Boston, 1934), especially chap. 3. The problem is, of course, the basis of Kluckhohn's "Parts and Wholes in Cultural Analysis," 111–33.

thinking and arts of a time that they believe typify the whole culture. Because such a portrait is often derived from the arts or from formal culture, it is also called the style of a civilization.[30] Essentially, this method hypothesizes the configurational unity of a society's culture and asserts that it is derivable from the few pervasively dominant or basic value orientations that are found in one sector of that culture.[31]

If this view of a culture as organized into a consistent hierarchy constituting a unique configuration were true, cultural analysis would be an immense aid to the historian in accomplishing his goals. He could proceed with greater certainty in the analysis of historical evidence, because paucity of documentation would not constitute the obstacle it now does to his task. He could easily expand a relatively few pieces of data into a whole culture by merely reconstructing their place in the total configuration of the time. On the levels both of documentary analysis and of factual synthesis (and even perhaps on the level of explanation of those facts), he could move easily from a few scraps of evidence about a few culture bearers to their entire culture.

Such an intellectual paradise would enable the historian to reconstruct the past behavior of men much better than he could otherwise. But, alas, the definition of culture assumed in this holistic configurational view rests upon one of the great value-orientations or ideologies of our time—the concept of system. We can examine cultural

[30] Meyer Schapiro, "Style," in Alfred Kroeber, ed., *Anthropology Today: An Encyclopedic Inventory* (Chicago, 1953), 287–312; Alfred Kroeber, *Style and Civilization* (Ithaca, N.Y., 1957).
[31] Modes of cultural integration are surveyed by Bidney, *op. cit.*, 365–415. The efforts of Voltaire, Guizot, Burckhardt, Lamprecht, Huizinga, and Ortega y Gasset to depict a total culture are analyzed by Karl J. Weintraub, *Visions of Culture* (Chicago and London, 1966).

CULTURE AND THE
STUDY OF THE
ACTOR'S VIEWPOINT

holism no further without a careful inspection of what may turn out to be the most culture-bound and mythical (i.e., false) of notions, but one that grips the contemporary scientific world. So important is the concept of system in today's behavioral theory that I shall devote two later chapters to it.

Yet even without assuming a culture to be a wholly integrated hierarchical system of basic value orientations or even a fully self-conscious and explicitly espoused set of ideations, there remains much in the culture concept of considerable use to the historian for interpreting past group behavior. If half of the dual function of the historian as pointed out in Chapter 3 is to try to understand the actions of past men as they understood them in their world at their time, then the notion of culture even as empirically established shared ideation explicitly forces the separation of actors and observers to the benefit of historical analysis. The historian assessing his evidence with a *self-conscious* concept of culture will search more for dissimilarity than for similarity of the past with the present. In fact, if anything, the whole perspective of the historian changes as a result of his concern with establishing a culture. Instead of constructing genetic connections of past with present-day phenomena, he will increasingly come to construe history in terms of the times he is studying. Only through such a reconstruction will the historian be true to the goal of his craft—not to impose current ideas upon the past. And keeping faith with the aim of the historical guild means not only seeing the actions of the past through the eyes of the actors but also seeing their categories of experience in terms of their conceptions. The idea of cultural components—knowledge, belief, values, norms—as well as their patterning into complexes of orientations affords a valuable corrective to the ethnocentrism of time, which could be called temporocentrism. Without an explicit, self-conscious concept of culture, the historian is more likely to derive and synthesize facts in terms of his own cultural framework than in the perspective of the ideation of the past people he is studying.

In addition to helping the historian avoid temporocentrism by reinforcing the actor-observer distinction, the concept of culture offered here also enables the analyst of the past to distinguish past group ideation and behavior more carefully. The distinctions between beliefs, knowledge, values, and norms in combination with consciousness and self-consciousness offer a convenient checklist of the possibilities in interpreting evidence. The historian will view past group ideation according to the conceptual categories of its time, and he will see behavior in terms of that conceptualization instead of today's. Cultural theory enables the historian to understand more readily past group ideation in such a way that he can estimate the behavior it should and did produce with greater probability so that he can talk about past actual behavior with greater confidence than he could without the theory. At the same time, the various types of values and norms, considered as ideal and operative, caution him against making overly simplistic connections between the two on the basis of his partial data. All in all, the historian has everything to gain and little to lose by adopting even the most problematical conception of culture.

IMPLICATIONS OF THE CULTURE CONCEPT FOR HISTORICAL ANALYSIS

My contention about the worth of the culture concept in historical analysis is proved best by its application in a series of examples. These examples range from giving a more precise meaning to words frequently found in documents or employed by historians in their syntheses to a new understanding of past man's assumed relationship with his physical and social environment at a given time. The conception of a culture can even lead to the reinterpretation of a whole period. As the following examples will show, an appreciation of culture can revamp the historian's conception of the role of ideas in men's lives and therefore promote a new approach to historical causation.

Words possess connotations and contexts founded in the culture of their users, and so documentary analysis must take into account the cultural assumptions of the producers of historical sources. Far too often historians interpret the words they read, particularly the abstract nouns, as meaning what they do to a reader today rather than what they meant to the writer then. Thus, for example, Thomas Jefferson's words are interpreted as those of a twentieth-century liberal or the Bill of Rights is pictured as guaranteeing civil liberties as they are argued at mid-twentieth century. Only recently have historians reread the documents of that period as their writers intended them, and neither Jefferson nor the Bill of Rights can be portrayed as part of present-day democratic liberalism if the analyst would be true to the past. So the "darker side" of that era, as some liberals today view it, is revealed to be the true picture when the historical analyst seeks to understand past usage as the users understood it.[1]

Only recently have historians turned their attention to the history of words as an important indicator of history itself. Donald Fleming asks that historians produce a sort of "natural history" of words as a clue not only to changes in past societies' ways of thinking but also perhaps as an explanation of those changes. Such a natural history should seek to answer, "Why should this word arise in this sense at this time? Why exfoliate into different forms of speech, and explode into radically new meanings; why flourish and dwindle?"[2] As an example of such research, he traces the word "attitude" from its earlier use to designate a posture of the human body to its modern meaning to denote a state of mind. He argues that the transformation of the word from bodily to mental attribute accompanied and embodied the whole new conception of man that has arisen in the past century. New psychological, political, and moral images of man caused a new meaning for an older word, and in turn that new meaning is one component of the new image. Raymond Williams, likewise, has been concerned about the larger social and cultural context of changed language usage. In his book on *Culture and Society, 1780–1950,* he examines the almost simultaneous redefinition of such words as "culture," "industry," "art," "democracy," and

[1] The reinterpretation of both Jefferson and conceptions of the Bill of Rights in this way is presented vigorously by Leonard Levy, *Legacy of Suppression: Freedom of Speech and Press in Early American History* (Cambridge, Mass., 1960), and *Jefferson and Civil Liberties: The Darker Side* (Cambridge, Mass., 1963).

[2] Donald Fleming, "Attitude: The History of a Concept," *Perspectives in American History,* I (1967), 287, but see also the whole article, 287–365.

THE CULTURE CONCEPT
AND HISTORICAL ANALYSIS

"class."[3] In the late eighteenth century, all of these words suddenly assumed their modern meanings, and he shows how this change reflected the rise of industrialism and the new social and political ideas and organization of the time. The historian may conclude that these words appearing in a document dated earlier than the 1770s meant something different than now, or that the application of these words' modern meanings to a period prior to the 1770s falsifies the actors' view of their own era.

148

To avoid such errors, historical analysis in general and documentary investigation in particular must include an historical semantics so as to appreciate ideation as it once was. Just as anthropologists have only recently started to develop more sophisticated techniques to try to reconstruct the values and beliefs that lie behind the meaning of words when employed by a man in a given culture at a certain time, so historians must do more in this direction than they have previously. Historians, too, should employ componential analysis, contrast-level study, programmed specifications, and other techniques of the linguistic anthropologists to overcome the many barriers imposed by time to cross-cultural understanding of a language. Anthropologists call their general effort to eliminate linguistic solipsism ethnographic semantics,[4] and I should think historical analysts must supplement their traditional documentary techniques with the same sophisticated approach, which I shall christen historiographic semantics. ("Historiographic" because historical semantics is already a well-recognized branch of linguistics, and although the historian might borrow something from historical semantics, still his purpose is far different, in the end, from that of the linguist.)

[3] Raymond Williams, *Culture and Society, 1780–1950* (New York, 1958), especially xi–xviii, but see the entire book.
[4] A good introduction to the subject is B. N. Colby, "Ethnographic Semantics: A Preliminary Survey," *Current Anthropology*, VII (1966), 3–32.

A BEHAVIORAL APPROACH TO HISTORICAL ANALYSIS

Such close linguistic attention to the cultural background of historical evidence will not only bring forth new facts from the sources, but it will also promote greater precision in the vocabulary used by the historian to designate the thinking and the action of past peoples. The historian should clearly distinguish between those terms he uses as the actors meant them and those he utilizes according to his own society's usage. Simple as this distinction may seem, Richard Koebner has shown the false senses implied by the words "empire" and "imperialism" when used to label what historians presumed to be similar phenomena over much of human history. By careful historical analysis of these two words, he demonstrates the error of applying them in the general sense in which they are employed in most history texts.[5] After reading his books, no historian can use either these two words or for that matter any other words without wondering whether he is not implying far more than users of such words did in their time. Likewise, all the many catch words of the historian to denominate events and eras by words adopted from the past become suspect. The difficulties in using the word "Progressivism" to designate a period have already been examined in another connection. Or, an even better example, do we really know whether Northerners at the end of the American Civil War used "Reconstruction" in the same way history books now do?[6] Such catchwords imply that actors' and observer's conception of the phenomena are the same, but is such really the case? Only thorough research can prove each instance, and all such historian's terms should undergo as rigorous an analysis as any of the events said to constitute their significance.

[5] Richard Koebner, *Empire* (Cambridge, Eng., 1961) and, with H. D. Schmidt, *Imperialism: The Story and Significance of a Political Word, 1840–1960* (Cambridge, Eng., 1964).
[6] So far as I know there is no published analysis of the origins and development of the word "Reconstruction" but one of my students once indicated the possibilities in a term paper.

THE CULTURE CONCEPT
AND HISTORICAL ANALYSIS

Behind words denoting place lie conceptions of environment, and again the historian must be careful to point out what was meant by a place name or a more general term designating an area at the time of use. In short, the historian must discover the perceptual geography of the time and people he studies before asserting what environmental terms connoted to the users.[7] Historians have long produced or are familiar with the studies that trace Europeans' changing conceptions of the earth through the history of maps or reports of discoveries and explorations, but these books lack the analytical rigor demanded by the culture concept.[8]

As a result of such a cultural approach to geography, Edmundo O'Gorman has devoted his scholarly life to show-

[7] What I call perceptual geography is treated under the term *cognitive behavioralism* by Harold and Margaret Sprout, *The Ecological Perspective on Human Affairs; with Special Reference to International Politics* (Princeton, N.J., 1965), chap. 7 (originally published as "Man-Milieu Relationship Hypotheses in Context of International Politics" [1956]). It is also called *behavioral environment* by William Kirk, "Historical Geography and the Concept of the Behavioral Environment," *Indian Geographical Journal*, XXVI (1951), 152–60, and "Problems in Geography," *Geography*, XLVIII (1963), 357–71. Compare Alexander Spoehr, "Cultural Differences in the Interpretation of Natural Resources," in William L. Thomas, ed., *Man's Role in Changing the Face of the Earth* (Chicago, 1956), 93–102. Perceptual geography is not to be confused with the general subject of cultural geography. Both use the culture concept but in quite different ways; only perceptual geography approaches physical environment from the actors' view alone. A brief but good analysis of cultural geography as a subject is the Introduction to Philip L. Wagner and Marvin Mikesell, eds., *Readings in Cultural Geography* (Chicago, 1962), 1–24.

[8] Compare the various approaches to portraying the actors' view of geography taken by the following recent books: Ralph Brown, *Mirror for Americans: Likeness of the Eastern Seaboard, 1810* (New York, 1943); Lloyd A. Brown, *The Story of Maps* (Boston, 1949); Boies Penrose, *Travel and Discovery in the Renaissance, 1420–1620* (Cambridge, Mass., 1952); Douglas R. McManis, *The Initial Evaluation and Utilization of the Illinois Prairies, 1815–1840* (Department of Geography Research Paper no. 94, University of Chicago, 1964); and William Goetzmann, *Exploration and Empire* (New York, 1966).

A BEHAVIORAL APPROACH
TO HISTORICAL ANALYSIS

ing that America was not discovered but "invented." He argues that Columbus could not have landed in America in 1492 in terms of the actor's view, because the "Admiral of the Ocean Sea" neither purposed such nor realized he had. Rather the idea of an "America" evolved as the explorers and people of the time came to realize that an empirical entity, a great land mass, existed in contradiction to their traditional image of the earth's geography. Thus the idea of a "new world" evolved, or was "invented" in O'Gorman's term, and it in turn transformed man's image of himself in relation to the universe. He maintains the confusion about this simple matter occurred because historians imposed upon the actors of the past their own certain knowledge of the Western Hemisphere, thus distorting the historical cicumstances of the "discovery."[9]

Even less attention has been paid to the conceptual bases of more abstract environmental terms of past men. A prime example referred to frequently already is the idea of the frontier. Although historians long appeared to believe that Turner utilized a notion of the frontier held by Americans from the time of the Revolution, John Juricek demonstrates that the word as Turner meant it could only have been used in that manner by Americans of Turner's time. Before his time, the overall connotations of sequence and evolution were lacking in the precise sense Turner saw them operate in frontier settlement.[10] An even better example of

[9] An English summary of O'Gorman's work by himself is *The Invention of America: An Inquiry into the Historical Nature of the New World and the Meaning of Its History* (Bloomington, Ind., 1961). Wilcomb Washburn, "The Meaning of 'Discovery' in the Fifteenth and Sixteenth Centuries," *American Historical Review*, LXVIII (1962), 1–21, feels the problem is more complex than O'Gorman's presentation indicates.

[10] John T. Juricek, "American Usage of the Word 'Frontier' from Colonial Times to Frederick Jackson Turner," *Proceedings of the American Philosophical Society*, CX (1966), 10–34.

THE CULTURE CONCEPT
AND HISTORICAL ANALYSIS

the difficulty of ferreting out the meaning of past men's environmental assumptions is Cecilia Kenyon's "Men of Little Faith."[11] Opponents of the United States Constitution worried among other things about the ability of the proposed government to stretch so far as to encompass the loyalties of men in the physically dispersed thirteen states. No republic before had ever been so large in area as that urged by the Constitution's advocates. Apparently because it was so prevalent at that time, this provincial notion of political geography is one of the specific items refuted in the *Federalist*. Obvious as this idea now is, not one of the many students of that era pointed it out before Miss Kenyon did in 1955. This peculiar environmental notion is also the basis apparently for Jefferson's proposal of laying out small-sized states in the trans-Appalachian West after the Revolution. He deliberately made them small so their inhabitants could achieve a republic. Like many other advocates of state over federal government at that time, Jefferson feared the inability of representative government to operate over a large space.[12]

Jefferson and the other politicians of his era, like men at all times, had images of man and how he acts individually and collectively. The fact that the famous political documents of the new United States are based upon a few particular images of man is so well known that even elementary school texts depict the struggle between Jefferson and Hamilton in terms of such an ideology. The supposedly cynical view of man entertained by Hamilton as opposed to the happier notion of human nature held by Jefferson is even

[11] Cecilia Kenyon, "Men of Little Faith: The Anti-Federalists on the Nature of Representative Government," *William and Mary Quarterly*, 3d ser., XII (1955), 3–43.
[12] Robert F. Berkhofer, Jr., "Providing for the Expansion of a Republican Empire: From Jefferson's Ordinance of 1784 to the Northwest Ordinance," in manuscript.

made to appear the basis of each man's personality as well as his actions. Regardless of the accuracy of this picture, it does reinforce the point that men and the documents they produce are founded upon values and beliefs about themselves and other people as products of human nature. What men believe about the opportunities and limitations of human nature influences their actions as well as their ideals and expectations. The historian must discover these images in order to assess his evidence as well as to depict the cultural ideation of the times.

Men also see the institutions of their culture in a certain way, and the historian must attempt to portray these institutions as their participants saw them in addition to how he as observer understands their operation. Antebellum slavery is once more a good example. No matter how clever econometric analyses of slavery's profitability may be, historians must still determine what the slaveholders thought on the subject. If the slaveowners believed the disadvantages versus the worth of owning Negro bondsmen must be gauged by considerations beyond mere profit or loss as computed by an accountant (especially one of today), then the historical analyst too must note this fact in his consideration of the subject. In this circumstance, slave owning may have been seen by the actors of the era to possess so many implications for the entire South that it became a whole subculture in American society, or a "peculiar institution" as they said. As a result, they may have weighed factors of social accounting in their measure of slave profitability that no econometrician would take into his accounting.[13] A conception of culture reminds and aids an analyst to see the function and structure of institu-

[13] This seems to be what Eugene Genovese is arguing among other things in his *Political Economy of Slavery: Studies in the Economy and Society of the Slave South* (New York, 1965).

THE CULTURE CONCEPT
AND HISTORICAL ANALYSIS

tions as the actors perceived them by viewing their evaluation in terms of the values, norms, and value orientations of
those participating in them.[14]

A cultural perspective is even more useful in reminding
historians to look at relations among institutions as the people of the time viewed the connections. The historian
should attempt to be true to the cultural configuration as
reflected in the institutional nexuses of a period. The merit
of this approach as opposed to judging institutional relationships by present-day standards is readily exemplified in the
long-standing controversies about the connection between
economic and other institutions in Europe during the various centuries of the modern period. What was the participant's view of the relation between economics and religion
in sixteenth- and seventeenth-century European life? Did
they see the Protestant Ethic as promoting, reinforcing, coexisting with, or irrelevant to the spirit of capitalism?
Would not answers to these two questions have a significant
bearing upon the argument over Weber's thesis?[15] What
was the tie between economics and politics in the eighteenth century? Did the middle class in Europe and America revolt solely or even mostly for economic reasons in
their own eyes, or did they see governmental rights and
liberties in a broader context than do many of their modern

[14] The failure to distinguish between different actors' perceptions of the
functioning of institutions may be seen in Stanley Elkins, *Slavery: A
Problem in American Institutional and Intellectual Life* (Chicago, 1959).
In Chap. 3, "Slavery and Personality," he implies that masters and
slaves defined and interpreted their relationship the same way. He
comes to this conclusion upon the basis of evidence about masters' attitudes and psychological theory. He fails to allow for a Negro slave
subculture other than the Sambo one enforced by white brutality.

[15] The most recent book in this long debate is Kurt Samuelsson, *Religion and Economic Action: A Critique of Max Weber*, E. Geoffrey
French, trans. (New York) 1961).

[16] An effective and comprehensive presentation of this view of the many
revolutions is Robert R. Palmer, *The Age of Democratic Revolution:
A Political History of Europe and America, 1760–1800* (Princeton, N.J.,
1959, 1964), 2 vols.

*A BEHAVIORAL APPROACH
TO HISTORICAL ANALYSIS*

interpreters?[16] Lastly, in the nineteenth century what relationship must be sustained between economic and other institutions in order for a nation to industrialize? Are the participants' views of this connection the same as those of the observer, and if not, what consequences did that fact possess for historical events?[17] It is not proposed to answer here these profoundly important questions other than to point out how they all revolve about the notion of cultural configuration and integration. Furthermore, an observer's view of these institutional relationships may obscure or, more likely, conceal the nature of and the actual influence of the participants' attitudes and actions. The desirability, even the necessity, of relating economic institutions to the broader cultural framework is amply demonstrated by the latest trends in economic development theory.[18]

The connections between institutions according to an overall cultural configuration held by the participants leads the analyst to consider the total conception of a society as envisioned by its members. By doing just this, American historians are moving toward a whole new interpretation of the early period of American history and, as a further

[17] Does not the dispute among those who argue about the comparative advantages and disadvantages of industrialism in European and particularly in English history concern to a large extent this issue? On the argument, see Friedrich A. Hayek, ed., *Capitalism and the Historians* (Chicago, 1954). Walt W. Rostow, *The Stages of Economic Growth: A Non-Communist Manifesto* (Cambridge, Eng., 1960), argues that a people's attitudes must change for the take-off into industrialism and that all sectors of a society must accommodate to industrialization in both ideas and action. A sociological analysis of industrialization in England is Neil J. Smelser, *Social Change in the Industrial Revolution: An Application of Theory to the British Cotton Industry* (Chicago, 1959).

[18] A good introduction to this side of industrialization is Wilbert E. Moore, "Social Aspects of Economic Development," in Robert E. L. Faris, ed., *Handbook of Modern Sociology* (Chicago, 1964), 882–911. An historian's comments on the subject is Thomas Cochran, *The Inner Revolution: Essays on the Social Sciences in History* (New York, 1964), 110–43.

THE CULTURE CONCEPT
AND HISTORICAL ANALYSIS

result, are altering profoundly the traditional image of American history so long expounded by historians and teachers. American historians, from Bancroft to those of the present day, have conceived of the founding of the United States in terms of the democratic ideology of the Jacksonian period. Therefore the Declaration of Independence, the Constitution, and all the other many famous documents of early United States history were read and analyzed explicitly or implicitly in relation to the future democracy. In the last decade, historians have increasingly believed such an approach erroneous and tried to read the sources afresh as their writers meant them. As a result the term republicanism has returned to the vocabulary of American history with the meaning that the founding fathers intended. The Americans of that period are now portrayed as creating not only a newly independent nation but also a new kind of nation that was in their opinion *novus ordo seclorum,* as the Great Seal of the United States adopted in 1782 proudly proclaimed. This new approach to old data has resulted in a new perspective on institutions, man-environment relationships, conceptions of society and history, and words and phrases of the early national era. If historians worked with a more explicit conception of culture, they would see that the economic, religious, social, intellectual, political, artistic, and architectural trends of the period formed a coherent whole quite unlike that of the democracy that followed 1815 and different from the society and culture of the earlier eighteenth century. This period of the new American nation can only be fully understood on its own cultural terms as an age of republicanism.[19]

[19] No one book gathers together all the aspects of this theme, but some of the various strands that must be combined may be found in the following recent works: Stow Persons, *American Minds: A History of Ideas* (New York, 1958), 129–43; Felix Gilbert, *To the Farewell Ad-*

Perhaps the greatest transformation wrought by this view of the early national era is the change it forces in the traditional image of American history. According to the previous synthesis instigated by Turner and Beard, American history from 1763 to the 1930s was a continuous struggle between two groups of people differing in economic worth and hence in social rank and political power. Inevitably, according to this standard version of the American past, the liberals, or the have-nots, and the conservatives, or the haves, must possess differing ideologies and must oppose each other because of their economic background. With these assumptions about society and man, historians pictured American history as the same old story of conflict, except new names kept filling old roles as time flowed. On one side were the Tories, opponents of the Articles of Confederation, advocates of the Constitution, Federalists, Whigs, Republicans, and Robber Barons; on the other side were Whigs (at least some), pro-Articles men, opponents of the Constitution, Jeffersonians, Jacksonians, and Democrats, except for the conservative ones. History marched in straight file from Hamilton to Hoover in one camp and Jefferson to F. D. Roosevelt in the other camp. Now with the emergence of an age of republicanism, the genetic continuity of the two socioeconomic sides is destroyed. Ideological consistency based upon economic power is denied, and new sides form with each new issue with frequent crossover of participants from one side to the other. Under this new impression of the American past, Thomas Jefferson, for example, shared more values and beliefs with John Adams and even Alexander Hamilton than with Andrew Jackson. Thus an implicit attempt to understand a culture

157

dress: *Ideas of Early American Foreign Policy* (Princeton, N.J., 1961); Sidney E. Mead, *The Lively Experiment: The Shaping of Christianity in America* (New York, 1963), 16–71.

THE CULTURE CONCEPT
AND HISTORICAL ANALYSIS

on its own terms forces a whole new view of early national and of all American history.

To say that American historians are altering their image of their country's past as a result of today's view of culture does not, of course, modify the fact that Americans have held other versions of their past as a result of their own culture. The economic determinist view of the American past was, or still is, part of Americans' image of their past, just as the reinterpretation of republicanism will be part of it in the future. History as written is as much cultural ideation as other facets of thought, and so a cultural perspective on the past should include the actors' view of their history. Later Americans, for example, seem to have glorified the early Republic in such a way that they could use that image as a measure of their society's deviation from that of the previous golden age. Andrew Jackson and his followers lamented the loss of republican virtues in the 1820s and hoped to restore them by his administration.[20] Later in the nineteenth century, Populist farmers bemoaned the loss of the earlier republican virtues—this time of the age of Jackson—and advocated economic and governmental reforms to return the United States to the ways of the beloved agrarian society of the past.[21] Finally, the Progressives again saw the Republic in peril and again employed the vision of the earlier Republic as a yardstick to measure the economic and political corruption in an industrialized United States.[22] From these three incidents, and others, an analyst could construct the theme of the "dying Republic"

[20] This is a major point of Marvin Meyers, *The Jacksonian Persuasion: Politics and Belief* (Stanford, Calif., 1957), especially 3–32.

[21] Richard Hofstadter has stressed this theme as part of the "folklore of Populism" in his *The Age of Reform: From Bryan to F.D.R.* (New York, 1955), 60–93.

[22] In no writer of the period is this more apparent than in Herbert Croly, *The Promise of American Life* (New York, 1909).

A BEHAVIORAL APPROACH TO HISTORICAL ANALYSIS

as one of Americans' many uses of their past, and then show how history is part of the cultural ideation of a given period.

As is evident from these examples, a conception of culture not only provides aid in reconstructing the ideation of the past but as a result of doing that must also possess implications for analysis of historical causation. If past group behavior is partly the response to shared interpretations of situations, then reconstruction of historic cultural ideation is a partial explanation of why some things happened the way they did in the past. To the extent that group action is collective (as this term is defined in Chapter 4) and based upon cultural interpretation, then an explanation of the resultant action would depend upon an analysis of that aspect of the people's culture. Obvious as this statement is, the implications are far-reaching for the causal analysis of many traditionally debated phenomena. For example, in discussing the American Revolution, must the historian attribute causation according to the actors' categories of experience? If so, does this mean that the long discussion over economic versus political causes of that event are beside the point because the actors of the period could only see a combined politico-economic category and not separate ones? Before the era of laissez-faire theory, there was only political economy and often that was considered a branch of moral philosophy. What we after the nineteenth century see as separate categories and therefore different disciplines was earlier viewed as one category. Hence to divide the causes of the Revolution into economic and political falsifies the thinking of the revolutionists.[23]

[23] A longer version of this argument is my "Taxation and the Causes of the American Revolution," *Bulletin of the Minnesota Council for the Social Studies* (Winter, 1963), 40–44. Compare, however, Gordon S. Wood, "Rhetoric and Reality in the American Revolution," *William and Mary Quarterly*, 3d ser., XXIII (1966), 3–32.

What this brief example shows is the necessity for conceiving of causation in actors' as well as observers' framework, and a culture concept is a significant clue to analyzing the actor's framework.

Because the concept of culture and its importance for causation as well as for all analysis has been perceived—consciously but not self-consciously, to use my terms—by many historians, these men stress the significance of studying past intellectual constructs in order to understand the past. Increasingly symbolic interpretations are superseding the so-called "objective" ones as historical analysts attempt to understand the facts of the past as the people who lived them understood them. Thus not only is the American Revolution seen as being fought for political rights, but the War of 1812 is once more seen as caused by American concern over neutral rights and preservation of the Republic.[24] In many ways, these very new interpretations sound old-fashioned, for they look like refurbished patriotic slogans. This is neither strange nor reprehensible. Nor are these new interpretations an attempt to purvey a glorious heritage at the expense of historical truth. Rather, they are efforts to relate causation to the conceptual categories of the actors, and so it is not peculiar to say that Americans of that time acted partly for the reasons they said they acted, nor therefore to use the words they once used. Such interpretations may be old-fashioned in phraseology, but they are not old in the sense that they imply that the same moral

[24] The standard version of this interpretation for the Revolution is the little book by Edmund Morgan, *The Birth of the Republic, 1763–89* (Chicago, 1956), 1–77; and now Bernard Bailyn, *Ideological Origins of the American Revolution* (Cambridge, Mass., 1967), states the case even more strongly. Two recent books viewing the causes of the War of 1812 in this manner are Roger Brown, *The Republic in Peril: 1812* (New York, 1964), and Patrick C. T. White, *A Nation on Trial* (New York, 1966).

judgments past actors made on these events must also be made by us today.[25]

The ramifications of the culture concept for so many aspects of historical analysis point to a broader conception of intellectual history than is traditional. Intellectual history from a behavioral orientation must be cultural history as the notion of culture has been developed in this and preceding chapters. To serve this important function, intellectual historians must widen the scope of their subject matter and utilize new methods appropriate to the study of cultures. No other conception of the tasks or techniques of intellectual history will serve the needs of history or of other historians, for historians in other fields must know the cultural context of the behavior they study. On the other hand, all historians perforce must become intellectual historians to some extent, if the reconstruction of the actors' viewpoint is so crucial to understanding action. Insofar as the intellectual historians can lift this burden from their colleagues they should, for that would clear the decks for further research. But all historians must work for written history that accepts explicitly and self-consciously the difference between present-day cultural ideation and past cultural ideation, and such written history can only be achieved with a modern, explicit notion of culture.

This conception of intellectual history raises the question of just how important ideas are in determining the course of history. The problem revolves about two points: What specific influence can be attributed to ideas as such in in a given case of analysis? What are the limits of using ideas to explain the overall situation being studied? In other

---

[25] This distinction between actors' and observer's moral judgments is made very carefully in one example of the genre, Cecilia Kenyon, "Republicanism and Radicalism in the American Revolution: An Old-Fashioned Interpretation," *William and Mary Quarterly*, 3d ser., XIX (1962), 153–82.

words, the historian must investigate not only what ideas were present but also how they acted and what else in addition explains the behavior in the situation under analysis. Even if the analyst accepts ideas as necessary to the explanation of a case, he must still establish their degree of sufficiency, or limits, as explanation. Our behavioral analysis thus far has addressed itself obliquely to these points, but we must confront the issue squarely now. A brief discussion of public opinion will provide a focus for our conclusions about the role of ideas in history.

The modern notion of the significance of public opinion has a definite historical context, which pinpoints both the limits and utility of that conception. This term, like so many others we use today, gained its contemporary connotations in the last quarter of the eighteenth and first quarter of the nineteenth centuries. This view of public opinion rests as much upon the desirability as upon the existence of the people's influence in the formulation of governmental policy. The desirability of public opinion in the determination of governmental affairs came with the evolving ideal of a *res publica* in the seventeenth and eighteenth centuries. This moral conception of public opinion's worth would make no sense, however, unless technology and social organization created a "public," allowed it to have "opinions," and fostered the influence, or feedback, of those opinions to government officials. Increased literacy, cheap cost of mass communication by book or newspaper, and coffee-house or salon gatherings, among other things, were all therefore as necessary to the creation of public opinion as was the idea of its desirability. The printing press provided the mass medium to unify an aggregative public into the collective or at least conjunctive publics of salon and coffee house. Even the financing of the public debt by public creditors may have fostered attention to public opinion as much as a changing conception of the people's relation to government. One of the first theoretical treatises on the subject of public opinion was by Jacques Necker, the French Minister of Finance under Louis XVI, who also published the first governmental financial statements. Both his book and his rendering of public accounts acknowledged the importance of public opinion in relation to public credit.[26]

Thus it can be seen that the notion of public opinion has social structural and normative connotations in addition to its ostensible meaning. Opinions rather than opinion exist because the society is presumed pluralistic, that is, divided by interests, occupations, educational levels, and other indexes of social diversity. This diversity creates publics rather than *a* public. Not only must the society be socially differentiated but that society must have the technological means of at least one mass medium to place issues before the public or publics. Lastly, if we are to have the modern meaning of public opinion, that society must espouse values of individualism, majoritarianism, and probably equalitarianism to give heed to public opinion in addition to acknowledging its existence.

While modern public opinion studies may seem far removed from these historical origins of the term's significance, a closer look at any of the standard texts on the subject reveals the continuing concerns of what ought to be as well as what is a "public" and what is "opinion" in a

[26] This brief history of the conception of public opinion is based upon these references: Paul A. Palmer, "The Concept of Public Opinion in Political Theory," in *Essays in History and Political Theory in Honor of Charles H. McIlwain* (Cambridge, Mass., 1936), 230–57; Hans Speier, "Historical Development of Public Opinion," *American Journal of Sociology*, LV (1950), 376–88; and Wilhelm Bauer, "Public Opinion," Edwin R. A. Seligman and Alvin Johnson, eds., in *The Encyclopedia of the Social Sciences*, vol. 12 (1934), 669–74.

complex social structure. These concerns are reflected in the definitions of public opinion. For example,

164

> The term public opinion is given its meaning with reference to a multi-individual situation in which individuals are expressing themselves, or can be called upon to express themselves, as favoring (or else disfavoring or opposing) some definite condition, person, or proposal of widespread importance, in such proportion of number, intensity, and constancy, as to give rise to the probability of affecting action, directly or indirectly, toward the object concerned.[27]

Although concern for markets today prompts public opinion polling as much as political candidates and issues, still many public opinion researchers are as interested in the quality and desirability of bringing public opinion to bear upon government as they are in studying its formation and effects.

Regardless of the normative connotations of the term, analysts are concerned with the social organization that permits, facilitates, or produces public opinions. Thus analysts and pollsters explore such social characteristics as class background, institutional affiliations, and primary group relations for clues to the formation, constancy, intensity, and other characteristics of public opinions. From this network of social relations, they extract ideas about the role of leaders of opinions, sections of the public more attentive than others, and the flow of communication in general in a society.[28]

[27] Floyd H. Allport, "Toward a Science of Public Opinion," *The Public Opinion Quarterly*, I (1937), 23.
[28] Recent texts are Harwood L. Childs, *Public Opinion: Nature, Formation, and Role* (Princeton, N.J., 1965); Bernard C. Hennessy, *Public Opinion* (Belmont, Calif., 1965); Robert E. Lane and David O. Sears, *Public Opinion* (Englewood Cliffs, N.J., 1964); and V. O. Key, Jr., *Public Opinion and American Democracy* (New York, 1961). Two anthologies on the topic are Bernard Berelson and Morris Janowitz, eds., *Reader in Public Opinion and Communication* (rev. ed., New York,

A BEHAVIORAL APPROACH
TO HISTORICAL ANALYSIS

This brief examination shows that culture and social organization must be considered together in order to determine the role of ideas in history. Ideas are not only items in *a* culture, but their influence is facilitated or stymied by the nature of social relationships prevailing in *a* society. Ideas operate within the limits of what a social structure allows as well as what the culture permits or prescribes. Ideas gain expression through groupings and social organization as well as through intellectual media, and so communication in its broadest sense flows along the network of social relations as well as containing a message in a culture. Thus how ideas affected the lives of past peoples will depend as much upon a society's social relationships as upon its cultural ideations.

The necessity of exploring this connection in assessing the significance of ideas in the making of history is confirmed by Ernest May's latest reinterpretation of the United States's sudden acquisition of overseas colonies in 1898–99.[29] Despite much previous work by him and others to account for the intellectual background of this imperialist thrust for colonial empire, he feels the question of timing is still unanswered. Why did the people of the United States support such imperialism at that time when they did not do so before or after the 1890s? To him this question can only be answered by a consideration of the social processes by which intellectual currents are focused upon foreign policy

1953); Daniel Katz et al., *Public Opinion and Propaganda* (New York, 1954). An important article in clarifying my thinking was John W. Riley, Jr., and Matilda W. Riley, "Mass Communication and the Social System," in Robert K. Merton, Leonard Broom, and Leonard S. Cottrell, Jr., eds., *Sociology Today: Problems and Prospects* (New York, 1959), 537–78. Appearing too late to influence the writing of these paragraphs was the important article by Lee Benson, "An Approach to the Scientific Study of Past Public Opinion," *Public Opinion Quarterly*, XXXI (1967), 522–67.

[29] Ernest May, "American Imperialism: A Reinterpretation," *Perspectives in American History*, I (1967), 123–283.

decision making. Essentially, he hypothesizes the social structure of public opinion formation and influence in regard to United States foreign policy during the late nineteenth century.

1. The public interest in foreign policy then, as now, was far smaller than the whole population, and it was composed of the comparatively well-off, well-educated, and politically active citizens. It was probably urban-based and numbered perhaps three million in all.

2. This "attentive" public can be divided into a few "opinion leaders" and many "talkers," or those who talk about other people's opinions. Included in this latter category was most of the press.

3. The opinion leaders had local or cosmopolitan perspectives and influence, but always had access to some public means of conveying their ideas and/or access to political decision makers.

From this simple hypothetical social structure of the communications flow, here further simplified for presentation, May offers new conclusions about the timing of colonial expansion. After deciding that the test of an opinion leader would be a function of citation in newspapers, he reconstructs the Boston, New York, Chicago, and Indianapolis opinion elites and their national and local significance in opinion formation.

Following the views of these leaders from the late 1860s through the first decade of the twentieth century, he concluded that only serious division in the usual consensus among these leaders about the undesirability of colonies permitted the "Great Aberration." As he says, "In 1898–99, the absence of consensus among the establishment resulted in the transfer of leadership to wider circles. The public became larger. Effective opinion, heard in Washington, was cacophonous, and the level of rationality within it declined."[30] Thus imperialist expansion sentiment for once gained concrete fulfillment outside the continent. Only with a model of the social relationships underlying foreign policy ideas could May have reached such an interesting answer to the question of timing.

The connection between ideas and social relations points to the limits of the culture concept in historical analysis. To the extent that social relationships are based upon cultural ideation, then a knowledge of a culture will provide clues to the flow of communications as well as to what is communicated. If social relationships only partially reflect cultural ideation, then the analyst will not know how a culture is manifested and lived, so to speak, if he only knows the cultural ideation. The less coincidence between a culture and a society, the less the construction of that culture will tell the analyst about that society, and the less important a knowledge of only the ideas will be in understanding the role of ideas in the history of that society. Whatever the connection between a society and a culture in any given historical case, the historian must reconstruct each culture and each society individually if he would determine the role of ideas in historical situations, for ideas act in social structures as well as containing cultural content.

This necessity of relating a culture to a society points to the ultimate limitation of ideas and the culture concept in historical analysis. No matter how well the historian understands past cultural ideation, it is still the actors' viewpoint. And that is at best only half of the job of historical analysis as defined in Chapter 3. The historian must go on

[30] *Ibid.*, 276, but see whole article for conclusions as well as method.

to analyze the total situation according to the observer's view as well. This observer's view concerns the overall structure of the situation, of which the actors' viewpoints may be oblivious or only partially knowledgeable. The investigation of the overall situation involves the analyst in the knotty problem of relating actors' views and observer's view into one coherent whole.

Regardless of the nature of an historian's specific investigation, he must make some assumptions about the way the things he studies fit together. If the historian would adopt the behavioral approach advocated in this essay, the problem of conceiving of wholes becomes all the more urgent. The behavioral analyst of past human activity must organize the totality of relationships he studies, whether it is a set of actors' constructs or observer's constructs, into an interpretative unity. Thus the historian, like the social scientist, is constantly faced with the problem of wholes and parts. Not only must he attempt to specify the relationship between the parts and the whole in his studies, but he, like any student of human behavior, must also cope with the even greater difficulty of identifying what are the parts and what are the wholes in each case. The perplexities involved in these problems were encountered by us particularly in the preceding chapters on culture and society, but they are met by historical analysts in all areas. In the end, any social analyst must organize the totality of relationships he studies.

This problem of organization of the entities into a whole is today at the very center of disputes over behavioral theory. As a result, all discussion of the problem is deeply shrouded in controversy. In an attempt to resolve the difficulties, theorists have become increasingly interested in the ideas of system and model. Because these ideas concern the problem of wholes, they too are engulfed in heated debate about their specific use, their general applicability, and

MODELS AND SYSTEMS AND THE PROBLEM OF WHOLES

whether they indeed do advance the study of the behavioral whole.[1]

The words "system" and "model" have each acquired a wide variety of definitions; yet as used by behavioral theorists today, they are frequently given the same or closely related meanings and are even substituted for the word "theory" at times. That all these terms seem synonymous to many theorists indicates the ultimate goal they espouse for the social sciences. System and model can be defined similarly only if system is intended to mean a set of interrelated entities, and if model suggests that the study of these entities may be interpreted so as to correspond in some way to some other object or objects that the analyst already understands better than that which he desires to understand. In other words, the analyst seeks to learn about one system by comparing it to another system that is already familiar to him and that he believes can serve as a model of the more unfamiliar one. For these two words to be used as equivalent to "theory" would indicate that the analyst thinks theories are propositions about a system of entities said to be a model of the objects desired to be studied and that these propositions are specified in a formal manner, preferably mathematical.[2]

Most social theorists would admit that their work falls

[1] Daniel Lerner has edited a symposium, *Parts and Wholes* (New York, 1963), that shows the approaches of various disciplines to this perplexing subject. Many of the articles cited in this and the following chapter are now brought together conveniently in an anthology edited by N. J. Demerath, III, and Richard A. Peterson, *System, Change, and Conflict: A Reader on Contemporary Sociological Theory and the Debate Over Functionalism* (New York, 1967).

[2] The best guides to clarifying the use of "model" and "theory" are May Brodbeck, "Models, Meaning, and Theories," in L. Gross, ed., *Symposium on Sociological Theory* (New York, 1959), 373–403; Abraham Kaplan, *The Conduct of Inquiry: Methodology for Behavioral Science* (San Francisco, 1964), 258–326; and Richard Rudner, *Philosophy of Social Science* (Englewood Cliffs, N.J., 1966), 23–28.

far short of such a goal but that nevertheless the goal is worth pursuing. Some of them would even maintain that the present deplorable condition of their craft will only improve by assuming that what they study can be best understood in terms of systems and models—even if such an assumption is untested by results.[3] In other words, these men would strive to achieve ideal ends with the present imperfect means by acting as if the means were better than they really can be at the present time. For them to attempt such work, however, both the nature of system and the conception of model must change in actual use from highly abstract and formal usages to less precise and more metaphorical meanings. Yet these new meanings trade upon the prestige of the more abstract connotations associated with the words. We could end the whole affair here but for the prevalence of these words in modern behavioral analysis and, even more importantly, the significant results that are claimed to be emerging from these assumptions about system and model.

Though systems analysis, as its advocates call it, originated in biology and engineering, its proponents feel that its highly general approach to phenomena allows it to cut across all disciplines. Through analysis of the abstract concept of system itself, the advocates of this "new science" hope to establish similarities among entities as diverse as atoms, organisms, societies, and galaxies. In the eyes of its most enthusiastic prophets, systems analysis seeks to reintegrate the natural and social sciences and, in fact, all knowledge. These hopes were expressed succinctly by the econ-

[3] The most vigorous assertion of this position is David Easton, *A Framework for Political Analysis* (Englewood Cliffs, N.J., 1965). This would also seem Talcott Parsons' chief defense of his work, for which see his own statement and various analyses of his work in Max Black, ed., *The Social Theories of Talcott Parsons* (Englewood Cliffs, N.J., 1961).

MODELS, SYSTEMS, AND
THE PROBLEMS OF WHOLES

omist Kenneth Boulding when he dubbed general systems theory "the Skeleton of Science."[4] Although many social theorists may not claim as much nor even acknowledge the origins of systems theory, they do use the word frequently and many still possess high hopes for its use in behavioral analysis.[5] A reader can find the word combined into such phrases as the social system, the economic system, the political system, and even cultural and personality systems.[6]

The word "system" possesses several meanings, and systems analysis depends upon a combination of at least two of these meanings. A system, according to the dictionary, is "an assemblage of objects united by some form of regular interaction or interdependence; an organic or organized whole." A more scientifically rigorous definition based upon this meaning is that of anthropologist Anthony F. C. Wallace, who is talking about a "sociocultural system."

A system may be defined as a set of variable entities (persons, objects, customs, atoms, or whatever) so related that,

[4] Kenneth Boulding, "General System Theory—The Skeleton of Science," *General Systems*, Yearbook of the Society for the Advancement of General Systems Theory, I (1956), 11–17. For an essay on the subject by one of the founders of the approach, see Ludwig Bertalanffy, "General Systems," *ibid.*, 1–10. Its utility as the basic approach in the social sciences is proposed by James G. Miller, "Toward a General Theory for the Behavioral Sciences," in Leonard D. White, ed., *The State of the Social Sciences* (Chicago, 1956), 29–65. Criticism of this article specifically and of the approach in general is R. C. Buck, "On the Logic of General Behavior Systems Theory," in Herbert Feigl and Michael Scriven, eds., *The Foundations of Science and the Concepts of Psychology and Psychoanalysis* ("Minnesota Studies in the Philosophy of Science," vol. 1 [Minneapolis, Minn., 1956]), 223–52.
[5] David Easton does so explicitly in *A Framework for Political Analysis.* Compare, on the other hand, the articles in Roy Grinker, ed., *Toward a Unified Theory of Human Behavior* (New York, 1956).
[6] Talcott Parsons popularized the use of social system in his book of that title (New York, 1951), but it was used earlier as were many of the other terms in Parsons and Edward Shils, eds., *Toward a General Theory of Action* (Cambridge, Mass., 1951). Easton popularized the political system in the book he wrote with that title (New York, 1953).

first, some variation in any one is followed by a predictable (i.e., non-random) variation in at least one other; that there is at least one sequence of variations which involves all of the entities.[7]

We may term this meaning an empirical system, because the relations of the entities, though abstracted, are found supposedly in reality. At the same time, system is also said by the dictionary to mean "a complete exhibition of essential principles or facts, arranged in rational dependence, or connection; also a complex of ideas, principles, etc., forming a coherent whole." This definition may be designated an analytical, or theoretical system, for it is the construction of the thinker and not dependent upon reality.[8] The goal of system analysis is to apply a theoretical system of the latter sort to the abstracted relationships of an empirical system. If the abstracted relationships of the empirical system simplify reality in order to comprehend it, then the empirical system is also said to be a model by most social theorists. Furthermore, if the combined analytical-empirical system should contain the principles of the relationships expressed in a series of precisely defined interrelated propositions, then the social theorists would say they also possessed a theory.

Everett E. Hagan, an economist, has summarized the "Logical Requirements of General Systems Analysis" in just such a manner so that model and system and by implication

[7] Anthony F. C. Wallace, *Culture and Personality* (New York, 1961), 31–32.

[8] Compare my use of analytical and empirical systems with Parsons and Shils, eds., *op. cit.*, 49–51; Talcott Parsons, "The Present Position and Prospects of Systematic Theory in Sociology," in Georges Gurvitch and Wilbert E. Moore, eds., *Twentieth Century Sociology* (New York, 1945), 43; Easton, *The Political System*, 96–97; Easton, *A Framework for Political Analysis*, 35–45; A. R. Radcliffe-Brown, *A Natural Science of Society* (New York, 1957), *passim;* and Everett E. Hagan, *On the Theory of Social Change: How Economic Growth Begins* (Homewood, Ill., 1962), 505, 506, n2.

MODELS, SYSTEMS, AND THE PROBLEMS OF WHOLES

theory are all intermixed in use because they all possess similar meanings. Thus he starts off his list of requirements,

174

1. An analytical model is defined by defining the elements and their interrelations. The relationships among the elements of a system are statements of the alternative values (magnitudes) or states of one of the elements associated with alternative values or states of one or more of the other elements. Because the elements are assumed to vary in magnitude or state, they are termed variables—which, broadly, includes constants—that is, the variation in some may be zero. If two variables are related in this way, each is said to be a function of the other without regard to the direction of causation between them. While the flow of causation between any two elements may be in one direction and not the other, among all the elements taken as a group, apart from the impact of forces from outside the system, all depend upon all. . . . [9]

The supposed power of systems analysis to advance knowledge is beyond showing mere analogy and homology among various phenomena. It is nothing less than the assumption that systems *qua* systems regardless of the entities composing them exhibit certain fundamental similarities. Thus in systems analysis, theorists concern themselves with those problems common to all systems, such as, What is the system? What are its boundaries? What are its components? Are there subsystems? Why does the system persist as a system? What is the system's relationship with its environment? Supposedly every system should and can be studied in this manner. In the behavioral sciences two fundamental sets of answers have been given for these questions depending upon the basic model used for the system.

Throughout the history of Western social thought two basic models of society have persisted, and the latest

[9] Reprinted by permission of The Dorsey Press from Everett E. Hagan, *On the Theory of Social Change: How Economic Growth Begins,* copyright 1962 by the Massachusetts Institute of Technology; p. 506.

*A BEHAVIORAL APPROACH
TO HISTORICAL ANALYSIS*

phase, systems analysis, seems no exception to this generalization. From the Greeks onward, men have attempted to comprehend the complexity of societal relationships by likening the totality of that network to either a mechanism or an organism. If society is pictured as an organism, then the theorist stresses the wholeness of the society as more than the mere sum of its parts, just as the living organism seems to consist of a complexity greater than the mere aggregation of its components. The mechanistic model of society likens social relationships to the mechanism of classical physics, in which the whole is the functioning of its parts. Although the invention of servo-mechanisms such as thermostats and engine governors that administer their own regulation has confused somewhat the formerly clearcut boundary between mechanism and organism, systems analysts still lean toward one or the other basic model in their theorizing.[10]

175

Both approaches to systems analysis study the patterns of relationships that compose a whole, but they go about their analyses in quite different ways as a result of their fundamental assumptions about the working of their respective models. Not all the social sciences are internally divided by disputes over the merits of the two models, but some disciplines do have heated controversy among their own practitioners. Economists, for example, have always utilized a mechanistic model for their study of wholes, but sociologists still argue among themselves about the merits of functionalism in general and structural functionalism,

[10] For a history of the two models, see Werner Stark, *The Fundamental Forms of Social Thought* (London, 1962). Recent analyses of modern social theory in terms of the two models are Karl Deutsch, *The Nerves of Government* (New York, 1963), 27–34; Karl Deutsch, "Mechanism, Organism, and Society," *Philosophy of Science*, XVIII (1951), 230–52; Paul Meadows, "Models, Systems, and Science," *American Sociological Review*, XXII (1957), 3–9.

MODELS, SYSTEMS, AND THE PROBLEMS OF WHOLES

essentially an organismic model, in particular. Since the two basic models have such great implications for the type of analysis performed on wholes and the results believed attained, it would be well to examine each model at length, particularly in the words of its proponents, in order to discover the assumptions of each side and also the diverse meanings behind sometimes similar terminology. Therefore, following the precept preached in the last chapter on value orientations, I shall quote lengthy excerpts of the authors on each side so that I will not distort their categories of analysis.

Talcott Parsons, a leader in introducing the concept of system into sociology in the United States, uses both a mechanistic and an organic model in explaining his use of that term. He begins his elaboration of the concept with the traditional mechanistic example of the solar system, but then he turns to biology for the further implications he wishes to draw about a notion of system.

The most general and fundamental property of a system is the interdependence of parts or variables. Interdependence consists in the existence of determinate relationships among the parts or variables as contrasted with randomness of variability. In other words, interdependence is *order* in the relationship among the components which enter into a system. This order must have a tendency to self-maintenance, which is generally expressed in the concept of equilibrium. [Footnote: That is, if the system is to be permanent enough to be worth study, there must be a tendency to maintenance of order except under exceptional circumstances.] It need not, however, be a static self-maintenance or a stable equilibrium. It may be an ordered process of change—a process following a determinate pattern rather than random variability relative to a starting point. This is called a moving equilibrium, and is well exemplified by growth. Furthermore, equilibrium, even when stable, by no means implies that process is not going on; process is continual even in stable systems, the stabilities residing in the interrelations involved in the process.

A particularly important feature of all systems is the inherent limitations on the compatibility of certain parts or events within the same system. This is indeed simply another way of saying that the relations within the system are determinate and that not just anything can happen. Thus, to take an example from the solar system, if the orbit of one of the planets, such as Jupiter, is given, it is no longer possible for the orbits of the other planets to be distributed at random relative to this given orbit. Certain limitations are imposed by the fact that the value of one of the variables is given. This limitation may in turn be looked at from either a negative or a positive point of view. On the one hand, again using the solar system as example, if one of the planets should simply disappear, the fact that no mass was present in that particular orbit would necessitate a change in the equilibrium of the system. It would make necessary a readjustment of the orbits of the other planets in order to bring the system into equilibrium. This may also be expressed in the statement that there is a change in the structure of the system. On the other hand, the same problem may be treated from the standpoint of what would happen in the case of the coexistence of "incompatible" elements or processes within the same system. Incompatibility is always relative to a *given* state of the system. If, for example, the orbits of two of the planets should move closer to each other than is compatible for the maintenance of the current state of the system, one of two things would have to happen. Either processes would be set up which would tend to restore the previous relations by the elimination of the incompatibility; or if the new relation were maintained, there would have to be adjustments in *other* parts of the system, bringing the system into a new state of equilibrium.

These properties are inherent in all systems. A special additional property, however, is of primary significance for the theory of action. [This is Parson's approach, and here he turns to the organismic model.] This is the tendency to maintain equilibrium, in the most general sense stated above, within certain boundaries relative to an environment—boundaries which are not imposed from outside but which are self-maintained by the properties of the constituent variables as they operate within the system. The most familiar example is the living organism, which is a physiochemical system that is not assimilated to the physiochemical conditions of the environment, but maintains certain distinct properties in relation to environment. For example, the maintenance of the constant body temperature of the mammal necessitates processes which indicate the interdependence between the internal and the external systems in respect to temperature; these processes maintain constancy over a wide range of variability in environmental temperatures.

The two fundamental types of processes necesary for the maintenance of a given state of equilibrium of a system we call, in the theory of action, *allocation* and *integration*. By *allocation* we mean processes which maintain a distribution of the components or parts of the system which is compatible with the maintenance of a given state of equilibrium. By *integration*, we mean the processes by which relations to the environment are mediated in such a way that the distinctive internal properties and boundaries of the system as an entity are maintained in the face of variability in the external situation. It must be realized that self-maintenance of such a system is not only maintenance of boundaries but also maintenance of distinctive relationships of parts of the system *within* the boundary. The system is in some sense a unity relative to its environment. Also, self-maintenance implies not only control of the environmental variations, but also control of tendencies to change—that is, to alteration of the distinctive state—coming from within the system.[11]

The additional assumptions—we might almost call them imperatives, they seem so forced upon the theorist by his model—demanded by the organismic analogy may be seen even more clearly in A. R. Radcliffe-Brown, the anthropologist who was so influential in the spread of functionalism in his field. He admits quite candidly that the concept of function in the social sciences must be based upon analogy between social life and organic life[12] and he is explicit in developing the analogy in his work. In the quotation that follows, he establishes first the nature of the

[11] Reprinted by permission of the publishers from Talcott Parsons and Edward Shils, eds., *Toward a General Theory of Action*, Cambridge, Mass., Harvard University Press. Copyright, 1951, by the President and Fellows of Harvard College; pp. 107–8 (author's italics).

[12] A. R. Radcliffe-Brown, "On the Concept of Function in Social Science," *American Anthropologist*, new ser., XXXVII (1935), 394.

A BEHAVIORAL APPROACH
TO HISTORICAL ANALYSIS

organism as such and then he applies his scheme to societies.

For the further elucidation of the concept it is convenient to use the analogy between social life and organic life. Like all analogies it has to be used with care. The animal organism is an agglomeration of cells and interstitial fluids arranged in relation to one another not as an aggregate but as an integrated whole. For the biochemist, it is a completely integrated system of complex molecules. The system of relations by which these units are related is the organic structure. As the terms are here used the organism is not itself the structure; it is a collection of units (cells or molecules) arranged in a structure, i.e., in a set of relations; the organism has a structure. Two mature animals of the same species and sex consist of similar units combined in a similar structure. The structure is thus to be defined as a set of relations between entities. (The structure of a cell is in the same way a set of relations between complex molecules, and the structure of an atom is a set of relations between electrons and protons.) As long as it lives the organism preserves a certain continuity of structure although it does not preserve the complete identity of its constituent parts. It loses some of its constituent molecules by respiration or excretion; it takes in others by respiration and alimentary absorption. Over a period its constituent cells do not remain the same. But the structural arrangement of the constituent units does remain similar. The process by which this structural continuity of the organism is maintained is called life. The life-process consists of the activities and interactions of the constituent units of the organism, the cells, and the organs into which the cells are united.

As the word function is here being used the life of the organism is conceived as the *functioning* of its structure. It is through and by the continuity of the functioning that the continuity of the structure is preserved. If we consider any recurrent part of the life process, such as respiration, digestion, etc., its *function* is the part it plays in, the contribution it makes to, the life of the organism as a whole. As the terms are here being used a cell or an organ has an activity and that *activity* has a *function*. It is true that we commonly speak of the secretion of gastric fluid as a "function" of the stomach. As the words are here used we should say that this is an "activity" of the stomach, the "function" of which is to change the proteins of food into a form in which these are absorbed and distributed by the blood to the tissues. We may note that

179

the function of a recurrent physiological process is thus a correspondence between it and the needs (i.e., necessary conditions of existence) of the organism. . . .

To turn from organic life to social life, if we examine such a community as an African or Australian tribe we can recognize the existence of a social structure. Individual human beings, the essential units in this instance, are connected by a definite set of social relations into an integrated whole. The continuity of the social structure, like that of an organic structure, is not destroyed by changes in the units. Individuals may leave the society, by death or otherwise; others may enter it. The continuity of structure is maintained by the process of social life, which consists of the activities and interactions of the individual human beings and of the organized groups into which they are united. The social life of the community is *here* defined as the *functioning* of the social structure. The function of any recurrent activity, such as the punishment of a crime, or a funeral ceremony, is the part it plays in the social life as a whole and therefore the contribution it makes to the maintenance of the structural continuity.

The concept of function as here defined thus involves the notion of a *structure* consisting of a *set of relations* amongst *unit entities*, the *continuity* of the structure being maintained by a *life-process* made up of the *activities* of the constituent units.[13]

With this exposition of wholes and parts as developed by the social theorists who base their system upon organismic analogy, we can understand now more clearly the mechanical model underlying the frequently abstract language of those who would call themselves more strictly systems analysts. If we return to Hagan, who defined a total system as composed of its elements and their relationships, we can see the fewer assumptions and the greater abstraction of the current mechanistic approach to systems in language about the components and the overall system as Hagan defines them.

[13] *Ibid.*, 394–6, his italics; reprinted in his *Structure and Function in Primitive Society* (New York: The Free Press, 1952; London: Cohen & West, 1952), 178–9, 180. Compare his *A Natural Science of Society.*

A BEHAVIORAL APPROACH
TO HISTORICAL ANALYSIS

2. The variables of a system must exist either in conceptually measurable amounts, or in one or another set of definable states. It is impossible to conceive of variation in one element associated with variation in another if the two cannot be conceived of as varying by measurable amounts, or from one state or structural form to another. If a variable (such as "community spirit" or "love of family") is not defined so as to be conceptually measurable or as existing in one or another set of definable states, it cannot have a precise reasoning, in an analytical model or otherwise.

A variable is a single dimension of an entity, not the entity itself. Thus a variable is not a physical body but one of its qualities, for example, length; in a model of society it is not an individual, but say, each value and need (motive) attributed to him and each component of his perception of the nature of the world. The individual as a group of interacting elements may be a subsystem within the model.

3. A system which is interacting with its environment is an open system; all systems of "real life" (concrete systems) are therefore open systems. For analysis, it is necessary to assume in the intellectual construct that the operation of the system is affected only by given conditions previously established by the environment and not changing at the time of analysis, plus the relationships among the elements of the system. . . .

Elements of the system whose magnitudes are wholly determined by the environment, and which are therefore constant rather than variable so long as the system is insulated from change in the environment, are termed *parameters*. For example, in some analyses in economics the size of the population and per capita income are parameters, that is, it is assumed that they remain constant. . . .[14]

The contrast between the two models of system is even more striking when Hagan discusses equilibrium.

4. It is often useful to construct a model which is in equilibrium, and in stable rather than unstable equilibrium.

Equilibrium in its simplest sense refers to a condition in which the variables in the system are in such a relation-

[14] Hagan, *op. cit.*, 506–7.

ship to each other that all remain constant in value, not by assumption, but by their interaction.

Suppose that some external force that directly affects one variable in the system changes in magnitude temporarily, then reverts to its previous magnitude. The change this temporary disturbance causes in one variable will necessarily cause at least temporary changes in the magnitudes of other variables, because of the functional relationships among them. (If the change in one variable affects no other variable, then that one variable is not in any significant sense a part of the system.) These changes will in turn react on the magnitudes of the variable which first changed, and on each other. The equilibrium of the system is stable if the final result of this reaction is a return to the initial values. The equilibrium is unstable if a temporary disturbance causes the values of some or all variables to move cumulatively farther from the initial equilibrium.

The equilibrium of the system may, of course, be stable with respect to one type of disturbance and not with respect to another. Further, the equilibrium of a system may be stable with respect to a small disturbance ("stability in the small") but not with respect to a large disturbance ("stability in the large"). Stability of equilibrium, moreover, implies only that the equilibrium values of the variables will remain unchanged as long as the system remains closed except for temporary "disturbances." If permanent changes in the environment are communicated to the system, there will be corresponding permanent changes in the equilibrium values of the variables in the system (that is, the values they will have when the system has settled down into the new equilibrium), even though the equilibrium is stable.[15]

The various assumptions about the nature of wholeness and the different conclusions about relationships among

[15] *Ibid.*, 507. Compare John S. Chipman, "The Nature and Meaning of Equilibrium in Economic Theory," in Don Martindale, ed., *Functionalism in the Social Sciences: The Strengths and Limits of Functionalism in Anthropology, Economics, Political Science, and Sociology*, monograph no. 5 of the American Academy of Political and Social Science (Philadelphia, 1965), 35–64.

*A BEHAVIORAL APPROACH
TO HISTORICAL ANALYSIS*

components that arise from using one or the other model of system emerge clearly in the extensive quotations from the proponents of each side. Although both groups of theorists are concerned with the boundary and nature of a system, those who postulate a mechanistic model see magnitudes of interrelated variables, open and closed systems, and parameters, whereas the devotees of the organismic model assume a more concrete, organized structure with definite boundaries and a complicated, patterned internal differentiation. For the former, a function is simply as defined in mathematics, $y = f(x)$, whereas for the latter, a function is the contribution a concrete part makes to the persistence of the whole. The mechanistic model may or may not be in equilibrium, and if it is, then equilibrium is merely a state of balance among opposing forces, a state of mutually dependent variables. The organismic model, however, depends upon that special case of equilibrium known in biology as homeostasis, in which the whole maintains within itself relatively stable conditions by means of its own regulatory mechanisms. In the mechanical model, the whole is the result of the aggregate relations of its parts, but in the organismic model the whole is not only a product of the functioning of its parts but also, as a result of its wholeness, is a regulator of the relations among those parts.

Under these impressions of the whole, the theorist of the organismic model must postulate some further assumptions about the persistence of the whole that the mechanistic model-builder finds unnecessary. Parsons, for example, creates certain categories of functions that will provide for the maintenance of the internal structure and the external boundary of systems as he views them. He has developed four broad classes of such functions—or "functional requisites," as he calls them—that are necessary for maintaining a system in a stable state. First, the system must preserve its basic pattern so that the parts remain in a certain relation to each other and thus to the whole. This function he designates "pattern-maintenance." The system must also relate to its environment by adaptation so as to preserve its wholeness. He calls this either "adaptation" or "boundary-maintenance." Then, too, the system itself has an overall function in relation to other systems or its environment, and that he denominates "goal-attainment." Lastly, there is the allocation of functions and coordination of internal parts to permit smooth overall functioning of the system, which he terms "system-integration." The system as a whole is thus integrated in terms of its goal and its self-maintenance.[16]

Parsons believes that such a general approach to systems means that his theory is applicable on every level of human behavior. It applies just as readily to intrapersonal as to interpersonal relationships—to parts of one man, to one man, to many men, or to a whole society. He further believes that systems are composed of subsystems that also have all the requirements of systems and can be treated as such in their own right. The relation of a system to one of its subsystems is one of systematic exchange; the output of the subsystem is the input of the system on the next higher level. For example, the goal attainment and adaptation of a subsystem become part of the functional requisites of the more inclusive system. In this way, Parsons moves from the smallest unit (the role) to groups ("collectivities" of roles), to institutional sectors (such as the economy or the polity) to the total social system. Perhaps systemic exchange as used by Parsons is the latest form of

[16] Parsons has used sundry terms at different times as his thought developed. Recent statements are "Some Highlights of the General Theory of Action," in Roland Young, ed., *Approaches to the Study of Politics* (Evanston, Ill., 1958), 282–301, and, with Neil Smelser, *Economy and Society: A Study in the Integration of Economic and Social Theory* (New York, 1956), 16–19.

A BEHAVIORAL APPROACH
TO HISTORICAL ANALYSIS

the chain of being, for it certainly resembles that value-orientation in its hierarchy of positions on a graded scale.[17]

Though some of Parson's disciples question the applicability of systems analysis to anything less than a total society, they do not deny the significance of functional requisites to maintaining the persistence of a social system nor of functional prerequisites to the coming into being of such a system. Because they pay particular attention to structure as an on-going organization of parts and because they believe that the function of these parts is to preserve the structure, Parsons, Radcliffe-Brown, and others who hold similar organismically based models of social system are called structural functionalists. Although these theorists differ somewhat in their views, still all postulate in common certain conditions for the creation and the continued existence of a given social system.[18]

Just how valuable the elaborate taxonomy and terminology of the structural functionalists will prove in the long run and whether such an approach actually explains anything in a scientific sense is best left to the intellectual marketplace, but this analytical scheme has already made heuristic contributions to modern social science. This contribution is particularly clear if one separates the method of approach from the substantive theory. Its chief benefit has been to make behavioral scientists aware of the complex interrelationships within and among social, political, eco-

[17] Almost any work of Parsons will show this, but see particularly his *Social System.*

[18] Among many, Radcliffe-Brown, *A National Science of Society*, and Marion J. Levy, Jr., *The Structure of Society* (Princeton, N.J., 1952), especially 27–197. Illuminating discussions of structural-functionalism from this as well as other viewpoints are Walter Buckley, "Structural-Functional Analysis in Modern Sociology," in Howard Becker and Alvin Boskoff, eds., *Modern Sociological Theory in Continuity and Change* (New York, 1957), 236–59, and Alvin Gouldner, "Reciprocity and Autonomy in Functional Theory," in Gross, ed., *op. cit.,* 241–70.

MODELS, SYSTEMS, AND
THE PROBLEMS OF WHOLES

nomic, cultural, and other behavioral phenomena. Once again, analysts have focused their attention upon the whole, particularly the overall organization of society, as a result of structural-functional analysis instead of treating individual or partial manifestation in their particularity with

no concern for their place in a total system. By explaining the functions of structural parts to the maintenance of a whole, these analysts have drawn explicit attention to the long-range effects, particularly unintended consequences, of recurring intended actions in a way no other theorists have. Furthermore, their approach has tended to treat ideas and activities as part of one analytical system to the benefit of social observation and theory. In this latter case some proponents of the approach even assert that their method "has excluded speculation about human motives and introduced objectively determinable factors" into the study of behavioral phenomena.[19] If this is so, then structural functionalism is purely an observer's construct in the end despite its seeming application to the structural viewpoint of the actors under study.

To claim all these contributions to social theory in the name of structural functionalism may be fair, although some might demur; but to assert that they can be achieved only as the result of using such an approach is definitely not true. Some of these benefits flow equally from other forms of systems analysis. Therefore, it is worthwhile to sort out the amount of commitment an analyst must make, first to systems analysis as such and then to the respective mechanistic and organismic models, in order to achieve what kind of observational and theoretical benefits in his study of wholes.

In the literature, the exploration of this commitment

[19] Especially Ian Whitaker in Martindale, ed., *op. cit.*, 127–43, but the whole booklet is on pros and cons of functionalism.

A BEHAVIORAL APPROACH
TO HISTORICAL ANALYSIS

has led to distinctions between heuristic method versus substantive theory or to divisions of theorists into systems analysts, loose or eclectic functionalists, and strict structural functionalists. This argument in many ways really concerns the difference between an organic or mechanical model of systems as we have developed it here. Rather than repeating the vitriolic accusations in a controversy still not dead, it would seem more profitable to examine what implications the various positions on (1) the nature of relationship among parts, (2) the nature of persistence or equilibrium of the whole, and (3) the nature of explanation involved might possess for the historian's task of studying men's past behavior. Leaving the last item for the philosophers debating explanation,[20] we will deal in the next chapter with the theoretical space of coexisting entities and in the succeeding chapter with theoretical time as the persistence of the relationship of these entities.

[20] On the validity of functional analysis as explanation, see Carl G. Hempel, "The Logic of Functional Analysis," in Gross, ed., *op. cit.*, 271–307 (reprinted in his *Aspects of Scientific Explanation* [New York, 1965], 297–330); Ernest Nagel, *Structure of Science: Problems in the Logic of Scientific Explanation* (New York, 1961), 520–35; Richard Rudner, *op. cit.*, 84–111; Ronald P. Dore, "Function and Cause," *American Sociological Review*, XXVI (1961), 843–53.

SYSTEMS ANALYSIS AND THE ORGANIZATION OF THE OBSERVER'S VIEWPOINT

The only choice denied the historian among the assumptions about the nature of the whole is no choice at all. The historian like any other analyst of human behavior must adopt some conception or model of the whole. The question merely remains, Which conception or model? The answer depends upon the purposes of the study as well as the nature of the behavior studied. An examination of the type of integration presumed by various models of systems analysis with their application to specific historical situations will clarify some of the choices available to the historian in the interpretation of the whole.

All social analysts are interested in discovering relationships among the phenomena they study. If systems analysis and functionalism merely meant the search for connections among human behavioral phenomena, then every analyst would subscribe to such an approach. But systems analysts and both brands of functionalists go beyond this point and claim to relate part to part and the parts to a whole. Many theorists can still agree with this stand, and to that extent they are all functionalists, if one intends by that term to mean a theorist who believes in the possibility of studying a whole systematically and conceives of function in its mathematical sense. The dispute arises in defining the nature of the whole. The mechanistic systems analysts see the whole as the interrelationship of the parts, and the behavior of the system is predicated upon the aggregate behavior of the parts. On the other hand, the structural functionalists, as we have seen, not only treat the system as a whole but seek to explain its behavior in terms of its own goals and what maintains it in such a way that the functional interdependence of the parts creates the total system, which in turn guides the functioning of those parts. It is this step that many systems analysts and even so-called "loose" functionalists refuse to take, because they argue that the structural functionalists postulate as given much that should be assumed problematical and subject to proof. If functionalism must mean what it does to the structural functionalists, then few social theorists will lay claim to the title.[1]

In this debate over functionalism, the historian is presented with a variety of choices. First, he should decide whether connected parts can be studied as wholes or not; in other words, can historical phenomena be grouped as systems? If he decides in favor of a system concept, then he must determine the nature of the whole. Should the number of parts and their relationship be presumed problematical and therefore to be established empirically, or should they be postulated as connected according to some model? Even if some model is used, how tight an integration should be assumed? Should the integration be conceived of as mechanistic or organic? Regardless of which approach to system is used, the historian must still determine upon what levels of generalization he can employ the idea of system. Is systems analysis applicable, for example,

---

[1] A particularly confused analysis of these points is the widely cited article by Kingsley Davis, "The Myth of Functional Analysis as a Special Method in Sociology and Anthropology," *American Sociological Review*, XXIV (1959), 757–72. A clear analysis of the nature of commitment is Alvin Gouldner "Reciprocity and Autonomy in Functional Theory" in Llewellyn Gross, ed., *Symposium on Sociological Theory* (New York, 1959), 247–70.

SYSTEMS ANALYSIS AND
THE OBSERVER'S VIEWPOINT

to all levels of social interaction from two people to an entire society? Or is it more beneficial or even applicable only on one or another level of social complexity? Lastly, and crucially for the historian, what implications does a concept of a system, particularly as structure, have for the study of time? Does systems analysis involve necessarily a state of equilibrium, hence an atemporal dimension? If so, can the historian use a systems analysis in any but the most limited cases?

Faced with these choices, the historian should, I would argue as I have so often before, adopt a stance of methodological toleration. To assume few or no wholes can be studied systematically in past time would defeat the goals of the historian as much as it does those of the behavioral analyst of the present. To accept as the sole way to study wholes, on the other hand, the tight organic integration assumed by the structural functionalists seems equally unnecessary in either theory or method. Methodological toleration leaves open all options, and pure utility to the historian's purposes at hand should determine which choices he makes in any given analytical circumstance. In line with this reasoning, it would seem useful at this point to examine some of the possibilities by example with an eye to seeing the method of application and the resultant benefits to historical analysis.

That an assumption of system can aid the historian to solve problems he could not otherwise answer has been demonstrated dramatically in the argument over the profitability of slavery in the ante-bellum United States. Before the recent study by Alfred Conrad and John Meyer, authorities differed over profitability according to the random research they had done in the relatively plentiful but still far too few surviving account books. Conrad and Meyers constructed a model of slave-holding returns from general market prices as well as specific plantation costs in order to patch out their data. They could only combine these factors by assuming that slave owning fit into an overall Southern economic system that was reflected in cotton and slave prices in the marketplace. For slavery to be profitable to the slave-owner in the less fertile upper South, he had to receive income from slave breeding as well as from field production. In order for the two economists to prove their contention, therefore, they had to demonstrate that such breeding and selling were practiced by Virginians and other planters in the upper South, despite their explicit condemnation of the practice as opposed to the cavalier code of *noblesse oblige*. They showed that the prices for female slaves and the age distribution of slaves within the South conceived as an operating economic system could only be explained by the presence of widespread transport of slaves from the upper to lower South. By treating the entire South as one system, they immediately could show that the similarity of prices in different slave centers indicated a free market, and thus planters even in the upper South operated profitably by selling their excess slaves.[2] While their results are controversial, they have so changed the entire argument by their assumption of system that one historian of slavery has called their work a "conceptual breakthrough."[3]

[2] Alfred H. Conrad and John R. Meyer, "The Economics of Slavery in the Ante-Bellum South," *Journal of Political Economy*, LXVI (1958), 95–130, reprinted in their book, *The Economics of Slavery and Other Studies in Econometric History* (Chicago, 1964), 43–92.

[3] Stanley M. Elkins, *Slavery: A Problem in American Institutional and Intellectual Life* (Chicago, 1959), 234. A recent article summarizing the arguments over profitability since the days of slavery is Harold Woodman, "The Profitability of Slavery: A Hardy Perennial," *Journal of Southern History*, XXIX (1963), 303–25. A more analytical approach to the question is Stanley L. Engerman, "The Effects of Slavery upon the Southern Economy: A Review of the Recent Debate," *Explorations in Entrepreneurial History*, 2d ser., IV (1967), 71–97.

*SYSTEMS ANALYSIS AND
THE OBSERVER'S VIEWPOINT*

An even better example of the results for historical analysis of an assumption of system is the iconoclastic work of Robert Fogel, *Railroads and American Economic Growth*. By an elaborate econometric analysis of the United States economy at the end of the nineteenth century, he refutes the long-held belief that the railroads played an indispensable role in the development of that economy. In order to prove his contentions, Fogel constructs a statistical model of the United States economic system in 1890 and then shows that an alternative means of transportation would have done as well as railroads. Americans could have achieved nearly the same level of prosperity with, he says, artificial waterways as they did with railroads. In this manner, Fogel denies the unicausal hypothesis so long associated with the railroad in American history and replaces it with a multicausal model of economic development based upon a conception of system.[4] Although Fogel's results or even his counterfactual approach to railroad indispensability may be questioned, his methodological assumption of system must remain the foundation of the debate he started.[5]

In these examples, the systems' integration was mechanistic, for the behavior of the whole was established from the interrelations of the parts. The functionalism was mathematical, and the entities were magnitudes of variables. The systems were observers' constructs of what seemed to fit together. All these characteristics are common to systems analysis and model construction in economics and,

[4] Robert W. Fogel, *Railroads and American Economic Growth: Essays in Econometric History* (Baltimore, Md., 1964).
[5] Vigorous opposition to Fogel's analysis is voiced by Stanley Lebergott, "United States Transport Advance and Externalities," *Journal of Economic History*, XXVI (1966), 437–61. Compare, however, Albert Fishlow, *American Railroads and the Transformation of the Ante-Bellum Economy* (Cambridge, Mass., 1965).

*A BEHAVIORAL APPROACH
TO HISTORICAL ANALYSIS*

therefore, not surprisingly, to the so-called "new economic history" of which these two illustrations are now famous cases.

An analyst can switch the meaning of function from its strictly mathematical sense to its organic sense of contributing to the persistence of a system without thereby making a full commitment to structural functionalism. A "loose" or "half-hearted" functionalist connects a part to its context of a whole without really stressing the organic qualities of that whole. Such is the method followed by Robert Merton in his now-classic "Paradigm for Functional Analysis in Sociology."[6]

According to him, the steps for such an analysis are as follows:

1. The selection of the item or items to which the analyst would impute functions. "The basic requirement is that the object of analysis represent a standardized (i.e., patterned and repetitive) item, such as social roles, institutional patterns, social processes, cultural pattern, culturally patterned emotions, social norms, group organization, social structure, devices for social control, etc."[7]

2. The separation of such subjective dispositions as motives and purposes of the individual actor or actors involved from the objective consequences of the actions as seen by the observer and upon which the function will be based.

[6] Robert K. Merton, *Social Theory and Social Structure* (2d ed., New York, 1957), 50–54, but see all of chap. 1. Ernest Nagel, "A Formalization of Functionalism with Special Reference to Its Application in the Social Sciences," in his *Logic Without Metaphysics and Other Essays in the Philosophy of Science* (New York, 1956), 247–83, asks many valuable, clarifying questions during the process of analyzing Merton's paradigm.
[7] Merton, *op. cit.*, 50.

3. Distinguishing the various categories of objective consequences. The consequences which make for "adaptation or adjustment of a given system" are called "functions"; those which do not are termed "dysfunctions." Functions may be divided into "manifest" or "latent" depending upon whether the functions performed are recognized and intended by the actor(s) in the system or whether they are neither intended nor recognized by the actor(s). Latent functions differ from simple unintended actions by their recurring persistence in maintaining the system. Dysfunctions can be either latent or manifest also.

4. The unit served by the function must be specified, and this means there is

5. A specification, tacit or explicit, of the functional requirements or needs of the system examined.

6. Complete analysis also requires that the analyst specify the mechanisms that operate to perform the function or functions, and in social analysis, these must be social mechanisms, "e.g., role-segmentation, insulation of institutional demands, hierarchical ordering of values, social division of labor, ritual and ceremonial enactments, etc."[8]

7. To avoid the assumption of "functional indispensability of [particular] given social structures," Merton mentions the possibility of functional alternatives or equivalents to serve the postulated functional requisite equally well.

8. Yet the variability of items to fulfill the designated function cannot be unlimited in this theoretical framework because of the interdependence of parts. The demands of the whole would seem to limit the number of functional alternatives. As a result, the structural constraints restraining the number of items should be specified.

[8] *Ibid.*, 53.

*A BEHAVIORAL APPROACH
TO HISTORICAL ANALYSIS*

9. How are strains and instability contained so as not to disrupt the structure of the system? This may be studied dynamically as tension management, in which case an equilibrium is produced, or as social change. If the analyst knows the strains, can he predict the nature of the dynamics, whether equilibrium or change?[9]

Essentially Merton wants analysts to construct an observer's conception of a structural function. To the extent that the actors recognize the item as serving to promote structural persistence then he calls it a manifest function; to the extent they do not recognize explicitly its function in the overall structure, then he terms it a latent function.

The "half-heartedness," as some see it, of Merton's systems commitment is revealed in his own analysis of the old-time political machine.[10] He inquires into the paradox of bossism in America. Why did bosses like Tweed, Vare, Crump, Flynn, and Hague, who were condemned as bad by so many people, continue so long in power in violation of both the legal and moral codes of their day? Merton feels that the role these men and their political organizations played in the society of their time can be understood only by examining two sociological variables.

(1) the structural context which makes it difficult, if not impossible, for morally approved structures to fulfill essential social functions, thus leaving the door open for political machines (or their structural equivalents) to fulfill these functions, and (2) the subgroups whose distinctive needs are left unsatisfied, except for the latent functions which the machine in fact fulfills.[11]

By the first variable, Merton means the American political organization of the period with its constitutionally speci-

[9] Merton's steps ten and eleven are irrelevant to our purposes here.
[10] Merton, *op. cit.*, 71–82.
[11] *Ibid.*, 72.

fied decentralization of power. Such a structure contained no centralized responsible leadership, because decision making was scattered among many persons under the system of checks and balances and the haphazard rise of agencies. Thus the boss could step in to provide the necessary leadership, and his organization could be more "human" because it was extralegal, that is, an unofficial structure that could flaunt the laws for special purposes. The machine served functions for a wide variety of subgroups whose needs were not met under the legal government. It humanized abstract governmental procedure and justice with its middle class emphasis on the rules in favor of the poor native-born American or immigrant lower class, who received among other things food baskets, peddlers' licenses, and protection from the law they did not understand. Big and small businessmen, whether legitimate or illegitimate, understood the law, but they needed exemptions from laws geared to a small-town America so that they could pursue their legal or illegal ends in the large city. Thus contractors bought building permits and gamblers purchased police protection from the boss and his organization. Participation in the machine itself offered social mobility to the disadvantaged, who were not white Anglo-Saxon Protestants in the big metropolis. All these functions of the machine explain, then, why reform attempts were so short-lived if they were successful at all. Unless a new structure was substituted to serve the functions of the old one, the machine was bound to revive in the circumstances. According to this analysis, social security and unemployment insurance, not any increase in morality among the populace, rang the death knell of the old-time political boss.

The looseness of Merton's analysis from the strictly structural-functional viewpoint is obvious. He never really specifies the systemic context of the political machine other than by vague references to the decentralized political organization of the time. He does not even treat the political machine as a subsystem or system in its own right. Neither does he show that the machine filled all of the needs of the overall sociopolitical system, only that it satisfied some of the needs. Nor does he demonstrate that only the machine could fulfill those functions that he said it served. In all these ways, Merton's analysis and even to some extent his paradigm fall short of a rigorous structural-functional analysis. Yet, quite obviously, his treatment of the machine is illuminating, and so for the historian he pursues a legitimate strategy in regard to functionalism and systems analysis.[12]

The value of the approach taken by Merton was recognized long ago by Thorstein Veblen and Max Weber. Veblen's examination of conspicuous consumption is functional analysis à la Merton, because he too did not define the overall system carefully. Although he asserts that in the modern capitalistic system the real function of consuming expensive goods is not for direct use and gratification but to symbolize the social status of the purchaser, he does not construct a model of that system.[13] In the same manner, Max Weber describes how the Protestant Ethic fostered the spirit of capitalism without proving the system within which this operated. The ascetic Calvinist practiced his calling with sobriety, frugality, and industry with the manifest function of achieving salvation; the latent function of the Protestant Ethic was capital accumulation, given the socioeconomic system of the times. Although Weber's essay is usually considered an example in the use of ideal types, it is just as good an illustration of functional

[12] Alvin Gouldner, *op. cit.*, 242–44, discusses Merton's commitment to functionalism.
[13] Merton uses Veblen as an example of his scheme of analysis in *op. cit.*, 57–8, 69–70.

SYSTEMS ANALYSIS AND
THE OBSERVER'S VIEWPOINT

analysis according to the option of not defining the system thoroughly.[14]

Because Veblen and Weber like Merton never explicitly establish the overall system with which they work, they can only be called loose functionalists. They emphasize the relationship of a part to a whole, but they never define the whole fully or carefully show that the relationship they assert was the only possible one given the overall system. This lack of emphasis on the wholeness of the system and even the wholeness of the part as a subsystem differentiates their analyses, useful as they may be, from those of the strict structural functionalists.

The difference between Merton and a strict structural functionalist can be seen in their orientation and procedure. According to Marion Levy, another Parsons student like Merton, the two basic questions an analyst pursuing a "structural-functional requisite" analysis must ask are, "What must be done if a unit of the sort chosen is to persist?" and "How must what must be done be done?"[15] In more formal language and at somewhat greater length he outlines four basic steps of approved procedure.

> 1. One must define the unit to be discussed. For these purposes the unit must be a unit in terms of which operations (or processes) can or do take place. . . . [It must be an empirical system?]
> 2. One must discover (at least by hypotheses) the factors setting the most general limits of possible variations for the type of unit chosen. . . .

[14] For this reason, it is perhaps appropriate that Talcott Parsons translated the work into English. The Protestant Ethic was no longer so latent once Benjamin Franklin apotheosized the "obvious" into almanac homilies.

[15] Marion J. Levy, Jr., "Some Aspects of 'Structural-Functional' Analysis on Political Science," in Roland Young, ed., *Approaches to the Study of Politics* (Evanston, Ill.: Northwestern University Press, 1958), 53.

3. One must try to determine what general types of conditions must be met if the unit is to persist as defined within these limits. These conditions are the functional requisites.

4. One must then determine what patterns of action must be present if operation in terms of them is to result in the production of functional requisites. These patterns are the structural requisites.[16]

Never once in setting forth the program does Levy neglect the systemic wholeness of the structure under study, and so the reader can see in even this brief excerpt the difference between the strict structural functionalist and the loose functionalist.

To find a strict structural-functional analysis relevant to the traditional concerns of the historian is difficult, but fortunately from our viewpoint, Neil Smelser, another of Parsons' students, chose to apply his theoretical framework to the industrialization of English textile production.[17] More specifically, as the title of his book suggests, *Social Change in the Industrial Revolution: An Application of Theory to the British Cotton Industry*, Smelser studies the increasing differentiation of social units in the production of cotton goods from about 1770 to 1840. He aims to show that when one social role or social organization becomes outmoded under changing historical circumstances, differentiation occurs by a "definite and specific" sequence of events to divide the unit into two or more roles or organizations that are functionally equivalent to the original but structurally distinct from each other. In order to establish such a point, Smelser postulates a definite sequence of steps applicable to any structural differentiation and a general theory of systemic functions as the bases of those changes.

[16] *Ibid.* Also see his glossary in back of book, xv–xvi.
[17] Neil J. Smelser, *Social Change in the Industrial Revolution: An Application of Theory to the British Cotton Industry* (Chicago, 1959).

SYSTEMS ANALYSIS AND
THE OBSERVER'S VIEWPOINT

Although the theoretical timing sequence is particularly interesting to an historian, it is not as germane to this chapter as the functional analysis *per se*.

Smelser's book proceeds from general theory to specific application in a series of redundant structural-functional analyses applied ever more concretely to the problems at hand. On the most general level, he postulates the usual four functions of any social system: latent pattern-maintenance and tension-management, goal-attainment, adaptation, and integration. Applied to any given industry, goal-attainment concerns the various decisions to produce and the control of production in general. The adaptive function involves the decisions to capitalize and the procurement of capital facilities. The integrative function includes the decisions to organize or the control of industrial organization. And the latency- and tension-management function covers the implementation of those decisions or the problem of technical production. Essentially, structural differentiation results from dissatisfaction with existing modes of accomplishing these functions that causes the evolution of new organizations and roles to fulfill the function more satisfactorily.

In order to show the possible directions for such differentiation, Smelser studied the subsystems of each function, for each function may in turn be studied in terms of the four basic systems. The possibilities are indicated most quickly by reproducing Smelser's diagram (Figure 9–1), in which C stands for the cotton industry and the small letters are the initial letters of each function: adaptation, goal attainment, latent pattern-maintenance, and integration. The roles of, for example, C_{Gg} are those that decide how much and what to produce and may represent concretely many forms such as independent producer, master manufacturer, cotton-spinning capitalist, the man-

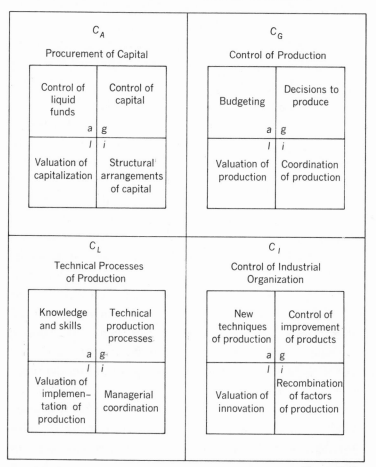

201

Figure 9—1

ager, and the powerful consignee. Differentiation occurs along the axis of a boundary exchange between one functional requisite of a system and one of the subsystem. Again the possibilities are indicated by diagram in Figure 9–2.[18] By these means Smelser produces an elaborate taxonomy

[18] Figures 9–1 and 9–2 reprinted from pp. 43 and 46 of *Social Change in the Industrial Revolution* by Neil J. Smelser by permission of The University of Chicago Press. Copyright 1959 by Neil Smelser.

SYSTEMS ANALYSIS AND
THE OBSERVER'S VIEWPOINT

to study social change by differentiation along functional lines.

Because the taxonomy is further complicated by the addition of a sequence of seven possible steps in each instance of differentiation, even the overall conclusions of

the book are too detailed to summarize. Suffice it to look at one small example and then his general accomplishment. In the putting-out industry, or the so-called "domestic system," the control of fixed capital C_A was not separated from production processes C_L, for both were encompassed in the same person or persons and therefore the same role in the household. The factory system represented these functions among other things by greater specialization of labor and therefore by more differentiated roles and larger numbers of persons. "The *functional* problems of capital control and production remained invariant; the structure of the industry differentiated, however, along the C_A-C_L axis."[19] By postulating many such functional interchanges, Smelser is able to provide a coherent account of such varied items as the invention of machinery, the disciplining of labor, the decisions of entrepreneurs, or the protests to Parliament that accompanied the shift of cotton carding, spinning, and weaving from the home to the factory. Analyzing the family as an economic unit in the same manner, he accounts for the strikes, the agitation to limit factory hours, the rise of trade unions and cooperative societies, and the appearance of savings banks by the structural differentiation of family functions as its members (and roles) left home for the factory.[20]

[19] *Ibid.*, 403.
[20] Compare Smelser's analysis of family functions with Marion J. Levy, Jr., *The Family Revolution in Modern China* (Cambridge, Mass., 1949). A more general application of Smelser's theoretical framework with brief historical examples is his *Theory of Collective Behavior* (New York, 1963).

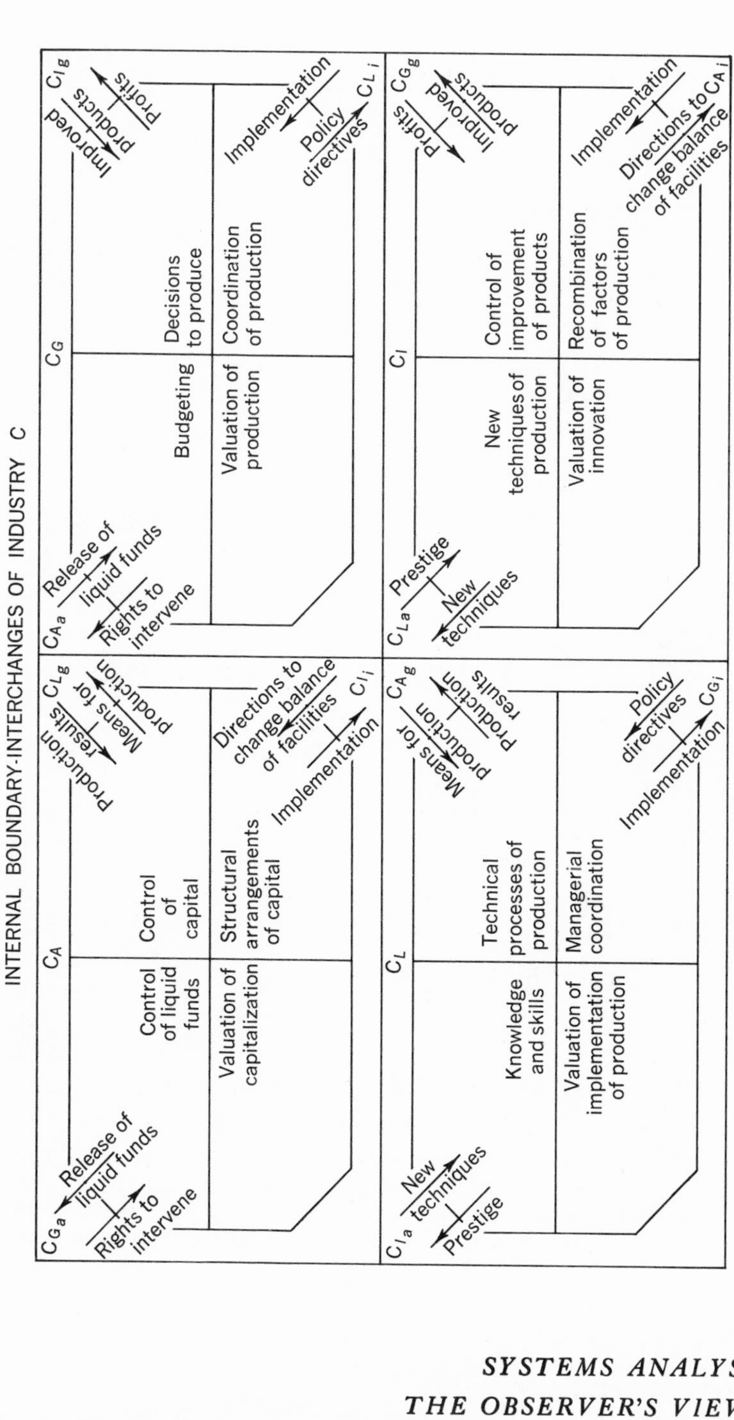

INTERNAL BOUNDARY-INTERCHANGES OF INDUSTRY C

Figure 9–2

SYSTEMS ANALYSIS AND
THE OBSERVER'S VIEWPOINT

Even this very brief summary of Smelser's elaborate analysis reveals the limits as much as the advantages of a structural-functional framework in historical work. The tight organismic integration that lies at its base seems applicable only to certain historical subject matter. This limitation, however, affords no reason to reject the approach out of hand. As Smelser's book demonstrates, the analytical framework works particularly well if the social organization is highly goal-directed by design or by nature and therefore the functions are fairly obvious and the parts serving those functions can be readily distinguished. Historians of armies and churches as well as those of industries should find the theories of Parsons, Levy, Smelser and other structural functionalists particularly useful because goals, pattern maintenance, and integration are the special concerns of such groups.

If the structural functionalists claimed only what we allowed here, then there would be far less controversy about their approach. But they maintain that their assumptions about system are particularly appropriate to the study of the most general levels of social organization, the institutional sector, such as the religious or political systems, and the total society. As a result of their postulating according to the organismic model what others believe problematical at best, we must now abandon at this level of complexity our methodological toleration.

The problems posed by the organismic model, difficult enough on a less general level of social organization, become insuperable on the most general level of a total society. Even an attempt to study a society, or for that matter a culture, as a whole involves a large leap of methodological faith, for such a step implies that there is an overall organization of parts that produces a working whole of a certain sort. Thus just to speak of a society or a culture as a system, or even to study an economy or the political organization of a society as a system, involves an assumption about the nature of the whole that is refractory to proof and difficult to observe. Therefore it seems foolhardy to postulate such wholeness as given. To go beyond this step and assert that an organic integration of a mulitude of societal components comprises the true nature of a social or cultural system seems more than foolhardy. In the best of circumstances, the historian can only presume a problematical interdependence of parts with maybe the possibility of holism. The nature of that whole and its integration must remain open to empirical study. In this approach the analyst leaves open the possibility of discovering varying degrees of interrelationships among the parts. He must be prepared to discover unintegrated social and cultural wholes composed either of some autonomous unrelated parts or of conflicting parts as well as integrated wholes of various degrees of integration. Whether the autonomy or conflict within the system is functional or dysfunctional in any one case is also an empirical question.[21]

The nature of a society considered as a whole is an area of major controversy in social theory today because theorists still argue whether conflict or harmony is the more natural state of men in society. Some opponents of functional analysis maintain that functionalists, both loose and strict, bias their studies toward the internal harmony of the system because of their stress on goal-attainment, tension- and pattern-maintenance, and integration. As a result, these opponents argue, the functionalists minimize or even exclude from study and therefore from a society all factors that cause internal dissension. Furthermore, by

[21] Again see the important essay by Gouldner, "Reciprocity and Autonomy in Functional Theory," in Gross, ed., *op. cit.*

emphasizing ideal and expected norms and values in their search for system-integrating functions, the functionalists neglect actual behavior that does not meet prejudged standards. Thus these critics accuse the structural functionalists in particular of seeing only cohesion and consensus among the people in a society instead of the conflict and dissension also normal in any group of men. At the same time, by concentrating on a homeostatic equilibrium of internal regulation to achieve structural persistence, the structural functionalists, charge their opponents, cannot explain change by factors other than those external to the system. If they assumed conflict was a usual state, then they could more readily account for the changes that baffle them so under their present assumptions.[22]

On their side, these opponents of functionalism see change as natural because they believe conflict between groups within a society is normal behavior. Different groups are presumed to have different interests and hence they must clash in one way or another in an attempt to achieve their ends in relation to each other. As a result of their assumption about conflict within a society, any general societal adherence to common norms is seen by these theorists as the coercion of the less powerful by the more powerful. Consensus on common values does not and cannot exist in a complex society, and any common norms are the result of authority, not belief. To these theorists, conflict rather than consensus and willful use of power rather

[22] The best presentations of these criticisms are Ralf Dahrendorf, *Class and Class Conflict in Industrial Society* (rev. [English] ed., Stanford, Calif., 1959), and John Rex, *Key Problems of Sociological Theory* (London, 1961), especially 115–155. Other works on this side are Ralf Dahrendorf, "Out of Utopia: Towards a Reorientation of Sociological Analysis," *American Journal of Sociology*, LXIV (1958), 115–27; David Lockwood, "Some Remarks on the Social System," *British Journal of Sociology*, VII (1956), 134–46; and C. Wright Mills, *The Sociological Imagination* (New York, 1959).

A BEHAVIORAL APPROACH TO HISTORICAL ANALYSIS

206

than voluntary adhesion to societywide goals and beliefs are the usual state of a society. For these reasons, the conflict theorists, as they are called, believe change is as natural to a society as the functionalists think persistence is.

Because functionalists stress normative integration, equilibrium, and social cohesion, some of their opponents have accused them of political conservatism. Their ideological opposition argues that their scheme of analysis supports the political status quo by their concern with stability and consensus. Merton feels the sting of this attack sufficiently to devote several pages in his essay on functionalism to refuting this senseless charge.[23] The charge seems to result from confusing the normative in an ideational sense on the actors' level with the normative as an ideological ideal on the observer's level. Functionalists in general and structural functionalists in particular do, however, have difficulty in accounting for changes, as the conflict theorists assert.[24]

Interestingly enough, many conflict theorists do not abandon systems analysis or even functional analysis; they only reject the application of these to a total society in the manner of the organic functionalists. To the conflict theorists, the various interest groups may be treated systematically and functional analysis applied to the systems or even to the system combining the conflicting entities. Thus one of these theorists could study *The Functions of Social*

[23] Merton, *op. cit.*, 37–46.
[24] For attempts to retain the structural-functional framework for the study of change, see Francesca Cancian, "Functional Analysis of Change," *American Sociological Review*, XXV (1960), 818–26; David Lockwood, "Social Integration and System Integration," in George K. Zollschan and Walter Hirsch, eds., *Explorations in Social Change* (New York, 1964), 244–57; and Alvin Boskoff, "Functional Analysis as a Source of a Theoretical Repertory and Research Tasks in the Study of Social Change," in *ibid.*, 213–43.
[25] Lewis A. Coser, *The Functions of Social Conflict* (New York, 1956).

SYSTEMS ANALYSIS AND
THE OBSERVER'S VIEWPOINT

Conflict, as he titled his book.[25] To the extent that these analysts postulate a total conflict system, they use the same unproven theoretical assumptions as the theorists they accuse of being in error. In other words, both sides argue only about the nature of a society; they proceed about its analysis in much the same manner.

The historian cannot accept the overall approach of either the structural functionalists or the conflict theorists, for both assume, ironically, only one kind of society in every possible case. There seems to be no more room for variation between these two models of society in the minds of each side than the lack of variety they see within all societies; both sides presume what they ought to prove. Only research will establish the possible existence of either of these two models in any given historical case, and, more likely, such research will show other possibilities as well. The historian must keep an open methodological mind about the concept of system on any level, but particularly on the level of an overall society.

From these comments the reader can understand the problems involved in studying the whole of a society and a culture that were posed in the preceding chapters. The unity or integration of a whole society or a whole culture is at best an hypothesis that must be proven in a specific instance. To assert that a certain totality of social relationships or cultural entities is fully integrated and constitutes a special type of whole by theory alone is to deny an empirically based science. Rather, patient research must carefully construct larger and larger wholes from precisely defined, empirically researched parts. The nature of the overall organization of the totality studied will and can only be determined by the examination of the final parts and their relationships.

The active controversy over the nature of the whole in the behavioral sciences has not carried over into the historical guild in any form, except perhaps in the new economic history. Yet surely the question of cultural or social holism is as important to students of past societies as it is to analysts of present-day ones. More importantly, the question of system as applied to social change is as central to the historian's task as it is to that of the sociologist, political scientist, or economist. Historians must have some idea of the whole of a nation's history, for example, when they write a freshman or sophomore textbook, but we never find the criteria for determining the whole discussed explicitly there or elsewhere. The historian has long recognized interconnections in the history of a society or a culture but with little self-conscious idea of the possibilities involved in such a search. Even less understood is the problem of dividing history by space and time wholes. Explicit notions of systems analysis will aid the historian in all these tasks.

With this position adopted, the argument about wholes and parts and the organization of the observer's viewpoint would seem to end, but the historian still needs to examine the idea of system from the perspective of time. Regardless of the model used as a foundation for analysis, for there to be a system at all its parts and their relationships must persist through some period of time. The conception of time thus becomes an important consideration in the analysis of all systems, but the theorists of this persuasion, except for the economists, have written surprisingly little upon the subject. While other analysts may omit time, or treat it as an independent variable, or, even worse from the viewpoint of the historian, deal with it in a highly abstract fashion, the historian places that dimension of human existence at the very center of his discipline. No matter how valuable systems analysis may be to historical analysis, it is as nothing if it fails to take time into account. Because of this crucial significance of time to the historian, the whole next chapter will be devoted to an examination of that topic.

Moreover, even granting for the moment the utility of systems analysis to the study of wholes in historical research and writing, the historian is still left with a crucial problem. To what extent can the past be studied holistically? This question inquires not only about what wholes there are to be studied in history, but also, and more significantly, about what way the historian can examine the flow of past events as a whole. In essence, how comprehensive a system is what we call *a* history? Can a part of the past be studied as a system as the word "history" would seem to imply? Again these questions presume the study of the nature of time covered in the next chapter.

The reader must not leave this and the previous chapter, however, with the impression that he has examined very many of the models used by behavioral theorists,[26] or that systems analysis is the sole approach to the study of the whole. Rather this and the preceding chapter are an attempt, in brief scope, to call the attention of the historian to the general problem of the whole that he must face like every other behavioral analyst. The arguments between the consensus and conflict theorists, furthermore, should not obscure the central point that all these analysts believe in and use the idea of system in their research and writing. And historians, by becoming aware of the problem, can only profit from their newly gained knowledge.

[26] A nontechnical discussion of such models is the previously cited Deutsch, *The Nerves of Government*. See also Oran R. Young, *Systems of Political Science* (Englewood Cliffs, N.J., 1968).

Historians presume a notion of time so fundamental to their studies that they rarely discuss it. They divide time all the time, but any explicit statement about how they do it is infrequent. Generations, periods, eras, and epochs pass without careful delineation in history volumes, and years, decades, and centuries possess much more meaning for historians

than their nominal definitions would ever indicate to the layman. In fact, one could accuse most historians of being quite careless about the chief differentia of their discipline. As a result of their carelessness, they utilize in their writings few of the many varieties of time conceptions available to them.[1]

Social theorists provide little help in this situation, for they either assume time as an independent variable and therefore unimportant to their studies or they treat it far too abstractly for the historian's comfort. The nature of time, at least in relation to systems, has been developed

[1] Books on historical methods rarely discuss the nature of time nor do recent philosophies of history except for Nathan Rotenstreich, *Between Past and Present: An Essay on History* (New Haven, Conn., 1958), who bases his whole book on the concept. No historians were represented in two recent symposia on the subject of time (except for the art historian George Kubler): J. T. Fraser, ed., *The Voices of Time: A Cooperative Survey of Man's View of Time as Expressed by the Sciences and by the Humanities* (New York, 1966), and "Conference on Interdisciplinary Perspectives of Time," held January 17–20, 1966, in New York. Beiheft no. 6 of *History and Theory* on "History and the Concept of Time" contains articles by three historians, but they really deal with past historiography as much or more than with how the historian today can or should deal with time.

most consciously and most fully by the economists under the concept of equilibrium. Equilibria may be static or dynamic, stable or unstable or moving, partial or general, long- or short-term, among many possibilities in the economists' lexicon. Stable equilibrium refers to the tendency

of the system to react to change in such a way that it returns to the initial condition of equilibrium. A system may be stable in regard to one kind of disturbance but not to another, or it may be stable in reference to a small disturbance but not to a large one. If the disturbance shifts the value of the variables but the basic relationship still holds, then the equilibrium is said to be stable but not static; it is a dynamic equilibrium. A comparison of equilibrium positions under differing parameters is called comparative statics. If the path of this change is followed, then it is termed comparative dynamics.[2]

From even this brief description, it is obvious that the structural functionalists employ only one kind of equilibrium. Organismic functionalists assume homeostatic equilibrium, in which, as was mentioned in the last chapter, the equilibrium is maintained in a steady state through the self-regulation of internal mechanisms postulated by the

[2] Terminology is diverse and variously used, but consult Fritz Machlup, *Essays on Economic Semantics* (Englewood Cliffs, N.J., 1963), 9–72; John Chipman, "The Nature and Meaning of Equilibrium in Economic Theory," in Don Martindale, ed., *Functionalism in the Social Sciences*, monograph no. 5 of the American Academy of Political and Social Science (Philadelphia, Feb., 1965), 35–64; Sherman Krupp, "Equilibrium Theory in Economic and Functional Analysis as Types of Explanation," in *ibid.*, 65–83; Sherman Krupp, *Pattern in Organization Analysis: A Critical Examination* (Philadelphia, 1961), 32–50, 56–7; and the references they cite. For an analysis of equilibrium conceptions that both gives the historical background of such thinking in the United States and is relevant to our concerns here, see Cynthia E. Russett, *The Concept of Equilibrium in American Social Thought* (New Haven, Conn., 1966). A good basic discussion of equilibrium theory in social analysis is David Easton, *The Political System* (New York, 1953), 266–306.

A BEHAVIORAL APPROACH
TO HISTORICAL ANALYSIS

theorist. In essence, their model is stable, maybe even static, and always general according to the economists' terms. Perhaps, then, the difficulty in finding structural-functional analyses applied to history results from the nature of time assumed in organismic functionalism.[3]

The conception of time employed by the economists is overly simple and relatively unreal from the viewpoint of the historian. For economists, equilibrium refers more to a state of a theoretical system than to any empirical reality. Their assumption of equilibrium performs for them the role of controlled experiment through the manipulation of variables in a given theoretical model. To this extent their conception of time is purely a theoretical device. Even if economists explore what they call comparative dynamics, their analysis of change moves from one postulated theoretical steady state to another postulated theoretical steady state rather than providing a running account of the concrete occurrences historians concern themselves with in a study of change. Economists do not employ the concrete dated time of the historian in their analyses so much as movement from T_1 to T_2, to speak as symbolically as their conception is abstract. Because even these most sophisticated of systems analysts fail to deal with time as the historian understands it, we must start our examination of the subject upon the most elementary level and proceed to the implications of these basic points for historical analysis.

Ever since the ancient Greek thinkers pointed out

[3] For similar conclusions, see Alvin Gouldner, "Some Observations on Systematic Theory, 1945-55," in Hans Zetterberg, ed., *Sociology in the United States of America* (Paris, 1956), 38–42; Everett Hagan, *On the Theory of Social Change: How Economic Growth Begins* (Homewood, Ill., 1962), 510–13; and references in chap. 9, *n.* 25 of this book. A good example of such bias in organizational analysis is given by Krupp, *op. cit.*, 32–50.

CONCEPTIONS OF TIME:
THEIR VARIETIES AND USES

some of the paradoxes of time, philosophers have attempted
to reconcile the seeming antinomies of that evanescent dimension of human existence. Is time relational in that it is
measured and is to be understood by the events occurring
within it, or does time possess an absoluteness apart from
the events said to fall within it? How can time exhibit
change and constancy, sequence and duration at the same
time? Is the present a mere infinitesimal point, a knife edge,
between past and future, or do these three parts of time
fuse together? Or do they exist at all in reality? Is time
the interval between events or the duration of the event
or the moment of occurrence of the event? All these problems and many more beset the person who would ponder
the tenuous but suggestive concept of time.[4]

Essentially, all these riddles arise from the discrepancy
between man's notion of time as a concept and his experience of time as a feeling. From this discrepancy are derived
two basic dimensions of time, the external one of physical,
or measured, time and the internal one of subjective time.
Philosophers have tried to reconcile these two dimensions
for centuries, but they seem no closer to an ultimate solution now than when they first noted the discrepancy. In
such a case, it would be foolish to attempt here anything
other than an examination of some of the implications of

[4] Some basic analyses of the concept of time are Cornelius Benjamin,
"Ideas of Time in the History of Philosophy," in Fraser, ed., *op. cit.*,
3–30; Wilfred Sellars, "Time and the World Order," in Herbert Feigl
and Grover Maxwell, eds., *Scientific Explanation, Space, and Time*
("Minnesota Studies in the Philosophy of Science," vol. 3 [Minneapolis,
Minn., 1962]), 527–616; J. N. Findlay, "Time: A Treatment of Some
Puzzles," in Anthony Flew, ed., *Essays on Logic and Language* (Ox-
ford, 1951), 37–56; and L. S. Stebbing, "Some Ambiguities in Discussions
Concerning Time," in Raymond Klibansky and H. J. Paton, eds.,
Philosophy and History: Essays Presented to Ernst Cassirer (Oxford,
1936), 107–24. An interesting personal approach to the paradoxes of
time is Robert M. MacIver, *The Challenge of the Passing Years: My
Encounter With Time* (New York, 1962).

*A BEHAVIORAL APPROACH
TO HISTORICAL ANALYSIS*

what these two aspects of time and their resultant problems might possess for the historian in his work.[5]

Historians use physical time to date events. Dating is done with some absolute and universal time similar to what Isaac Newton postulated. Such time flows metrically and is irreversible. It is a conception of time derived and perfected from nature's supposed regularities. This concept of time embodies all events into one ordered dimension in which events may occur simultaneously but no two given instants can occur simultaneously, nor will they ever occur again. Time is portrayed as linear and nonrepeating. It flows uniformly and relentlessly in equally and infinitely divisible bits from past to future Nothing happens outside of time, but this kind of time is exterior to all that happens within it. It is a mathematical time as independent of events as it is of the human mind.[6]

Some such view of time would seem to be the foundation for historians' chronology in spite of the theory of relativity and the fourth dimension. To the historian dating is placement upon a metrical scale of absolute time. Time, in fact, is represented by a line—just as it was to Newton's teacher Isaac Barrow[7]—on which each point is an instant. Events can be marked at the same time-position following this scheme, but the line orders time in such a way that no instant and its events will repeat. According to the logic

[5] Stephen Toulmin and Jane Goodfield, *The Discovery of Time* (London, 1965), present a brief history of the development of the conception of time.

[6] Recent works in English on physical time are Hans Reichenbach, *The Direction of Time* (Berkeley, Calif., 1956); G. J. Whitrow, *The Natural Philosophy of Time* (London, 1961); Richard Schlegel, *Time and the Physical World* (East Lansing, Mich., 1961); and Adolph Grünbaum, *Philosophical Problems of Space and Time* (New York, 1963). Perhaps the best brief introduction to the subject is the review by Jacques Merleau-Ponty of some of these books and others, "Problems of Physical Time," in *Diogenes*, no. 56 (1956), 115–40.

[7] According to J. A. Gunn, *The Problem of Time* (London, 1929), 56.

CONCEPTIONS OF TIME:
THEIR VARIETIES AND USES

of dated chronology, time is treated as a continuous succession of equally divisible moments moving from past to present.[8]

As everyone knows—or feels—time also exists in a subjective dimension. This is time as experienced by people in all its swiftness of busy time or the slowness of waiting time. Time in this guise is not uniform; it is disjunctive and discontinuous. Past, present, and future may blend, and metrical irreversibility seems irrelevant or even invalid. At the same time the direction of time, or time's arrow, depends upon the subjective experience of time flowing from past to future. This is time as known to the human consciousness and therefore is neither absolute nor universal nor uniformly divisible. Events measure it as they are known to the actor.[9]

Writers and artists employ this aspect of time frequently but historians, even biographers, seldom do. The manipulation of internal time experience is familiar to most readers of Joyce, Proust, Stein, or Faulkner, to name but the very famous.[10] An important aspect of Cubism in paint-

[8] A linear conception of time is developed in schoolchildren by teaching chronology with time lines. See methods books in education, for example, Dorothy M. Fraser and Edith West, *Social Studies in Secondary Schools: Curriculum and Methods* (New York, 1961), 183–6.

[9] Phenomenologists and existentialists have been the philosophers most concerned with subjective time. See, among many, Edmund Husserl, *The Phenomenology of Internal Time-Consciousness*, Martin Heidegger, ed., James S. Churchill, trans. (Bloomington, Ind., 1964); Martin Heidegger, *Being and Time*, John Macquarrie and Edward Robinson, trans. (London, 1962); Maurice Merleau-Ponty, *Phenomenology of Perception*, Colin Smith, trans. (New York, 1962).

[10] On the literary treatment of time, see such commentaries as Hans Meyerhoff, *Time in Literature* (Berkeley, Calif., 1955); George Poulet, *Studies in Human Time*, Elliot Coleman, trans. (Baltimore, Md., 1956); and Wyndham Lewis, *Time and Western Man* (New York, 1928), especially 1–129. The well-known novelist J. B. Priestley attempts to gather together the many aspects of time in his book, *Man and Time* (Garden City, N.Y., 1964), which includes many pictorial representations of time as well as the more conventional written ones.

ing was an attempt to escape the limitations of time, external as well as internal, as everyone knows from even the most elementary of art appreciation courses. On the other hand, it is difficult to find historians who employ this side of time in their work. Although every biography must implicitly touch at least this dimension of time, it is never made the focus of the work as the novelists have done. Yet we know some men were very conscious of their place in time and how it therefore looked to them. George Washington had clerks put his Revolutionary War correspondence in order immediately upon the cessation of hostilities. While Minister to Berlin, Andrew Dickson White, the first president of Cornell University and also of the American Historical Association, even saved his fingernail clippings in dated envelopes for posterity.[11] But to what extent this internal time consciousness can be the basic framework rather than a mere incident of a biography is yet to be explored.

Time may have a subjective meaning for a whole society as well as for an individual. Such a social view may be termed cultural time. Different groups of people have differing orientations toward time. Middle-class Americans stress punctuality and the "saving" of time, for according to Benjamin Franklin, "Time is money." Most peoples, however, neither conserve time nor fidget about promptness. They little note its passage in personal terms, as Americans seem to do, by elaborate time-keeping devices on wrist and wall. Many people lack our notion of "lateness," and some do not even "keep" time in our sense.[12]

Cultural time also includes the general orientation of

[11] A graduate student arranging White's papers at Cornell University called my attention to these envelopes many years ago.
[12] A cultural approach to the variety of time conceptions is Edward T. Hall, *The Silent Language* (New York, 1959), especially chaps. 1 and 9.

a populace toward the dilemma of being and becoming. To some societies the present seems so insignificant compared to their traditions that the present is subordinated to the past in their lives. To middle-class Americans, on the other hand, the past is frequently held to be of very little significance in determining their lives, and they look to the future for ever bigger and better things. Hopes, not history, concern them. In a somewhat similar manner, societies can picture time in larger quantities as cyclic or unilinear or even as progress. In this cultural sector, religion and the sense of time combine to give meaning to the past, present, and future of a society.[13]

218

In accord with their time orientations, societies have sundry rhythms of social life. Different parts of the day and the changing seasons are defined as appropriate for certain social activities. The words "wintertime" and "summertime" conjure up immediately in most American minds images of seasonal activities just as night and day seem particularly appropriate for other activities. Historians generally accept such social time, as some analysts call this timing of social relationships, as given, but since it deals with recurrent activities, they do not usually deal with it in their histories.[14]

[13] Essays on various cultural approaches to time are contained in Fraser, ed., *op. cit.*, 77–135, and Joseph T. Campbell, ed., *Man and Time* (New York, 1958), 108–232. Also see A. I. Hallowell, "Temporal Orientation in Western Civilization and in a Preliterate Society," *American Anthropologist*, XXXIX (1937), 647–70, reprinted in the author's *Culture and Experience*, Philadelphia Anthropological Society Publications, no. 4 (Philadelphia, 1954), 216–35. Florence Kluckhohn makes time one of her five basic orientations for the comparative study of values in her book with Fred L. Strodtbeck et al. *Variations in Value-Orientations* (Evanston, Ill., 1961).

[14] The best introductions to social time are Pitirim Sorokin and Robert K. Merton, "Social Time: A Methodological and Functional Analysis," *American Journal of Sociology*, XLII (1937), 615–29; P. Sorokin, *Socio-Cultural Causality, Space, Time* (Durham, N.C., 1943); Wilbert E. Moore, *Man, Time, and Society* (New York, 1963); and Georges Gur-

Social historians may prove an exception. To the historian of an agricultural people, the seasonal activities of his actors may be of profound significance. Mildred Campbell in *The English Yeoman Under Elizabeth and the Early Stuarts* writes about the various tasks of her subjects through the seasons of the year.[15] Likewise, the historian of the ante-bellum South cannot fully understand slavery without knowing the yearly work pattern on the plantation.[16] The cycles of social time may involve the religious and ceremonial as well as the secular and mundane, and again it is the social historian, if any, who deals with this time specifically. A ceremonial day may receive incidental mention in other historians' works because it was the occasion of an important event, for example, the crowning of Charlemagne as Holy Roman Emperor on Christmas Day, 800, but such social time is rarely the subject of many books by other than social historians.

Rather than cyclic rhythms of activity, social time may be reckoned also in discontinuous events. Certain dates have a meaning to a society beyond their mere numerical reference. For Americans, 1776 and 1929 are two such dates. The mere mention of these numbers immediately recalls a certain cluster of happenings to most citizens of the United States. This is the social time of great events that are memorable to a people in terms of their myths and ideologies. Just as priests once kept the records of a society in order to perpetuate a certain collective memory of such

---

vitch, *The Spectrum of Social Time*, Myrtle Korenbaum, trans. (New York, 1963).

[15] Mildred Campbell, *The English Yeoman Under Elizabeth and the Early Stuarts* (New Haven, Conn., 1942), 209–10, but see throughout 156–220.

[16] The daily and seasonal activities of slaves are among the topics treated in chap. 2 of Kenneth Stampp, *The Peculiar Institution: Slavery in the Ante-Bellum South* (New York, 1956), 34–85.

time, so historians are supposed by many to serve a similar function in today's world. Many patriotic groups, such as the Daughters of the American Revolution and the American Legion, would have the *true* heritage of the glorious American past taught every schoolchild in the United States. Thus, Clio, the muse of history, was portrayed by the Greeks as both a recorder and an exhorter. Since historians frequently adopt a didactic or moral stance in their writings, they do recognize this other function, although they may perversely wish to inculcate the opposite of what they believe they are asked to do by the society at large.

220

To the extent the historian attempts to reconstruct the culture of past actors, he would be concerned with the belief a people had about their social time of great events, and, in fact, about their whole attitude toward their history. Societies studied by historians have myths and ideologies about their significant dates and their whole past. This discontinuous, subjective time of a people is a proper subject, like any other aspect of their culture, for the historian. What must be differentiated quite clearly, however, is the actors' sense of time as events and as history and the observer's sense of time as events and as history. Since historical documents tend to reflect the former more than the latter, the historian tends to depict the past reality of a people as that society thought it was rather than as it was in actual practice. We have already seen how easily Frederick Jackson Turner substituted the agrarian myth for the social reality of trans-Appalachian settlement. Although the historian must be ever on guard against such a practice, it does not mean that he should avoid, as unrelated to reality, all imagery, myth, and history as the actors see it. As we have argued previously, such actors' conceptions have important implications for history. The dying-Republic theme was a significant method of analysis for Americans and therefore the basis for propaganda by Jacksonians, Populists, and Progressives, as I pointed out in Chapter 5. Certainly the historian of religion must take account of the millennial dreams, apocalyptic hopes, or awesome fears of the movements he studies if he hopes to write their history.

Even though an historian makes careful distinctions between actors' times and observer's times, he as an observer is still the victim of his own cultural time. Our very conception of physical time is one of *our* cultural orientations! Yet we must use it to construct the chronology of the past. The dilemma of reconciling our metrical time with various cultural times is best seen in the use of our calendar for dating. Although historians in Europe and the Americas know our calendar is confined to our civilization, still they order all history according to Christ's birth. Some peoples cannot even conceive of the simultaneity of events, whereas to others time does not possess a single coordinate so that the years of one story need have no correspondence to the years of another story.[17] But if the historical guild were to adopt these orientations, then we would no longer be able to study the past and produce history as we know it now.[18]

[17] Even some of our time divisions are arbitrary. Years, months, and days would seem to have a natural basis, but the discrepancies among the recurrence of seasons, the phases of the moon, and the duration of sunlight and darkness forced men to intervene even here to establish arbitrary limits. The starting point of a day, a month, or a year is totally arbitrary as is the whole idea of a week, a decade, or century. Read, for example, the articles by H. Alan Lloyd and G. M. Clemence in Fraser, ed. *op. cit.,* 338–414.
[18] Query: Do societies that do not have an orientation similar to ours even study history? See Joseph Needham "Time and Knowledge in China and the West," in Fraser, ed., *op. cit.,* 92–135; John T. Marcus, "Time and the Sense of History: West and East," *Comparative Studies in Society and History,* III (1961), 123–39; and W. Von Leyden, "His-

CONCEPTIONS OF TIME:
THEIR VARIETIES AND USES

The dilemma of translating the time of one culture into that of another in order to write history (at least as we know it) seems inescapable, but to go beyond this point and base all writing only upon the implicit conceptions of time available in one's own society seems inexcusable today. Since the comparative study of culture is part of our culture, temporocentrism is remediable to the extent of that self-consciousness but only insofar as the remedy is reconcilable with the conception of time demanded by the writing of history as a craft today. By keeping in mind and by pointing out to the reader the difference between the actors' conceptions of time and the observer's historiographical framework of time, an historian should be able to avoid the worst gaucheries of cultural time bias.[19]

Besides the historiographical sin of commission in imposing our cultural time orientations upon other societies in the past, the other grave sin in the historian's treatment of time is one of omission. Historians tend to use in their work few of the possible analytical varieties of measured, or physical, time. On the whole, most history books utilize time only as a succession of moments and their events. As a result, these books expound change solely as a list of firsts and neglect continuity entirely. In some cases, time seems so real to the authors of some volumes that it produces change as some sort of coercive force, or at least nothing else is said to account for the innovations enumerated but not analyzed or explained. All of these short-

---

tory and the Concept of Relative Time," *History and Theory*, II (1963), 263–85.

[19] Compare the necessity for reconciling internal and external time in writing history as discussed by Siegfried Kracauer, "Time and History," in "History and the Concept of Time," Beiheft no. 6 of *History and Theory*, 65–78. For an interesting attempt by an economist to see time from the observer's view of the actor's moment, see G. L. S. Schackle's *Time in Economics* (Amsterdam, 1958) and *Decision, Order, and Time in Human Affairs* (Cambridge, Eng., 1961).

comings seem based upon historians' preference for time as static succession over time as dynamic sequence. An examination of the implications of both approaches to time should convince historical analysts that they must incorporate both kinds of temporal analysis into their studies if they would gain the fullest benefits for their reconstruction of the past.

Measured, or physical, time may be conceived as succession or as duration. To date an event, the historian usually places the event in a position on a linear time scale that shows a succession of time divisions. Essentially, he asks the question, When did what happen? And he answers with a time position. In theory, time conceived as successive positions may be infinitely divisible, but for the purposes of measuring human actions and historical events, the moments of time are "finite downward," to use one historian's borrowed phrase.[20] Time for the historian's purpose cannot be infinitely divisible into ever smaller bits, for the size of the division must apply to the duration of the subject considered. And for the historian, most historical events occur in relatively large-sized chunks of time.

Thus the historian rarely considers an event that takes place in less than, say, a minute or even an hour, and, more likely, the dated event, like a battle for example, occurred over a period of hours or even days. The dates we all memorized as children, still contained in so-called dictionaries or encyclopedias of history, show their finiteness by being precise only to the day or, more frequently in the case of wars and political occurrences, years. Intellectual trends may be dated in decades or longer. In this man-

[20] Alexander Gerschenkron, "On the Concept of Continuity in History," *Proceedings of the American Philosophical Society*, CVI (1962), 197–8, borrowing from Percy Bridgman. This is by far the best article on the subject of time by an historian.

ner duration is brought into the consideration of the action or event in time measured as succession. A dated event is therefore both a point in a succession of time instants on a linear scale and also an event of some duration measured on the same scale.

Dating is important to historical analysis beyond mere indication of time location. Placement upon a time scale answers to some degree the question why it happened in that manner at that time, because dating an event establishes its temporal context among other events. The historian answers this question by statements about a set of interrelated events presumed connected by more than mere temporal contiguity or coincidence. As W. H. Walsh, a modern philosopher of history, puts it, the historian assumes

that different historical events can be regarded as going together to constitute a single process, or whole of which they are all parts and in which they belong together in a specially intimate way. And the first aim of the historian, when he is asked to explain some event or other, is to see it as a part of such a process, to locate it in its context by mentioning other events with which it is bound up.[21]

Walsh calls this method of explanation by temporal context "colligation," reviving a term of William Whewell, a nineteenth-century philosophy professor at Cambridge. Chronology as dating on a time scale forms the foundation for the possibility of colligation, and so dates possess a more important aspect for historical analysis than merely nominal temporal placement. The placement establishes the context for the study of possible connections among past events, hence description and explanation.

[21] W. H. Walsh, *An Introduction to the Philosophy of History* (rev. ed., London, 1958), 23, but compare 62.

A BEHAVIORAL APPROACH
TO HISTORICAL ANALYSIS

Colligation may proceed along two lines depending upon the approach to metrical time. Because the historian usually orders time along a single linear coordinate, other events can be concurrent with a dated event or precede or succeed it. Although in many cases the merging of duration with succession in the timing of an event may becloud the precision with which the dating is done, the historian will nevertheless continue to conceive of other events as occurring before, after, or at the same time as the phenomenon he studies. Depending upon whether the historian emphasizes the simultaneity or the consecutiveness of events, he will employ time as a setting or as a sequence. In other words, when the historian attempts to answer explicitly or implicitly, why did the event occur when it did, he will most likely answer with a cluster of events happening at the same time setting or in a certain time sequence. In this manner he constructs a complex set of events using time as succession (sequence) or as duration (setting).[22]

When time is used as setting, actions and occurrences are grouped together as coexistent. The emphasis in this approach is on a pattern of events that correlate in time. An historical fact is given meaning in this method by being located in the overall pattern of coexisting events. Men and their actions are said to be placed in the context of their times, or their time setting, by this method of historical explanation. The answer to the question of why this occurred or why it occurred when it did is couched in those frequent phrases of the historian, *zeitgeist, climate of opinion*, or simply *the times*. Thus the biographer sets a man in his era, and the historian argues that certain events

[22] I owe these terms to Max Heirich, whose article "The Use of Time in the Study of Social Change," *American Sociological Review*, XXIX (1964), 386–97, is excellent.

must be understood in terms of their period. While Caesar, Napoleon, and Hitler are all political generals, what they did and how they did it the historian would assert is best understood by reference to their times.

The most general use of this explanatory method of time as setting is in periodization. Whether the historian uses the term decade, generation, era, epoch, or period, he conceives of the number of years under consideration as possessing a certain unity so that the time span designated is not purely arbitrary. Thus, for example, the decade of the 1920s or the 1930s in American history like the eighteenth or nineteenth centuries in European history convey to the historian a cluster of meanings beyond the mere numerical reference of ten or a hundred years. Supposedly, in each case a larger pattern or configuration of attitudes and actions exists that offers an explanation by its time setting of simultaneity, so as to enable the historian to use it as a short-hand vocabulary in his work. In spite of the usefulness, even necessity, of periodization by the historian, few explicit discussions of how to go about it exist.[23]

Arguments over periodization are not so much about what events occurred, for most historians will agree about this, but rather over the meaning of those events for an interpretive unity of a certain time span. A period should

[23] The methods of periodization are rarely discussed except in connection with specific suggested divisions. The longest work on the subject is in Dutch: J. H. J. Van Der Pot, *De Periodisering Der Geschiedenis* (The Hague, 1951), which really develops its points through a survey of historiography. Brief treatments are Oscar Halecki, *The Limits and Divisions of European History* (New York, 1950), 7–64, 145–84; Dietrich Gerhard, "Periodization in European History," *American Historical Review*, LXI (1956), 900–913; and M. I. Finley, "Generalizations in Ancient History," in Louis Gottschalk, ed., *Generalization in the Writing of History* (Chicago, 1963), 23–26. Also see Morris Cohen, *The Meaning of Human History* (Lasalle, Ill., 1947), 65–76, and Geoffrey Barraclough, *History in a Changing World* (Oxford, 1957), 31–63.

A BEHAVIORAL APPROACH
TO HISTORICAL ANALYSIS

display significant characteristics ramifying throughout it. For example, the "Age of Reason" or the "Renaissance" or the "Age of Jackson" or the "New Deal" designate more than the literature or art of the first two periods and the politics of the latter two. Periodization rests upon the belief that at a given duration of time a cluster of characteristics permeates many areas of life and supposedly relates diverse trends and events in a society. Since the culture concept attempts the same task, historians should periodize in line with the notion of culture developed in the preceding chapters. Periodization then would be based upon the shared ideation in a society. To the extent that such ideation accounts for the actors' behavior in a society, cultural periodization would unite the seeming diversity of *a* time in that society. By founding periodization upon the concept of culture, the historical analyst gains both the benefits and problems of that conception as we discussed them in preceding chapters. A period would be a unity to the degree that a culture may be proven a system of interdependent parts forming a whole. Certainly all attempts at historical periodization would benefit from the awareness of the perplexities involved in establishing systemic wholeness.

The holistic problem involved in time settings is best seen in relating one period to another. In theory one period would bear little or no relationship to another period because each would be a whole, but in the historical analysis of a society the second period must have been derived from the first because of the continuity of the society. The question for the historian becomes, in practice, When did the first period end and the second begin? In historical research there usually exists a time of transition that is blurred analytically but is nevertheless existent in the past of a society and important to the written history of that past.

In terms of cultural wholes, the entire history of a society should present some cultural continuity, but then do the various periods become different subcultures? The perplexities of distinguishing one period from another in the history of a society is particularly evident in the long controversy over the existence of the Renaissance. Should this era, once so proudly depicted as the beginning of all Western man cherished as modern, be seen as only the culmination of the Middle Ages rather than the commencement of the modern period? Were the traits once thought to be so new and such a break from earlier times only the continuous development of trends already well advanced in the High Middle Ages? In short, are the Middle Ages and Renaissance only two parts of the same period or two periods?[24] How can the historian solve this dilemma of continuity and change in periodization? Before we can explore this question further, we must examine the nature of change from the viewpoint of time as sequence.

In essence, the concept of time as setting is static, because it presumes a relationship based upon the correlation of events at one position or date (no matter how long) on a linear time scale. Even in the case of a period that might embrace many years' duration, for example, the passage of time as measured by change is held constant in order to study the configuration of that period. For this reason, the study of time as setting poses the same problems in regard to wholes and parts as any static or stable equilibrium study of a system. On the other hand, to the extent that knowledge of such systems is valuable in studying human behavior, it is also useful to the historian in studying the periodization of time in his discipline.

[24] Robert C. Stalnaker, "Events, Periods, and Institutions in Historians' Language," *History and Theory*, VI (1967), 166–76, reviews the issues and the literature briefly from this view.

A BEHAVIORAL APPROACH TO HISTORICAL ANALYSIS

Since periodization and other aspects of time as setting presume a stable relationship throughout a certain length of time, they are essentially atemporal conceptions when compared to time as flow. Furthermore, because settings are fixed in positions on a metric scale that orders time so that no moment duplicates another, the settings are assumed to be unique in their patterns. Thus conceiving of time as duration measured by a succession of moments can produce a notion of the uniqueness of historical events as well as a static view of change. So time is presumed everchanging by historians, but their major conception of time masks the phenomena of change and of recurrence.

If the historian works strictly with a conception of time as successive moments of duration, he is likely to see change as a series of "firsts."[25] Becoming easily passes into being according to the static conception of linear time. Change is measured by consecutive dated events on the time scale. Each event has a position on the scale, and the successive dated events are listed in the manner of the "one damned thing after another" school of narrative to show change. Change is then depicted not as a process or even a connected sequence so much as a mere catalog of selected events in succession. Yet positional dating and a succession of events shows almost nothing about change in reality. Crucial questions about rate, direction, and magnitude remain unasked, let alone answered. Ironically, the historians' implicit stress on being in this case contradicts their explicit concern over change. The history of dated events has to a large degree hidden the history of change. As a

[25] An extreme example of this type of historiography is Ronald Seth, *The First Time It Happened: Fifty Memorable Occasions in the Story of Man* (London, 1965), which includes among other firsts the first law code, the first Parliament, the first soccer club, and the first man to swim the English Channel.

CONCEPTIONS OF TIME:
THEIR VARIETIES AND USES

result change and continuity are rarely studied very carefully, and change is almost never measured except in the new economic history.

Consider, by way of example, the usual textbook treatment of American history before the Revolution. Change is indicated only by changing circumstances and so the treatment is really a catalog of dated events. If space allocation is an index of speed as well as significance, then little happened of significance or of difference between the founding of the colonies and the Seven Years War in the mid-eighteenth century. Implied in all these texts is the slow unchanging life of the colonists before the latter conflict and then the rapidly changing attitudes and activities of the new nationalists after that war. Length of text would seem directly proportional to speed of change. In diagram we could represent the actual passage of time by a line.

1607		1763	1776	1800

But to show rapidity of change, according to the space allocated to the years in survey texts, we would have to alter the line as follows

1607	1763	1776	1800

Historians usually depict change by filling in time, so to speak, with a multitude of activities. When times are dull, little is said; when times are fast, much is said. The filling-in is necessary if time is conceived as a succession of moments alone.

Time can be conceived as a succession of moments on a metrical scale and still be dynamic by considering sequence in addition to duration. Sequence can take two forms. Sequence can be unordered: Things occur after one another in a consecutive time sequence, but the events have no relationship to each other. Many historians would argue that accidents and coincidences comprise the true nature of history, and to that extent the past is an unordered sequence. If this were the case, then any chronological list of miscellany would qualify as history. Since it does not, then historians must assume that written history embraces through selection a more ordered set of relationships than mere accident, regardless of the possibility of a truly chaotic world. If the sequence is seen as ordered, that is, the events are depicted as following each other in some related way, then the historian presumes genetic or causal connections. Though historians frequently deny they establish genetic or causal sequences in their narratives, their implicit basis for selection, if it is not to use time as setting, must imply causal relationships. Here Hume's ghost rises to question the possibility of determining cause through mere time sequence, and present-day philosophers inquire whether genetic connections constitute another form of explanation than causality, but we shall leave all basic questions of explanatory connections to the last two chapters. Here all we need to claim is that historians operate with sequences ordered in some manner.

By combining ordered sequences with a metrical time scale, we can pose a series of questions to ask about change.

1. The delimitation of the sequence: When did it start? When did it stop for the purposes of investigation?

2. The order of the sequence in relation to time: What followed what?

3. The order of occurrence: Why did it happen in that sequence?

4. The timing of the sequence: Why did it occur when it did? Why did not something else occur? (These

questions help establish sufficient as well as necessary causes for the sequence.)

5. The rate of change: How fast did it take for the entire sequence? Were certain portions of it faster or slower than others?[26]

This list of questions inquires about timing of the sequence both as to the dating of the overall sequence and as to the components of the sequence. From the answers comes the measurement of change. Although full answers to these questions demand techniques of quantification not yet available to historical analysts in many cases, still the remembering of the questions as a checklist will produce better qualitative histories of changes over time.

For an example, let us once again look at the period prior to the American Revolution through the eyes of a content analyst who explored the subject of emerging American nationalism for the period from 1735 to the outbreak of conflict between England and her colonies.[27] In reaction to both those historians who asserted that the national identity of the colonists as American rose slowly but steadily through the eighteenth century and those who argued that nationalism suddenly sprouted during the War of Jenkins' Ear, or after King George's War, or even during the Seven Years War, Richard L. Merritt examined by quantitative content analysis the symbol usage of samples issues of five colonial newspapers. He counted the frequency of symbols denoting identity with either British or American political community. Such systematic analysis

[26] My analysis of sequence is modified from Heirich, *op. cit.*
[27] Richard L. Merritt, "The Emergence of American Nationalism: A Quantitative Approach," *American Quarterly*, XVII (1965), pt. 2, 319–35, and *Symbols of American Community, 1735–1775* (New Haven, Conn., 1966).

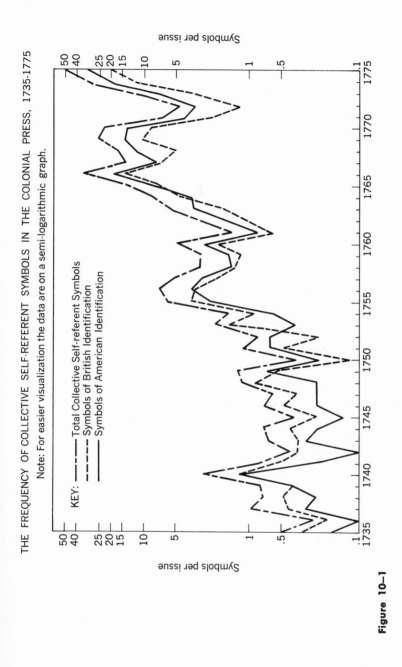

THE FREQUENCY OF COLLECTIVE SELF-REFERENT SYMBOLS IN THE COLONIAL PRESS, 1735-1775

Note: For easier visualization the data are on a semi-logarithmic graph.

KEY: ────── Total Collective Self-referent Symbols
     - - - - - Symbols of British Identification
     ─ · ─ · ─ Symbols of American Identification

Figure 10—1

CONCEPTIONS OF TIME:
THEIR VARIETIES AND USES

revealed that neither group of historians had been right. The sequence showed ups and downs of identification as well as ever greater usage of American symbols. His results are most quickly seen in his own chart (Figure 10–1).[28] From the chart it is obvious how important an analysis of sequence is to determine change. In essence, the chart establishes the points outlined in steps one through five above.

Like setting analysis, sequential analysis poses problems of wholes and parts but in a different manner. Upon what basis can the analyst select parts relevant to a whole sequence? How does he know what events should be connected to form a sequence? Once again a conscious conception of wholes is called for in the historical analysis of human behavior. The problem only becomes greater when we turn to exploring change and continuity.

Although for some historical analyses past time may be neatly divided into setting or sequence, more frequently the historian must treat both aspects of time together. Whether his topic is large or small, the historian must usually cope with both the breadth and depth of time simultaneously. Even a dated event, as we have seen, possesses both duration and a position in time as succession, and the problem of reconciling the two aspects only becomes more complex when the study involves a multiplicity of occurrences.

Since time as either setting or sequence poses problems of wholes and parts, the attempt to combine the two dimensions only multiplies the holistic problem and poses a certain indeterminacy in practice. The problem is best seen in the effort of social scientists to reconcile what they

[28] From Merritt, "The Emergence of American Nationalism: A Quantitative Approach," 335; reprinted by permission of the *American Quarterly.*

call a synchronic analysis of a whole with a diachronic analysis of its parts. As the etymology of the words would suggest, a synchronic analysis is the study of a cross section of the whole at one time; a diachronic analysis is the study of an item through time. Anthropologists particularly have been confounded in their attempts to combine a configurational or functional analysis of a culture (synchronic) with the historical analysis (diachronic) of the cumulative changes producing that culture. They see clearly that the configuration of the culture is the product of historical cumulation, but they cannot present the two topics simultaneously. Any social theorist is hard put to unite the two approaches, and usually one or the other method is chosen. Although nothing in theory as yet precludes the fusion of the two approaches to time, still in practice a study will emphasize one type to the virtual exclusion of the other. Thus most history volumes organize topically or by period or by a mixture of both. The apparent impossibility of writing simultaneously about the two dimensions of time might well be the historian's equivalent of the natural scientist's principle of indeterminancy.

A good example of such perplexity in historical writing is the work of Perry Miller on the Puritans and later Americans. If one reads Miller's major books not necessarily in the order of his writing them but in the order of the historical time he is writing about, one quickly sees that each volume is generally devoted to a synchronic or a diachronic analysis. Thus *Orthodoxy in Massachusetts, 1630–1650*[29] traces the Puritans from Old England to New England diachronically except for one chapter of synchronic analysis of the Puritan mind at mid-seventeenth

[29] Perry Miller, *Orthodoxy in Massachusetts, 1630–1650* (Cambridge, Mass., 1933).

CONCEPTIONS OF TIME:
THEIR VARIETIES AND USES

century. The latter topic later became the subject of a full-fledged volume devoted solely to a synchronic analysis in *The New England Mind: The Seventeenth Century.*[30] The diachronic analysis is resumed in *The New England Mind: From Colony to Province*,[31] which takes the history of the Puritan mind into the eighteenth century. At that point Miller portrays Jonathan Edwards' views as a microcosm of the New England mind in mid-eighteenth century.[32] In his biography of Edwards, Miller even has trouble reconciling the history of the man with the overall analysis of his philosophy. As a result he separates what he calls "the external biography" from the concepts of good, nature, sin, and other value orientations he attributes to Edwards. Despite its title, *The Life of the Mind in America from the Revolution to the Civil War*,[33] Miller's last uncompleted book, is really a synchronic analysis of the American mind shortly before the mid-nineteenth century. He does trace some of the development of each topic he sees in the configuration of American culture at that time, but the historical development is primarily an exposition of the configuration and not strictly a diachronic analysis. Historical analysis of the period between 1750 and 1850 had only appeared as articles up to the time of his death.[34]

236

[30] Perry Miller, *The New England Mind: The Seventeenth Century* (New York, 1939).

[31] Perry Miller, *The New England Mind: From Colony to Providence* (Cambridge, Mass., 1953).

[32] Perry Miller, *Jonathan Edwards* (New York, 1949).

[33] Perry Miller, *The Life of the Mind in America from the Revolution to the Civil War* (New York, 1965). I consider *The Raven and the Whale: The War of Words and Wits in the Era of Poe and Melville* (New York, 1956) to be part of this larger study for the sake of my analysis of Miller.

[34] Among such articles are "From the Covenant to the Revival" in James Ward Smith and A. Leland Jamieson, eds., *The Shaping of American*

Miller's failure to reconcile synchronic and diachronic analysis of American culture is a testimony to his analytical clarity, for an historian less clear about the interrelations of his facts would not have seen the impossibility of interpretation along both axes of time at once. At the same time, his inability to write both ways at once points up the giant historiographical problem of the incompatibility of treating time as setting and as sequence simultaneously.[35] Whether the indeterminancy dilemma can ever be solved is a matter of speculation at present, but nothing less than a solution should be attempted in light of the historian's goals to treat time as holistically as possible. The historical analyst's aim should and must be the study of a topic in the past in both the overall simultaneity and the sequence of time if he would follow the traditional aims in regard to time held by his guild.

Until a final resolution of the dilemma, the best the historical analyst can do in the presentation of a topic that involves both kinds of time is to work out possible compromises. He can attempt hybrid analyses from the viewpoint of analytical clarity. He might, for example, show setting as the result of several sequences producing a concurrence of configuration, although the sequences were not connected until the moment of the time setting. Perry

---

Religion. Religion in American Life, vol. 1 (Princeton, N.J., 1961), 322–368, and "From Edwards to Emerson," *New England Quarterly,* XIII (1940), 589–617, reprinted in *Errand Into the Wilderness* (Cambridge, Mass., 1956), 185–203.

[35] A graphic example of analytical inability to reconcile diachronic with synchronic treatment is Stow Persons, *American Minds: A History of Ideas* (New York, 1958), which divides American intellectual history synchronically into the colonial religious mind, 1620–1660; the Enlightenment mind, 1740–1812; the nineteenth-century democratic mind, 1800–1860; the naturalistic mind, 1865–1929; and the contemporary neo-democratic mind. Despite the dynamic appearance given by the dates, Persons finds it impossible to show the history of transition from one mind to another.

Miller seemed to be searching for this solution in his last book. An analyst could also show two different settings at two different times and treat sequentially the parts of the settings' whole in between. In this case, the historical synthesis would move from equilibrium at a certain time to equilibrium at a later date with the dynamics treated between the two wholes. Neil Smelser's book *Social Change in the Industrial Revolution: An Application of Theory to the British Cotton Industry*[36] seems to follow this pattern. He moves from the domestic system considered functionally to the factory system also considered functionally by means of his theoretical sequence of timing. In any case the trick demands avoiding a static presentation of the data while at the same time developing the configuration of the whole. Whatever the compromise and even final solution of the dilemma, we see how important a conscious concern about wholes and parts and about system is to the combination of description and explanation that is called written history.

For the historian concerned about change and continuity, certainly nothing less than attention to both aspects of time is necessary. A series of dated events may imply change at least, but such a list will never imply continuity. Such a list is a guide to innovation alone and not to persistence. Furthermore, such a static approach to change even conceals much of that phenomenon, as we have pointed out earlier. We agree for the most part with the art historian, George Kubler, who says in another context, "Calendrical time indicates nothing about the changing pace of events. Change in history is not yet a matter

[36] Neil J. Smelser, *Social Change in the Industrial Revolution: An Application of Theory to the British Cotton Industry* (Chicago, 1959).
[37] George Kubler, *The Shape of Time: Remarks on the History of Things* (New Haven, Conn., 1962), 83.

for precise determination."[37] Even a well-developed sequence answering the five basic questions posed earlier in this chapter does not show anything about continuity, and without a comparison to continuity, the analysis of change is not fully studied. The analysis of change in the fullest sense must therefore involve a study of continuity. This would seem to mean that change as sequence must be measured against continuity as setting and duration. Such an analysis of change would indicate change through a comparison of the change in relationship of the parts in the configuration of the whole or setting as well as by the change of the part or parts in sequence. The consciousness of configuration as setting would provide a basis for measuring both change and continuity. Analyzing change in this manner would produce more studies of changing interrelationships over time than mere catalogs of a succession of innovations or modifications.[38]

239

Some possibilities may be indicated quickly by diagram and by example. If we represent configurational wholes of time settings by circles and parts by letters, then we can quickly sketch a few alternatives, as shown in Figure 10–2. Smelser, for example, seemed to operate with alternative number three, but there are as many possibilities as there were variations in the past. An example of the utility of this approach for clarifying perplexing issues of change and continuity would be in regard to the debate over the decline of New England Puritanism. Because historians previously have not used explicit criteria for measuring change in this case, they have made various assertions about when and what constituted the decline of Puritanism. Estimates of decline range from the moment they landed, to the

[38] A much needed caveat on the customary usage of the term "continuity" by historians is Gerschenkron, *op. cit.*, 195–209.

CONCEPTIONS OF TIME:
THEIR VARIETIES AND USES

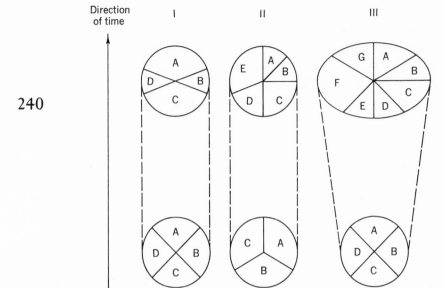

Figure 10–2

half-way covenant, or to the end of the seventeenth century.[39] Although we cannot present here a definitive solution to this problem of decline, the method of that solution can be sketched quickly. At least two distinctions must be made and then measured as well as possible. First, the overall cultural configuration must be established for the early period and then at successive time settings during the remainder of the seventeenth century. Miller, for example, derives his synchronic seventeenth-century New England mind willy-nilly from data scattered throughout the whole

[39] Perry Miller accepts the traditional date for decline sometime around the early eighteenth century in *The New England Mind: From Colony to Province*. Bernard Bailyn, *New England Merchants in the Seventeenth Century* (Cambridge, Mass., 1955), moves the decline back to the 1670s, and Darrett B. Rutman, *Winthrop's Boston: Portrait of a Puritan Town, 1630–1649* (Chapel Hill, N.C., 1965), believes the decline started immediately after the Puritans landed. Compare the explicit criteria each author uses to assert his choice of date.

period, and thus precludes any analysis of change. Perhaps configurations should be constructed for English Puritans also at the same points in time for an even better comparison. Second, the analyst must distinguish carefully between the ideal, the expected, and the actual insofar as he can in the society, so he will not assume that ideals preached in sermons typified actual behavior. By working up these configurations, the analyst should be able to determine more correctly than hitherto the nature and extent of the so-called decline. If many of the people said to be Puritan did not practice their ideals from the very moment of landing, then the whole issue is bogus. If the society gradually fell away from its ideals, then the decline could be stated more precisely than before, and so on for other possibilities.

This example, regardless of how little it may clarify the debate over Puritanism in New England, demonstrates above all how important explicit use of theory and particularly social theory is to an analysis of historic time. To study time as setting, the analyst must reconstruct the simultaneous pattern of attitudes and actions according to some theoretical framework. For this reason, the historian must depend consciously upon the conceptions of wholes and parts and system in general. In addition, he must also rely often upon social theories, because so much of his work deals with human behavior in its manifold forms. Similarly, the procedure for historical analysis presented earlier stresses the nature of group behavior as aggregative, collective, or conjunctive, because all three categories refer to a given pattern at one point in time but on different levels of analysis. The analyst must know whether what he studies results from observer's or actor's conceptions, and if the latter, whether it was performed consciously or not and as a group or not. Lastly, the procedure emphasizes whether the actors' actions resulted in intended or unintended consequences and how these were perceived on different occasions, because this side of group phenomena provides the dynamics in many sequences. In short, everything developed so far in this essay bears importantly upon the historical analysis of past time.

All in all, this brief survey of the varieties of time and their uses hopefully convinces the reader that the subject is indeed a large one deserving longer treatment. It should also be evident that most historians have neglected and therefore wasted many possibilities in their supposed chief interest by not discussing or thinking about the nature of time as used in historical analysis. Again George Kubler reminds us of the basic problem in regard to art objects in the past, but his words apply as well to other concerns of historians.

The number of ways for things to occupy time is probably no more unlimited than the number of ways in which matter occupies space. The difficulty with delimiting the categories of time has always been to find suitable description of duration, which could vary according to events while measuring them against a fixed scale. History has no periodic table of elements, and no classification of types or species; it has only solar time [universal physical] and a few old ways of grouping events, but no theory of temporal structure.[40]

Such a theory of temporal structure would seem to mean what social scientists call theories of social change. Does this mean that historians should or will become social scientists in the end? In order to answer this question we must examine what the relationship between history and the social sciences is in regard to time.

[40] Kubler, *op. cit.*, 96.

A BEHAVIORAL APPROACH
TO HISTORICAL ANALYSIS

Do historians treat time differently from social scientists, and if so, how? Must this difference exist, if it does exist, by necessity? And if any differences do exist, what implications do they have for explanation and analytical precision in history and the social sciences? To begin to answer these questions we must return to the nature of time as sequence.[1]

Sequences (and for that matter setting) may be either repetitive or unique, and supposedly the difference between the two types distinguishes history from the social sciences. If we combine the recurrence or nonrecurrence of a sequence of events with the factor of time duration as long- or short-term, for the sake of analysis, we see a possible ground for the distinction. A fourfold table reveals the combination of factors at a glance.[2]

Short-term, nonrepetitive occurrences are usually

Table 11-1

DURATION OF TIME	SEQUENCE OF EVENTS	
	Repetitive	Nonrepetitive
Short term	Process	Accident
		Series of events
Long term	Process	Trend
		History

[1] Compare my treatment of time and the discipline of history with that of space and the discipline of geography by Fred Lukermann, "Geography: *de facto* or *de jure*," *Journal of the Minnesota Academy of Science*, XXXII (1965), 189–96.
[2] Adapted from Wilbert E. Moore, *Social Change* (Englewood Cliffs, N.J., 1963), 49.

called accidents, whereas short-term, nonrecurrent series of events are termed just that. Long-term, nonrecurring sequences may be called trends or, in many cases, history. Recurring sequences are often termed processes regardless of duration. The terms I apply here may be controversial, especially the words "trend" and "history," but the exact terms are not so important as the points being made about them. Neither is the precise length of short- or long-term duration significant in the overall analysis, and therefore they are not determined with specific reference to actual time as measured duration.

In talking about processual sequences, we must add some questions to those asked about sequences in general.

6. The uniformity of the sequence: Does it follow the order invariably in each repetition?

7. The regularity of the process: How often does it recur?

In addition to these new concerns, the delimitation of the processual sequence becomes more crucial than for a nonprocessual sequence, because of its significance in determining just what does recur. At the same time, however, the repetitiveness aids the discovery of causality thanks to the possibility of comparison.

It is said that historians and social scientists diverge in their respective interests on the basis of these last questions about whether or not time can or should be treated as processual sequence. As Table 11–1 implies, historians are frequently thought to deal only with the unique whether as accidents, series of events, or as trends. The cumulation of these accidents, events, and trends is said to be the domain of history proper. The social scientist, on the other hand, seeks generalization and laws, and thus he looks to the recurrent, whether of short or long duration, for the comparisons necessary to establish his patterns. The historian tends to treat time sequences as unique series of events; so he accuses the social scientist of distorting time by ripping some events from their full context of coexistent setting and complex sequence in order to study the recurrent and produce generalizations. In this sense, the historian sees the social scientist as abstracting further from reality, hence warping the true nature of time, whereas he perceives himself as studying a manifold complex of concrete events and thereby preserving the true quality of time.

Such a perspective upon time and reality provides the basis for the well-known distinction between the idiographic and nomothetic disciplines, or between historical and scientific analysis. This distinction, which originated with Windelband, Rickert, Dilthey, and other thinkers following Kant's categorization, divides history as an individualizing subject from all sciences as generalizing subjects. On this basis, history is supposedly concerned with the particular, the concrete, and the unique, whereas the sciences, including today the social sciences, are interested in the general, the abstract, and the repetitive.[3]

To phrase the case for the difference between history

---

[3] The classic references are Wilhelm Dilthey, *Einleitung in die Geistestwissenschaften* (Leipzig, 1883); Wilhelm Windelband, *Geschichte und Naturwissenschaft* (Strassburg, 1894) and *Enleitung in die Philosophie* (Tübingen, 1914); Heinrich Rickert, *Die Grenzen der naturwissenschaftlichen Begriffsbildung* (Freiburg, 1896–1902) and *Kulturwissenschaft und Naturwissenschaft* (Freiburg, 1899). See also the symposium by R. B. Collingwood, A. E. Taylor, and F. C. S. Schiller, "Are History and Science Different Kinds of Knowledge?" *Mind*, N. S., 31 (1922), 442–66. A recent restatement of the position is Isaiah Berlin, "History and Theory: The Concept of Scientific History," *History and Theory*, I (1960), 1–31.

and the social sciences in terms of this ancient dichotomy is, like so many generalizations about the nature of disciplines, to state a half-truth at best. The sharp cleavage drawn between disciplinary goals and methods misrepresents the actual practice of scientists and historians and misconceives the nature of man's knowledge of reality. For the historian to claim an interest in only the unique and concrete in time and space involves him in a fundamental contradiction about his task and his method.

The historian cannot talk about something as unique without implicit or explicit comparison and generalization because of the very nature of language. Historical exposition presupposes the general and the recurrent to the extent necessary to give words meaning. For example, such common words in history books as war, revolution, priest, and king force the historian to make implicit comparisons upon the basis of categories so that he may generalize sufficiently to employ the words. Even if the historian wishes to show differences or uniqueness, he must still present history in terms comprehensible to others, and hence he must generalize and compare sufficiently to depict the differences he would show. The particular possesses significance only in the context of the general.[4]

4 Compare the positions of Alexander Gershenkron, "On the Concept of Continuity in History," *Proceedings of the American Philosophical Society*, CVI (1962), 195–209; W. H. Walsh, *Introduction to the Philosophy of History* (rev. ed., London, 1958), 34–47; Ernest Nagel, *The Structure of Science: Problems in the Logic of Scientific Explanation* (New York, 1961), 547–51; Quentin Gibson, *The Logic of Social Enquiry* (London, 1960), 7–11; Frederick J. Teggart, *Theory and Processes of History* (Berkeley and Los Angeles, 1960), 57–66; Alfred Conrad and John Meyer, *The Economics of Slavery and Other Studies in Econometric History* (Chicago, 1964), 4–15; William P. McEwen, *The Problem of Social-Scientific Knowledge* (Totowa, N.J., 1963), 199–203; Arthur C. Danto, *Analytical Philosophy of History* (Cambridge, Eng., 1965), 88–111; Carey B. Joynt and Nicholas Rescher, "The Problem of Uniqueness in History," *History and Theory*, I (1961), 150–

The philosopher Morris Cohen demonstrates how even a relatively simple statement of describing seeming uniqueness entails many implicit comparisons with the recurrent.

The absolutely unique, that which has no element in common with anything else, is indescribable—since all description and all analysis are in terms of predicates, class concepts or repeatable relations. Let us take a unique event, for example, that King John signed the Magna Charta at Runnymede on June 6th, 1215 A.D. Neither the individual John, the date, nor the specific act will occur again. Yet our statement identifies John as one of a class, the kings of England, who are defined as occupants of certain offices or as bearing certain relations to the various elements of the people of England. Magna Charta is significant as one of a number of political documents; and not only is the physical act of signing repeatable, but the motives which we assume compelled John to do it are recurrent ones in human experience. The date itself denotes a unique or repeatable state of the world. But note that it is defined in terms of a number of repeatable intervals, namely, years. Although language can never be self-sufficient and ultimately always depends upon a demonstrative element, i.e., a pointing to something which must be experienced, yet that to which the demonstrative points has its character determined by its abstract or repeatable traits.[5]

Just as the historian cannot talk about the unique and nonrepetitive without resort to the general and the recurrent, so he cannot *know* something or some moment is unique unless he consciously and conscientiously does the comparison to prove it singular. Far too frequently historians presume the object of their study is unique without

62; and Louis Gottschalk, ed., *Generalization in the Writing of History* (Chicago, 1963), especially 113-94. Folke Dovring's interesting little book, *History as a Science: An Essay on the Nature and Purpose of Historical Studies* (The Hague, 1960), revolves entirely about this distinction.
[5] Morris R. Cohen, "Causation and Its Application to History," *Journal of the History of Ideas*, III (1942), 21.

even bothering to establish the certainty of their presumption. Too often the historian assumes that the events of a particular time or the activities and physical objects in a specific place are unique without doing the necessary work to demonstrate this as fact. Thus, for example, what is unique about the American Revolution, American slavery, or American industrialization is only now being established in a tentative way by comparison with other revolutions at that time and later, with slavery in Latin America and elsewhere, and with industrialization in other nations.[6]

When the historian studies change and continuity, the repetitive and general must enter his study so that he knows where to look and understands what he finds. The study of continuity and change demands a framework of theory and of generality as we have argued earlier. If he would measure the duration of the continuity or the speed of the change, such knowledge is even more important than for the mere establishment of uniqueness.

The inability of the idiographic-nomothetic dichotomy to square with either the practice of historians or the nature of language indicates that it probably does not square with reality either. That ordinary language usage cannot differentiate the unique from the general or vice versa

[6] An interesting but somewhat misleading attempt by a sociologist to show the uniqueness of the beginnings of the American nation in a comparative framework is Seymour M. Lipset, *The First New Nation: The United States in Historical and Comparative Perspective* (New York, 1963), especially 15–98. Stanley Elkins in *Slavery: A Problem in American Institutional and Intellectual Life* (Chicago, 1959), renewed the old debate about the nature of ante-bellum Southern versus Latin American slavery. A recent example of the new debate is Herbert S. Klein, *Slavery in the Americas: A Comparative Study of Cuba and Virginia* (Chicago, 1967). All of the so-called "new economic history" depends upon a theoretical framework derived from comparison among modern economies. For an example of this genre in regard to American industrialization, see Douglass C. North, *The Economic Growth of the United States, 1790–1860* (Englewood Cliffs, N.J., 1961).

A BEHAVIORAL APPROACH
TO HISTORICAL ANALYSIS

without reference to the opposite condition shows an important truth about the nature of ontological reality insofar as men can know it. Reality as understood possesses two fundamental but seemingly contradictory features that cause the ambivalence reflected in ordinary discourse. On one hand, all events and things are unique in reality. Like snowflakes, no two atoms, bacteria, or amoebae are exactly alike, and supposedly recurrent phenomena like waves, quantum jumps, or chemical and physical experiments are each unique and different in some way. On the other hand, to individualize these uniquenesses requires that the observer know the generalities and recurrence among the objects he observes so that he knows they belong to the same class and possess similarities even in their individual differences. If an analyst can isolate the differences among some phenomena or moments to individualize them, then he must also have noted their similarities for the purposes of comparison.

Given the nature of time and reality as man can perceive them, any given moment or phenomenon can be viewed in either perspective depending upon the purposes of the investigator or the culture of the observer. According to this view of the universe, the distinction between the nomothetic and the idiographic dissolves into differing perspectives abstracted from the same reality. If the same moment or phenomenon may be viewed from either perspective, then to call one treatment of time and space more concrete, hence better, than another is to make a distinction without much substance based upon the nature of reality. To classify some thing or some time as singular and unique or recurrent and representative is in either case to remove that thing or moment from its context in space and time. In this sense, both modes of treatment are abstractions from reality as postulated. Man's perception of reality, then, determines whether a given phenomenon will be seen as singular or repetitive. The distinctions between the general and the particular, between the concrete and the abstract, and between the unique and the recurrent all reduce to a matter of analytical mode or, in the terms of the behavioral orientation adopted in this book, perceptual framework.[7]

Even the historian's stated goal of embracing all the events and actions in past time (insofar as they pertain to the historian's purposes) should urge him in the same direction as language, method, and the nature of reality as perceived, for time includes the recurrent as well as the unique and the accidental. According to both method and aim, the historian should and must study the recurrent, the general, and the abstract as well as the unique, the concrete, and the nonrecurrent so as to comprehend the fullness of historic time.

To say historians need to study the recurrent and use generalizations does not mean they must only look at the recurrent or only produce generalizations. Some historians, however, advocate and would practice comparative history based upon the deliberate study of the recurrent alone. For these members of the craft, history is more of a social science because its purpose is the study of causation. As Frederick J. Teggart, the earnest advocate of such a goal for history, has argued,

What we are given in experience is not one history, but a great number of histories. History is not unitary, but pluralistic. Every region and area has its own history, and the investigation of causation becomes possible when it is seen that the activities of men under different conditions may be compared.

Again, what we are given in experience is not change, but

[7] Compare Othmar F. Anderle, "A Plea for Theoretical History," *History and Theory*, IV (1964), 35–38, but the whole article is relevant to the material discussed in this chapter.

A BEHAVIORAL APPROACH
TO HISTORICAL ANALYSIS

evidence of changes, and changes may be investigated and compared. Further, what we are given in experience is not a series of events said to be "unique," but an infinite number of occurrences at different times and in different places. . . .

If we are to inquire into causation, it will be necessary to become familiar with the idea that there are classes of events, for where there are two or more occurrences which have features in common, these occurrences may be compared, and the possibility of comparison opens the way to induction.[8]

Whether induction from comparison establishes cause or only correlation may be left to another discussion, but for Teggart the aim of comparative history is to provide explanation as well as to produce description. Thus he not only argues the need of generalizations to study history, but he advocates that the study of history should produce generalizations as well.

Such comparative history can take many forms, however. Perhaps the most notable popular practitioner of history in this vein is Arnold J. Toynbee, with his study of civilizations, but the less broadly grandiose comparative treatments of revolution by Crane Brinton[9] and of industrial development by Walt Whitman Rostow[10] are also widely known examples of this genre of historical writing. Such statistical analyses as those of New York politics in the Jacksonian period by Lee Benson[11] and of the Vendée counterrevolution of 1793 by Charles Tilly[12] are also comparative history as correlation and causal analysis, although

[8] Frederick J. Teggart, "Causation in Historical Events," *Journal of the History of Ideas*, III (1942), 6–7.
[9] See Crane Brinton, *The Anatomy of Revolution* (rev. ed., New York, 1952).
[10] Walt Whitman Rostow, *The Stages of Economic Growth: A Non-Communist Manifesto* (Cambridge, Mass., 1960).
[11] Lee Benson, *The Concept of Jacksonian Democracy: New York as a Test Case* (Princeton, N.J., 1961).
[12] Charles Tilly, *The Vendée* (Cambridge, Mass., 1964).

their form and especially their techniques seem quite different from those of Toynbee, Brinton, or Rostow. Even William N. Chambers' *Political Parties in a New Nation* must use this type of historical analysis implicitly to assert that the United States was the first modern nation and therefore also had the first political parties in the history of the world.[13] If comparative history can take all these forms, then we should inspect more carefully its basis and its implications for historical analysis in terms of the problem posed in this chapter.

Regardless of whether the behavioral unit is a small community or a whole civilization, or whether the technique is statistical or otherwise, the goal of this form of comparative history is clear: the testing of one or more hypotheses about cause by a comparison of similarities and differences within units presumed comparable. Although the end is obvious, are the means to its accomplishment equally clear in theory and practice? As one would expect from our analysis of the particular and the general, comparative analysts must cope with the problem faced by the students both of the repetitive and of the unique.

Comparative history for the purposes of correlation and causation shares all the problems general to the so-called "comparative method" in the social sciences plus those difficulties peculiar to history. Although comparison is a fundamental procedure in all forms of causal analysis, the term comparative method as such is used to designate more specifically comparison employed as a substitute for experimentation. When an analyst cannot experiment with his subject matter through replication, establishment of controls, and the manipulation of variables, then he resorts

13 William N. Chambers, *Political Parties in a New Nation: The American Experience, 1776–1809* (New York, 1963).

A BEHAVIORAL APPROACH
TO HISTORICAL ANALYSIS

to the comparative method in the hopes of achieving the same explanatory results.

The basis of the method is the selection of units of analysis that manifest similarities and differences from case to case so that a comparison of these similarities and differences in the various cases produces significant generalizations about the relationships within all the units—just as if they had been experimented with. The procedure in the social sciences then becomes, in the words of one anthropologist,

. . . the analysis of social situations which are at first sight already comparable, that is, which appear to share certain features (modes of action, relationships) while differing in others, or to share their common features with some degree of difference. This first-sight impression will be rendered more precise by demonstrating the extent to which uniformities or differences in any one feature are accompanied by, or correlated with, uniformities or differences in others. Hence we are able, finally, to isolate the invariant relations between facts upon which all scientific explanations must rest.[14]

In other words, the analyst must seek a unit with some invariant frame of reference, so that he can determine in order of need (1) why despite differences the units are indeed comparable, (2) what are the similarities and differences within the units of analysis deemed comparable, and (3) what generalizations would seem to explain the nature of the units given those similarities and differences.[15]

[14] S. F. Nadel, *The Foundations of Social Anthropology* (New York, 1951), 222.
[15] The best references on the theory of the comparative method as such are Gideon Sjoberg, "The Comparative Method in the Social Sciences," *Philosophy of Science*, XXII (1955), 106–17; Edward A. Suchman et. al., "The Comparative Method in Social Research," unpublished manuscript, Cross-Cultural Methods Project (Cornell University, Feb. 1, 1955); and S. F. Nadel, *op. cit.*, 222–55. Robert M. Marsh, *Comparative Sociology: A Codification of Cross-Societal Analysis* (New York, 1967), contains

To find such units in behavioral analysis poses great problems. The worth of community studies, for example, would seem to depend upon the subject's typicalness in a society or its comparability to a whole society. But is "Yankee City" comparable to "Middletown," let alone to Boston or Chicago in regard to, say, social class? In other words, is the sample representative of the whole of which it is said to be part? In this sense, statistical sampling represents the problems of comparative method in microcosm. If comparison of units within the same society and culture presents problems, the selection of units across cultures or societies only increases the difficulties of comparison, because of the problem of finding "universal," nonculture-bound units. Can child-rearing practices in families in one society, for example, be said to be comparable to those of families in another society for the purpose of studying socialization and personality formation.[16]

The chief problem of using the method in behavioral

---

an up-to-date and extensive bibliography on theory, method, and practice in comparative studies as well as substantive chapters devoted to the subject. Compare the following historians on the problems and strategy of the comparative method, frequently with historical background of the method traced: Sylvia L. Thrupp. "Role of Comparison in the Development of Economic Theory," *Journal of Economic History*, XVII (1957), 554–70, and "History and Sociology: New Opportunities for Cooperation," *American Journal of Sociology*, LXIII (1957), 11–16; Fritz Redlich, "Toward Comparative Historiography: Background and Problems," *Kyklos*, XI (1958), 362–89; and Cyril E. Black, *The Dynamics of Modernization: A Study in Comparative History* (New York, 1966), 35–46. As its title suggests, Philip H. Bagby's *Culture and History: Prologomena to the Comparative Study of Civilizations* (Berkeley and Los Angeles, 1958), is entirely devoted to the topic of methodology in comparative history on the level Toynbee ought to practice it.

[16] The problems of cross-cultural analysis are explored in Frank W. Moore, ed., *Readings in Cross-Cultural Methodology* (New Haven, Conn., 1961). Compare Richard L. Merritt and Stein Rokkan, eds., *Comparing Nations: The Use of Quantitative Data in Cross-National Research* (New Haven, Conn., 1966).

A BEHAVIORAL APPROACH
TO HISTORICAL ANALYSIS

analysis, therefore, is the selection of units that are truly comparable from instance to instance. Ideally, according to John Stuart Mills' criteria, the units should be matched in all relevant and common attributes except the variable items from which the causation is inferred. But behavioral units rarely come in this form, and even if they did the inferred explanation would probably not be very interesting in most cases. As a famous comparative analyst notes in relation to developmental studies,

> The basic problem in comparative studies is not whether it is possible to construct such types [units] according to any relevant criteria but whether it is at all worthwhile to do so. The major test of worthiness is not only the extent to which such types with common characteristics can be discerned among various societies—something which may be to no small extent a matter of definition. The more important test of worthiness of such analysis is, first, whether common features delineate characteristics which are important for the understanding of the working of these types—as specialized, institutionalized systems, with boundary-maintenance and systemic problems of their own which differ from those of other systems. Second, such a test is greatly dependent on the degree to which it is possible to discern both the societal conditions common to different societies under each type of institutional system develops and becomes crystallized and the conditions of their change and transformation.[17]

Therefore to produce interesting generalizations requires complex units of analysis, but complex units of analysis increase the problem of establishing the comparability of the units.

As can be seen from even this brief discussion, the comparative method in the social sciences involves in the selection of a unit of analysis all the knotty problems of

[17] Schmuel N. Eisenstadt, *Essays in Comparative Institutions* (New York, 1965), 46-7.

determining a whole in behavioral analysis. Without comparable units, comparison is worthless, but the discovering of such units involves as much recourse to behavioral theory as it does to carrying out the actual research work and explaining the results. The identification of a unit always involves the isolation of some elements from the whole web of behavioral activity, and thus the selection must deal with, among other problems, those of contextual uniqueness versus abstracted repetition in both the actors' and observer's understanding of a behavioral whole.

One basic difficulty arises because obviously analogous behavior is not truly comparable from one group of people to another in the context of larger social and cultural patterns; to compare them results in a false comparison and a fallacious conclusion. What looks easily isolatable as similar behavior on the observer's level may not be seen in the same way at all by the actors from one unit to another. Two similar sets of child-training practices may have quite different meanings attached to them by the actors of two different cultures, so what does this similarity really indicate about the child training or the cultures? The analyst might be tempted to conclude from these formal similarities on the level of overt behavior some similarities about socialization and personality formation in the two societies and be quite wrong. On the other hand, the similarities must betoken something about the two cultures no matter how different they are otherwise. The real question here is not whether the analyst can compare but how he should compare.

Another basic difficulty stems from the level of specificity or abstraction upon which the units are selected. This difficulty is closely allied with the one of complexity of the unit. If formal analogies from easily observed similar behavior may be quite incomparable despite their concrete

likenesses, and even similar structures may produce erroneous comparisons, then upon what level of abstraction must
the analyst operate to find an invariant frame of reference
for the comparability of his units? In these circumstances,
structural functionalists argue that their approach provides
a sure-fire analytical scheme that allows true comparison.
Rather than being fooled by mere external appearances,
their functional X ray of the structure, so to speak, exposes
the processes similar to all units and hence provides truly
comparable units no matter how diverse they may be in
structure or appearance. Smelser's analysis of the many
organizations performing the same functions in England
during the initial stages of industrialism would seem to support their claims. Yet, if the basis of comparison must be
as abstract as the taxonomic entities of the structural functionalists, by what empirical indicators does the analyst
know his units of comparison? Do such schema presume
the basis of comparison they are employed to study? Once
again the analyst is caught in the dilemma between the
recurrent and the unique but now upon the level of
abstraction and in regard to the problem of the whole. The
only solution at this point in behavioral analysis would
seem to lie in the utility of a unit as proven by its worth in
repeated use.

The problems and hazards of the comparative method
in history are vividly seen in the failure of historians to
agree upon a definition of feudalism, the applicability of
that term to non-Western societies, and therefore the explanation of its occurrence in history. Until agreement
upon a definition, or the unit of analysis, is established, the
second and third cannot be accomplished. The accomplishment of the tasks are probably all interrelated in practice.

Any definition of feudalism must be an observer's construction because the word was not used as such until the

eighteenth century. In an attempt to find a meaning for the term, some historians have searched for its quintessential—or should I say ideal?—pattern in various parts of Western Europe from the eighth or ninth to the fourteenth or fifteenth centuries, so that extraction from a comparison of various degrees of feudalism would produce the desired meaning. Some historians would abandon the word as too vague to be useful at all after such a search. Others would confine the word to the "technical arrangements by which vassals became dependents of lords, and landed property (with attached economic benefits) became organized as dependent tenures or fiefs [feudum]."[18] Still another group of historians would employ the word to designate a general social situation, as would Marc Bloch, whose title *Feudal Society* indicates that he set out "to analyze and explain a social structure and its relationships." For him, feudalism involved

a subject peasantry; widespread use of the service tenement (i.e., the fief) instead of a salary, which was out of the question; the supremacy of a class of specialized warriors; ties of obedience and protection which bind man to man, and, within the warrior class, assume the distinctive form called vassalage; fragmentation of authority—leading inevitably to disorder; and, in the midst of this, the survival of other forms of association, family, and state, of which the latter, during the second feudal age, was to acquire renewed strength—such then seem to be the fundamental features of European feudalism.[19]

Both definitions run into problems of isolating the comparable units of analysis although both are supposedly derived from comparison. Even those historians who argue

[18] Joseph Strayer's definition in Rushton Coulborn, *Feudalism in History* (Princeton, N.J., 1956), 15.
[19] Marc Bloch, *Feudal Society*, L. A. Manyon, trans. (London and Chicago, 1961), 446.

for the first definition do not agree what behavioral relationships are involved from the observer's view let alone what meaning those relationships might have possessed for the actors. Some of the critics of this definition wonder whether the historians who propose it may not be fooled in thinking that similar words meant similar actions, thereby fallaciously substituting formal categories for functional ones. Other critics accuse the proponents of the narrow definition of really trading upon a larger social context than they admit to doing, and therefore not facing squarely the real issue of determining the unit of analysis. On the other hand, even historians who use the term in a general societal sense can be accused of not always differentiating carefully between what constitutes feudalism as such from the workings of that society in general. Regardless of which approach they use, many medieval historians would argue that feudalism existed only in Western Europe at a certain time. What seems to resemble it in Japan or elsewhere is not true feudalism.[20]

259

The debate now stands at this impasse. Further references to the documents will not really resolve the issues because the solution can only be an observer's construction of the behavioral whole to be called feudalism. Such a solution will more likely result not from further comparison among degrees of feudalism in various places and at various times in Europe but from comparison with other types of societies so as to delimit and delineate more clearly just what elements of the political, social, and economic organization must be involved together to produce a phenomenon

[20] In addition to Coulborn and Bloch, see for the recent debate, Frederic Cheyette, "Some Notations on Mr. Hollister's 'Irony,'" *Journal of British Studies,* V (1965), 1–14, and the articles by Hollister and Hoyt he mentions; also, J. W. Hall, "Feudalism in Japan—A Reassessment," *Comparative Studies in Society and History,* V (1962), 15–51.

TIME AND THE
DISCIPLINE OF HISTORY

called feudalism regardless of a narrow or broad definition. Surely any one of the elements of a warrior aristocracy, peasantry, manorialism, seigneurialism, or decentralized state authority is not enough in itself, or even a few together, to establish the conditions in which feudalism in either a narrow or a broad sense can be said to exist, for all alone or some together can be found elsewhere at other times. When this comparison of the nature of the overall societal conditions that produce the configuration of phenomena known as feudalism is done, then the argument over broad and narrow definitions will probably lose its relevance. Then also it can be quickly determined whether Japan and other societies were feudal at any time.

At one fell stroke by one process of comparison—no matter how laborious and complex the ultimate task of such an overall analysis of societal conditions—the twin problems of defining the unit and explaining its existence are solved. This is the goal of both those historians who would use comparison to study the unique and those who would use it to study the recurrent. Whether the analyst should then go on and use this analysis to produce theories about the nature of societies in general is another question we must still examine in our discussion about the relation of history to the social sciences.

As is readily seen from the example of feudalism, the comparative historian is always faced with the basic perplexities of the unique versus the recurrent, the general versus the particular in behavioral analysis, and for this reason the analyst cannot separate the selection of a unit for his comparison from the choice of a theoretical framework for its identification. So whether the analyst studies structure or process, form or function, change or continuity, he has that recurring dilemma of using a theory to find a unit of analysis and the unit to study the theory, but in the case of comparison the problem seems compounded of more difficulties than the usual case. Thus, when William Chambers argues that the first political parties had to arise in the United States rather than England, he must presume comparison with England and elsewhere, and this comparison rests upon a certain definition of a party system, that in turn depends upon a certain theory of parties. In the case of comparing revolutions and the stages of industrialism, the definition of the phenomena is dependent equally upon theory to establish the unit and upon the comparison of the units to produce the theoretical framework.[21]

In the end, both those historians who see the task of historical analysis to be the search for cause and correlation among the recurrent and those who oppose this end and believe history is the study of the unique must resort to comparison in their work. Thus the historical analyst, regardless of persuasion on this issue, must understand the nature and pitfalls of the comparative method. Because of the nature of his evidence, the historical analyst must be even more dependent upon a theoretical framework for comparison than the student working in living societies and cultures. Therefore, he must assume that the behavioral scientists' categories are valid across cultures in time as well as space.

But is this assumption justified? To what extent have the behavioral scientists avoided ethno- and temporocentrism in their work? Almost all the categories developed so far are derived from a small sampling of cultures in the United States and Western Europe. If the social and cultural variability posited by the behavioral theorists exists,

[21] Compare, for example, the approaches to revolution by Brinton, *op. cit.*, and Chalmers Johnson, *Revolutionary Change* (Boston, 1966).

then how many of these categories are valid? On the other hand, categories derived from intracultural and intrasocietal comparison can still be useful and valid. The real problem is just what or which categories are how narrow or how general in application.[22]

Only further comparison by the behavioral scientists and by historians testing the units can resolve this and other problems of the comparative method in the social sciences as well as in historical analysis. Since the behavioral categories were generated from the network of human activity by comparison of some sort, only continued comparison can establish what is truly invariant analytically over space and time from what is variable for the purposes of constructing categories that are neither ethno- nor temporocentric. Again, as urged so often before, conscious attention to the problem of the comparative method will alert the historical analyst of both the recurrent and the unique to the possibilities of that form of study for their respective purposes.

Does this conclusion mean that history is a social science because historians and social scientists must both use the comparative method? To the extent that both may use the same theories and the same methods, history could be classified as a social science. But to say that the aims of history are the same as the aims of the social sciences and therefore that history is a social science in that sense too would falsify the goals of many historians as they prefer to think of their task. The distinction drawn here can be seen in the way most social scientists as opposed to most historians approach the study of the past.[23]

[22] This is the whole point of Marsh, *op. cit.*
[23] Compare the nature of an historian's approach to an anthology on the topic, Edward Saveth, ed., *American History and the Social Sciences* (New York, 1964), with that of two sociologists, Werner J. Cahnman

Social scientists would use comparative history to produce theories of cultural and social change or of political and economic development.[24] At their most general, they would create neo-evolutionary analyses of societies ranked according to successive levels of sociocultural integration or of increasing structural differentiation and functional specialization.[25] The goal of such work is expressed well in the title of an article by the sociologist editor of a recent anthology upon the relation of sociology and history from the viewpoint of the former: "The Rise of Civilization as a Paradigm of Social Change."[26] At this level, the social scientists join hands with Rostow and Toynbee. Although historians might use theories of social change in their work, most would not profess the production of such theories as their task. It is this aspect of Toynbee's work

-----

and Alvin Boskoff, eds., (*Sociology and History: Theory and Research* (New York, 1964).

[24] This would seem the didactic thrust of Kenneth Bock's history of the comparative method, *The Acceptance of Histories: Toward a Perspective for Social Science*, University of California Publications in Sociology and Social Institutions, vol. 3, no. 1 (Berkeley and Los Angeles, 1956).

[25] Among anthropologists, see the work of Leslie A White, *The Evolution of Culture* (New York, 1959); Julian H. Steward, *Theory of Culture Change: The Method of Multilinear Evolution* (Urbana, Ill., 1955); and Elman R. Service, *Primitive Social Organization: An Evolutionary Perspective* (New York, 1962). Among sociologists, see the books by Talcott Parsons, *Societies: Evolutionary and Comparative Perspectives* (Englewood Cliffs, N.J., 1966); Marion J. Levy, Jr., *Modernization and the Structure of Societies: A Setting for International Affairs* (Princeton, N.J., 1966); and Schmuel N. Eisenstadt, *The Political Systems of Empires* (New York, 1963).

[26] Werner J. Cahnman in Cahnman and Boskoff, eds., *op. cit.*, 537–59. That not all theorists of social and cultural change attempt such bold schemes as those cited in this and the preceding note can be seen in the other articles by social scientists in *ibid.* and in Amitai Etzioni and Eva Etzioni, eds., *Social Change: Sources, Patterns, Consequences* (New York, 1964) and George K. Zollschan and Walter Hirsch, eds., *Explorations in Social Change* (Boston, 1964). Such a comparison will show, however, that all have the same basic goal.

that perturbs them as much as his carelessness of data and techniques.[27]

It is not the study of the recurrent as such nor the use of generalization that disturbs so many historians about comparative history on this plane. Many are not bothered by the necessity of using causal analysis or even the comparative method. Rather, they do not see the aim of all this to be the production of laws or lawlike generalizations as do the social scientists in their use of the past. The essential question for many modern historians is not whether or not to use generalizations, or to search for causes, or to employ comparison, but rather how to use these factors in the production of written histories that deal with the unique and the particular as well as the recurrent and the general.[28]

That most historians today would not and do not practice historiography as soley the study of the recurrent and the general points to some truth in the idiographic-nomothetic distinction drawn earlier, but this truth resides in the goals and perspective of the majority of historians and not in the nature of reality. Both history and the sciences deal with the unique and the general, the singular and the recurrent, but the goals of the practitioners of the two branches of knowledge result in different combinations of the two possible perspectives on time and reality. Usually the scientist explores the comparative in order to compre-

[27] Historians' views are among those collected by M. F. Ashley Montagu, ed., *Toynbee and History: Critical Essays and Reviews* (Boston, 1956).

[28] This is the major conclusion of the Committee on Historiography of the Social Science Research Council in Louis Gottschalk, ed., *Generalization in the Writing of History* (Chicago, 1963). I believe an investigation of the nature of work written by historians for *Comparative Studies in Society and History* would also confirm this impression of the aims of most historians. How little real comparison may be done by historians even under the rubric of comparative history is amply demonstrated by the authors in C. Vann Woodward, ed., *The Comparative Approach to American History* (New York, 1968).

A BEHAVIORAL APPROACH
TO HISTORICAL ANALYSIS

hend it into theory; only occasionally does he examine the unique for its own sake. To the extent that historic time includes the recurrent as well as the unique, the historical analyst can and must study this aspect of past life and use scientific theory and especially social scientific knowledge to understand what he studies. But in the end most his- torians are just as or more concerned with the unique aspect of past history, and this concern distinguishes them from the social scientists who prefer the comparative to the singular for their purposes of producing laws and theories.

When the historian studies past recurring behavior or events, he may borrow behavioral theory to aid his research and writing, but such borrowing need not make him a social scientist. The historian usually consumes social science generalizations; he does not seek to produce such generalizations. True, he may have to generalize to the extent that language, narrative, or even explanation demand it, but even then he is far from the goal of constructing the universal lawlike or lawful generalizations the social scientists hope to achieve. In his borrowing he may even test a theory like a scientist, but that is not usually his primary aim. His goal is far different. He seeks to treat all human events in time as holistically as possible regardless of whether they can be comprehended into scientific theories or not. Thus to the extent that this goal includes the recurrent, he may use social science theory and generalization; to the extent that time includes the unique, he must devise his own methods of understanding the past. The historian may study processes in history, but he cannot treat history as process in the sense we have given that word.[29]

[29] Compare Joynt and Rescher, *op. cit.*; Nagel, *op. cit.*, 547–606; and Louis O. Mink, "The Autonomy of Historical Understanding," *History and Theory*, V (1965), 24–47. That there is not and cannot be *one* theory of social change is the conclusion of Wilbert Moore after a sur-

In the end most historians, unlike social scientists, prefer to deal with the "time" or "times" as well as with timeless things. They study Napoleon or Caesar or Hitler, not just political generalship. That theories of political generalship might explain some things about these men is admitted, but that such theories, no matter how sophisticated they may ever become, will explain everything so as to preclude the idiosyncratic about these men seems highly doubtful to most historians at the present stage of knowledge. To the extent that a man is like all other men or some other men, to use Kluckhohn's famous statement, then the social sciences are useful and illuminating in historical analysis. To the extent, however, that a man is like no other man, and this variation cannot be accounted for by psychology alone, the social sciences are not valuable to the historian. Whereas the social scientist loses his interest at this latter point in a man, the historian's interest is only whetted. Likewise, many historians are fascinated with events as accidents or trends, whereas social scientists concern themselves with these events only insofar as they hope to order them into a theory. Until that time, they are content to leave these events to the field of the historian, who is glad to include them in his bailiwick.

The historian's attempts to study man's past actions as holistically as possible further distinguish history from the social sciences and also reinforce the tendency of historians to feel that they deal with the unique and nonrecurrent. Only history, unlike any of the social sciences, tries to deal with the totality of man's actions in historic time, analytically speaking. To say that historians study past time holistically does not imply they can or must study all of the

vey of the subject, "A Reconsideration of Theories of Social Change," *American Sociological Review*, XXVI (1960), 817–18.

A BEHAVIORAL APPROACH TO HISTORICAL ANALYSIS

human past, or even all of the human past that is documented. Rather it means that they try to bring a wider set of events into a single framework than do the social scientists, who only explore events insofar as they can be ordered into repetitive series. Historians therefore investigate aspects of time not yet amenable to "scientific" study, to return to Kant's distinction, in that we possess no generalizations, nor are we looking for generalizations, about events abstracted from reality in this way.

Although social scientists may study aspects of history in this sense now and then, not one of them professes this as a main, let alone as the sole, goal of their profession as historians do. As a result of espousing this goal, historians could be said to study past time in greater fullness than social scientists do. Since the historian does seek to study historic time in as great a whole as possible, he must stress the unique more, generalize less, and treat time less abstractly than the social scientist, if we understand this statement to mean that he feels the nonrecurrent is as or more significant than the recurrent, that he studies men's actions and attitudes whether or not they can or should be comprehended into a theory or generalization, and that he prefers to time events by an overall metrical scale rather than by repetitive cycles. For all these reasons, the historian must concentrate on time as dated chronology, because only by this means can he comprehend such diversity into one system so that he may treat it as holistically in study and in synthesis as he does. And this interest in time as a total dated system distinguishes the historian's concern as to both goal and method from those of the social scientists. At the same time, this holistic interest in time presents the historian with some of his greatest problems in analysis, for the diversity often presents him with irreconcilable dilemmas and always with an explanatory challenge.

The concern with the unique does not absolve the historian from the analytical precision demanded of all social analysts. He must specify what is unique even if he cannot explain fully why it is unique. If the unique is the result of a sequence, the historical analyst can show how it got that way, even if he cannot prove why it took that sequence. If the unique is the result of a configurative setting in time, then he can delineate the cluster as carefully and as fully as possible by attention to the assumptions of system. In either case, the historian is faced with the question of wholes and parts. For far too long the historian has trusted to implicit biases that he shared with his audience to provide the connections among the events he merely listed as concurrent or consecutive on the time scale of his narrative. Instead of presuming a unity by a narrative integration dependent alone upon a holistic conception of dated chronology, the historical analyst should prove the connections he usually only implies in his narrative. To the extent he does attempt this task, he will be more scientific in his reconstruction of the past than has been traditional in the craft. He will also find the task of research and synthesis far harder than it has been, because he will try to establish explicitly what heretofore was only assumed or not even seen as necessary to the writing of history.

Complete faithfulness to the craft's traditionally asserted goals of studying historic time as an analytical whole therefore requires that the historian use all the varieties of time as well as study all the various manifestation of past human behavior said to be historical. This new conception of the historian's task demands a greater awareness of models and systems, of explanations and theory, and of the levels and categories of historical analysis. The unique is still unique in this view, but the historian does not presume all phenomena in history are unique, nor even of those that are unique does he assume they are totally inexplicable. The recurrent also gains greater attention from the historian, because he seeks to prove the existence of the unique, to show change and continuity, and to study historical time as holistically as possible. The problems involved in such an enormous task show up in the historian's efforts at synthesis and explanation when he tries to incorporate all these analytically disparate items into one framework.

The goal of historical analysis, behaviorally oriented or otherwise, is a synthesis of the derived facts, or written history. In the end, the historian must organize all his theories and facts into some interpretation of the whole, and this interpretation of the whole presumes some form or forms of explanation. There is no synthesis without explanation of some kind, but the crucial question in historical analysis is what form of explanation. This is a particularly difficult problem given the disparate modes of analysis the historian is trying to incorporate into one framework. We must turn to the philosophers for possible solutions to this problem.

The problem of explanation is hotly debated in modern philosophy because of the controversy over the logic of asserting connections among statements about phenomena. Essentially an explanation seeks to render a statement about some phenomenon intelligible by linking it to other statements in a certain manner. Explanation consists paradigmatically therefore of an *explanandum*, or the statement to be explained, and an *explanans*, or the set of statements that are said to explain it.[1] The simplicity of this paradigm conceals the debate raging over the ways of validly accomplishing the connection. Although the criteria of what con-

---

[1] These terms, now general, are those of Carl Hempel, with P. Oppenheim, "Studies in the Logic of Explanation," reprinted in his *Aspects of Scientific Explanation and Other Essays in the Philosophy of Science* (New York, 1965), 247 and note.

stitutes a satisfactory connection are still being debated, the idea of explanation is so central to any discussion of methodology in a discipline that we must proceed at our own peril amidst the combatants. Explanation as used here encompasses what historians usually call causation but also includes many other possible types of connections, such as probability or functionalism. Because of the breadth of its meaning, the word "explanation" is preferable to the more specific "causation" in referring to the connections that historians must establish in their synthesis of derived facts.

Many historians do not believe explanation is part of their professed task, and certainly most of Clio's followers would not maintain that a knowledge of the technical criteria for explanation as discussed by philosophers is required in their work. At best these men would subscribe to some principle like historical understanding as the goal of their syntheses. According to their conception, written history is a skillful synthesis of description, evocation, and explanation—if provided—in artful fusion. Historical understanding in this sense is as dependent upon producing a feeling for the era under consideration as it is in accounting for what happened. Accounting for what happened, they believe, is to a considerable extent accomplished through evocation and the mere recounting of what did happen. Thus the traditional form of historical exposition is the narrative in which causal nexus is entwined in descriptive prose so as to evoke, to recount, and perhaps to explain simultaneously. In this view, the perfect historical synthesis is composed of a narrative exposition of chronologically ordered, factually true data about a part of man's past arranged so artistically that it helps to reproduce past reality in the mind of the reader at the same time as it perhaps explains man's past behavior within and by its organization. Such written history is considered both art and science by its admirers.[2]

Today the classic historical narrative fails from both an artistic and a scientific viewpoint. Modern novelists have pointed in new directions for story form as much as the new philosophers of science and history have indicated the possibility of greater explanatory precision. Historians who cling to a traditional narrative form based upon nineteenth-century models oversimplify the story of the past artistically as much as they omit the explanation of much of that

[2] Consider, for example, the tone and bias of Henry S. Commager, *The Nature and Study of History* (Columbus, Ohio, 1965). The heritage of this attitude may even be found in the otherwise sophisticated thinking of Henri-Irénée Marrou, *The Meaning of History*, Robert J. Olsen, trans. (Baltimore, Md., 1966) 192:

> This brings us to the essential point: explanation in history is the discovery, the comprehension, the analysis of a thousand ties which, in a possibly inextricable fashion, unite the many faces of human reality one to another. These ties bind each phenomenon to neighboring phenomena, each state to previous ones, immediate or remote (and in a like manner, to their results). One may rightfully ask oneself if real history is not just that: the concrete experience of the complexity of truth, a grasp of its structure and evolution, in which both are ramified in this way. This is a knowledge undoubtedly elaborated as deeply as it is broadly understood, but it is something which assuredly remains closer to actual experience than to scientific explanation.

Compare other historians on the nature of narrative: Frederick J. Teggart, *Theory and Processes of History* (Berkeley, and Los Angeles, 1960), especially 18–29, 51–66; Louis Gottschalk, *Understanding History: A Primer of Historical Method* (New York, 1950), 8–18, 193–208; G. J. Renier, *History: Its Purpose and Method* (London, 1950), 13–78, 169–256; and H. Stuart Hughes, *History as Art and as Science: Twin Vistas on the Past* (New York, 1964), 68–88. A classic admonition to historians about the purposes of narrative is Jean J. Jusserand et al., *The Writing of History* (New York, 1926), 1–32. Of more recent date but on the same subject is Samuel E. Morison, "History as Literary Art" in Oscar Handlin et al., *Harvard Guide to American History* (Cambridge, Mass., 1954), 44–49. For philosophers' analyses of historical narrative, consult citations in footnote 11 of this chapter. An important analysis of some great American narrative historians is provided by David Levin in *History as Romantic Art: Bancroft, Prescott, Motley, and Parkman* (Stanford, Calif., 1959).

A BEHAVIORAL APPROACH
TO HISTORICAL ANALYSIS

story. While novelists and philosophers have made great strides in method, the historians still too frequently allow the forms of the past to suppress the new knowledge of man.

The goal of producing an historical synthesis fusing feeling, chronological description, and explanation is no longer attainable, at least in the classic sense, in light of modern knowledge about human behavior. The complexity of behavioral interaction seen by modern social theorists disallows both the single narrative viewpoint and the haphazard explanation that have constituted traditional narrative history. Like other so-called "new" approaches to history, conscious stress on explanation delineates a behavioral approach from older types of history writing. A behavioral approach both depends upon precise explanation for its foundation and aids in making precise explanation. At the same time, the stress on explanatory precision and behavioral complexity has implications for the nature of exposition in historical synthesis to the point of demanding new artistic forms in order to be truer to this current knowledge. Because so much depends on the nature of explanation, we must examine at some length current philosophers on that subject, even at the risk of becoming embroiled in some of the battles.

One cannot study the problem of explanation in general and in history in particular without soon becoming aware of the immense literature that has been produced on the subject during recent decades in the fields of philosophy of science and philosophy of history. Whether or not these two fields are indeed separate ones depends upon whether historical explanation is a different form of explanation than the one denominated the scientific model. This question is of major concern to philosophers today and accounts for much of the literature.[3] Because so much of the recent critical, or analytical, philosophy of history (as opposed to the older speculative brand of Hegel, Marx, Spengler, or Niebuhr[4]) deals with the question in terms relative to the problems internal to the modern philosophy profession, the debate seems of little pertinence to practicing historians in their work.[5] Yet in spite of what appears like a purely internecine squabble among professional philosophers, the debate over the nature of explanation has important implications for historians. If the literature of the dispute is translated into terms applicable to the problems faced by the historian doing his work, then the relevance of the philosophers' debate becomes all too obvious. While we cannot attempt such a translation *in toto*, we will view this philosophical literature on explanation from the viewpoint of the behavioral approach adopted in this book.

In its current form, the philosophical dispute over the nature of history is not directly relevant to a behavioral approach to historical analysis. As could be guessed, its categories seem artificial and grossly oversimplified in light of current knowledge of human behavior. This occurs because the debate has divided into what seems to the disputants like two mutually incompatible models of the logic of explanation. One side argues that all explanation, if it really explains, must follow the scientific model whereby specific facts are deduced from a general "covering law," as it has come to be called. The opposition denies that historians use general laws at all in their syntheses. Usually the

[3] This point among many is made quite clearly in a review of Sidney Hook, ed., *Philosophy and History* (New York, 1963), by Marvin Levich in *History and Theory*, IV (1965), 329.

[4] This distinction between critical and speculative philosophy of history was drawn by W. H. Walsh, *An Introduction to the Philosophy of History* (rev. ed., London, 1958), 13–15.

[5] See, for example, the historians' comments in Hook, ed., *op. cit.*

opponents of the covering-law theorists subscribe to explanation by "rational action," by which they mean that man acts quasiphilosophically in selecting alternative modes of action.[6]

The most obvious defect apparent from a behavioral view in this debate is the quaintly outmoded model of man and society presupposed by the philosophers. The rational-action advocates seem to misunderstand or oversimplify the internal-external behavior relationship by restricting it on the whole to the purely rational-action sequence discussed in Chapter 3. Their opponents would seem to deny that this internal-external behavioral relationship is explanatory at all, because it cannot be used to predict invariably a given action by reference to any general laws. In fact, their model of explanation seems based upon observers' constructs alone. Both sides agree, however, that the internal-external relationship is something other than explanation by the scientific model. One school sees it as no explanation at all and the other views it as explanation according to means other than the scientific model. Yet to a person of behavioral persuasion, both sides simplify the explanation of human behavior by insisting that all kinds of human behavior be explained by their one favorite model of explanation.

[6] The two sides as they formed were argued by Patrick Gardiner, *The Nature of Historical Explanation* (Oxford, 1952), and William Dray, *Laws and Explanation in History* (Oxford, 1957). William Dray, *Philosophy of History* (Englewood Cliffs, N.J., 1964), is a brief college text organized mainly in these terms. Recent anthologies of modern views are Patrick Gardiner, ed., *Theories of History* (New York, 1959), 344–475; William Dray, *Philosophical Analysis and History* (New York, 1966); and the pages of the journal, *History and Theory*. A more complex presentation of the whole topic may be found in two recent books, Morton G. White, *Foundations of Historical Knowledge* (New York, 1965), and Arthur C. Danto, *Analytical Philosophy of History* (Cambridge, Eng., 1965).

EXPLANATION IN
HISTORICAL SYNTHESIS

In another sense both schools see the social sciences as either too much or too little scientific. The covering-law theorists, if they believe their model of scientific explanation applicable to history writing, must claim that general laws of human behavior do now exist or at least can be discovered; otherwise, written history explains in a way other than they advocate or it cannot explain at all. In either case, their model is prescriptive, for sufficient laws do not now exist, and if we are to await the development of such laws, then we have no historical explanation, hence job, as yet. On the other hand, their opposition claims that too few if any general laws exist in the social sciences that the historian can use for aid in explaining the past phenomena he studies, or that the use of such laws really makes history a social science and not history as they mean it. To a person of behavioral persuasion, these arguments credit the social sciences with either too much or too little accomplishment.

The debates among the philosophers seem as little in touch with current historical writing as they do with contemporary behavioral studies. The lack of contact is evident from the examples the philosophers select as paradigmatic of history writing. Far too frequently these examples are selected from writings of narrative historians following nineteenth-century traditions, such as George Macaulay Trevelyan or C. V. Wedgewood.[7] This is written history that had as its ideal the fusion of evocation and explanation within a descriptive chronology. Such examples confirm to both the rational-action and covering-law advocates what they contend the true nature of historical explanation to be.

[7] See for example the list of historians analyzed by Gardiner, *op. cit.,* 65–67, which includes besides these two writers Charles Seignobos, Benedetto Croce, Leonard Woolf, G. Plekhanov, Jacques Bainville, R. H. Tawney, H. Pirenne, and F. M. Stenton.

The covering-law theorists see "trivial laws"[8] or "explanation sketches"[9] at best in such examples; the rational-action proponents see empathy[10] and narrative sequence as explanation.[11]

That philosophers select older writers is significant because they tend to use the same few examples over and over once one is utilized in the debate. Thus a few examples became the chief sources for the philosophical analysis of historical explanation. As a result, the literature on what constitutes historical explanation appears old-fashioned and narrow to the eye of the modern historian, because the examples are so far out of touch with the best contemporary writing and so far from representative of the wider variety of historiographic styles available today.

The narrowness of the philosophers' debate from both the behavioral and the modern historiographical viewpoint makes it appear useless to today's historian. His perspectives seem broader to himself than those encompassed by the historians used by philosophers in their examples. His quest for explanation seems broader to himself than the philosophers are willing to allow or know they must comprehend. In this whole controversy, as in so many others, the best position for the historian is one of toleration so as to extract the maximum utility for historical analysis.

To say that the debate is overly narrow and often outmoded for the present-day historian does not exempt

[8] Karl R. Popper, *The Open Society and Its Enemies* (Harper ed., New York, 1963), vol. 2, 264.
[9] Carl Hempel, "The Function of General Laws in History," reprinted in Hempel, *op. cit.*, 238.
[10] Following the lead of R. G. Collingwood, *The Idea of History* (Oxford, 1946), especially 205–315.
[11] W. B. Gallie, *Philosophy and the Historical Understanding* (London, 1964), 22–125. Other philosophical analyses of narrative are White, *op. cit.*, 219–70, and Danto, *op. cit.*, 143–82, 233–56.

EXPLANATION IN
HISTORICAL SYNTHESIS

him from knowing about the criteria for precise explanation. Too often the historian, whether he is or is not sympathetic to the social sciences, is lax in his logic. Too often he feels that arduous research and well-written narrative are a substitute for precise explanation—if he is even aware that his assertion of connections is incomplete or even inconsistent resulting in or from faulty organization. A thousand well-confirmed facts cannot prove one proposition that is illogical or incomplete. No matter what historians claim to the contrary, they cannot escape showing causes or asserting connections; here, as argued before, explicit knowledge rather than implicit chance should produce better historical syntheses. Historians will and must enter where logicians fear to tread because of insufficient or even nonexistent evidence, but this mental carefreeness should never result from lack of acquaintance with the criteria for explanation as discussed by philosophers. What the "compleat" historical analyst needs to know, therefore, beyond the traditional historical methods and a modern behavioral approach is what constitutes explanation according to contemporary philosophers.

Yet to discuss what is explanation is to become embroiled in a heated controversy and the steadily increasing multitude of books and articles devoted to it. We have neither the space nor fortunately the necessity to undertake a complete examination of the subject. Rather we shall provide a lengthy footnote to the principal modern combatants and consider only those aspects most pertinent to the behavioral approach to history outlined in this book. In this way the reader is spared many of the polemics, and if he is interested, and he should be, he may read the controversy in the original sources, to use that favorite phrase of the historian. Even to consider only certain aspects of the argument, however, will necessitate our taking sides at times despite our stance of methodological toleration.[12]

Explanation is used by contemporary philosophers in at least two senses, one close to ordinary language usage and the other derived from the reconstructed logic of the physical scientists. In the words of one of the leading philosophers of science, Carl Hempel, who bases his model upon the latter, "to explain the phenomena in the world of our experience, [is] to answer the question 'why?' rather than the question 'what?' "[13] In his opinion the question "why?" can be answered satisfactorily only by logical deduction from a general empirical law or universal generalization after the initial conditions are given. As Karl Popper, who maintains a similar position, phrases it, "To give a causal explanation of an event means to deduce a statement which describes it, using as premises of the deduction one or more universal laws, together with certain singular statements, the initial conditions."[14] Now it is easy to see why these men are dubbed covering-law theorists, because they would explain a phenomenon by deducing it from the general law that subsumes or covers it. To them the nature of an answer to a why question is free of the context of asker's and teller's knowledge.

[12] In addition to Hempel, *op. cit.*, other important recent works are R. B. Braithwaite, *Scientific Explanation: A Study of the Functions of Theory, Probability and Law in Science* (London, 1953); Ernest Nagel, *The Structure of Science: Problems in the Logic of Scientific Explanation* (New York, 1961); and Israel Scheffler, *The Anatomy of Inquiry: Philosophical Studies in the Theory of Science* (New York, 1963). On explanation in the social sciences in particular, see Robert Brown, *Explanation in Social Science* (Chicago, 1963); Abraham Kaplan, *The Conduct of Inquiry: Methodology for Behavioral Science* (San Francisco, 1964); Quentin Gibson, *The Logic of Social Enquiry* (London, 1960); and Richard S. Rudner, *Philosophy of Social Science* (Englewood Cliffs, N.J., 1966).

[13] Hempel, *op. cit.*, 245.

[14] Karl R. Popper, *The Logic of Scientific Discovery* (Harper ed., New York, 1965), 59.

EXPLANATION IN
HISTORICAL SYNTHESIS

To a philosopher who analyzes ordinary language usage, the answer to a why question involves possibilities other than the model supplied by mathematical physics. Explanations in this sense may be definitions, justifications, fitting the unknown into a larger context, reinterpreting the unknown, explaining discrepancies, or a host of other possibilities dependent upon what the asker knows and wants to or needs to know.[15] Another philosopher therefore broadens the notion of explanation to include answers to "what?" "how?" "where?" and other questions involving interrogative words.[16]

The implications of the two positions for historical analysis can best be seen in the respective attitudes toward prediction and explanation. To the covering-law theorists prediction of the future and explanation of the past use exactly the same model of logic, for in both cases the analyst must deduce the desired statement from a law that covers the phenomenon studied. It does not make any real difference from their logical standpoint whether the outcome is known, as in the past, or unknown, as in the future, because the significant criterion is the general law. To covering-law theorists retrodiction, as they sometimes call it, and prediction are therefore similar operations.[17] According to their opponents, explanation of the past is quite a

[15] John Passmore, "Explanation in Everyday Life, in Science, and in History," *History and Theory*, II (1962), 105–23.
[16] Michael Scriven, "Truisms as the Grounds for Historical Explanation," in Patrick Gardiner, ed., *Theories of History*, 443–75, and "Explanations, Predictions, and Laws," in Herbert Feigl and Grover Maxwell, eds., *Scientific Explanation, Space, and Time* ("Minnesota Studies in the Philosophy of Science," vol. 3 [Minneapolis, Minn., 1962]), 170–230. Good introductions to the whole dispute are provided by Danto, *op. cit.*, 201–32, and Maurice Mandelbaum, "Historical Explanation: The Problem of 'Covering Laws,'" *History and Theory*, I (1961), 229–42.
[17] A particularly strong argument for this point is made by Adolf Grünbaum, *Philosophical Problems of Space and Time* (New York, 1963), 281–313.

A BEHAVIORAL APPROACH
TO HISTORICAL ANALYSIS

different operation pragmatically from prediction of the future, but, more importantly, the ability to predict does not necessarily entail the ability to understand the phenomenon in all cases from the viewpoint of explanation or vice versa.[18]

Brief as this exposition has been, we can now understand why contemporary philosophers focus so much attention upon the nature of historical understanding. Whatever it is that historians do or should do is of utmost importance to proving one or the other side on the logic of explanation. Yet this very pertinence of the topic to the philosophers' concerns makes their literature less useful to the working historian. The historical analyst is not interested in the nature of explanation as an issue in logic so much as he is concerned about writing history and what he needs to know about explanation to help him write it. Thus to be of any help to historians, we must examine the philosophers' arguments over explanation from the latter viewpoint.

From the argument presented so far we see that the controversy over a logic of historical explanation involves a differing conception of the questions asked of phenomena as well as of the logic of the connections said to be answers. In other words, the dispute centers upon whether a satisfactory explanation depends upon the phrasing of the question, what the asker already knows, and what he wants to know. The whole controversy is resolved according to Arthur Danto by remembering what he calls an "obvious and trivial point:"

Phenomena *as such* are not explained. It is only phenomena as *covered by description* which are capable of explanation, and when we speak of explaining them, it must be with reference to *that* description. So an explanation of a phenomenon must,

18 Scriven, "Explanations, Predictions, and Laws," 176–90.

in the nature of the case, be relativized to a description of that phenomenon. But then if we have explained a phenomenon E, as covered by description D, it is always possible to find another description D' of E, under which E cannot be explained with the original explanation. If there are indefinitely many possible descriptions of a phenomenon, there may be indefinitely many possible different explanations of that phenomenon, and there may, indeed, be descriptions of that phenomenon under which it cannot be explained at all.[19]

The point Danto makes about the relation of description and explanation has been exemplified in this book already. We could not clarify the nature and profitability of slavery, the nature of abolitionist and Populist mentalities, the myth and reality of the frontier, as well as many other impasses without stating our description of them and in that clarification also making clear our questions and the bases for the appropriate answers.

If we allow the argument that the type of description of a phenomenon determines the type of explanation needed for understanding that phenomenon, have we eliminated the distinction widely held by historians between chronicle and history as their goal? Traditionally, historians have believed that the ultimate basis for differentiating "mere" chronicle from "true" history (the adjectives indicate the historical profession's value judgments upon the two genres) was in the difference between description and explanation. Chronicles recount facts; histories account for those facts.[20] It is now apparent, however, that even the baldest chronological narrative both necessitates and implies explanatory connections in the selection of facts recorded.[21] Without some knowledge of the explana-

[19] Arthur C. Danto, *Analytical Philosophy of History* (Cambridge, Eng.: Cambridge University Press, 1965), 218, his italics.
[20] Walsh, *op. cit.*, 31–34; White, *op. cit.*, 222–25.
[21] Danto, *op. cit.*, 112–142, is quite convincing on this point.

tory connections, historians could neither derive facts from evidence nor synthesize those facts into some kind of written history. Just as there is no history, only historiography, given the nature of time, so there is no historiography on any level without some explanation, given the nature of reconstructing history. So the real question becomes, Is there any basis in the argument about explanation that would allow us to relate the philosophers' conceptions of explanation to the historians' conceptions of goals as expressed in their feelings about the difference between mere chronicle and history proper?

I believe the distinction can rest upon the seemingly inevitable gap, given the current state of knowledge, between described historical facts and explanatory statements concerning them. Even though the derivation of those facts depended upon some explanatory connections for their achievement, still the facts can be regrouped in such a fashion as to require explanations different from those that aided in their initial establishment. We can describe more than we can explain in this sense in light of current knowledge. In the social sciences, for example, the explanations of many behavioral phenomena are still shrouded in mystery, although the phenomena are describable in some ways. Until these sciences develop much more than they have to date, there will always be a gulf between the facts of history and their explanation, and so long as this is the case, we will have a basis for distinguishing between description and explanation, between chronicle and history in terms of current usage of those words by the historical profession.

In essence, this distinction must be founded upon the different questions asked about a set of derived facts so that different syntheses will emerge about the same past events. This difference may be viewed as distinguishing two different levels of historical explanation. On one level, we ask the questions,

1. Who was it?
2. What was it? (or What happened?)
3. When or where did it happen?
4. How did it happen?

On another level we ask why of the questions,

1. Why was this who or what involved?
2. Why did this happen when or where it did?
3. Why was it what or how it was, i.e., Why did this happen in this sequence?

Chronicle only asks the first set of questions and organizes answers at best into a narrative form; history proper in addition asks and attempts to answer in its synthesis the second set of questions. Thus the distinction between the two levels of historical explanation is not in regard to the derivation and description of a set of facts and the explanatory connections that produced them, but rather it is in the syntheses of those facts into either a chronological narrative or a proper history. Both steps of historical analysis use explanatory connections in their production, so the presence of explanatory connections as such is not the basis of the difference. The distinction applies solely to the step of synthesis and depends upon the kinds of questions asked and the answers demanded. Although chronicle and history shade into one another in practice, still the differing answers resulting from the two levels of questions eventuate in two distinctive forms of historical synthesis.

Clarifying the levels of explanation according to the basic questions asked and the resulting descriptions to be explained only poses more starkly certain problems facing the historical profession today. Should historians attempt to write only upon the second level of questions? In other words, is history proper the only proper history? Can the historian write only upon that level, even if he wants to, given his other assumptions? Lastly, is the Popper-Hempel covering-law model the only satisfactory form of explanation even on the second level of history proper? Or are other kinds of answers possible even upon that level?

This conscious emphasis upon explanatory criteria in general and the stress upon the second set of "why" questions distinguishes some of the newest trends in historical analysis. Nowhere do we see this trend better than in the new economic history as compared to earlier work in the same field. Examination of this field is therefore most likely to reveal the possibilities of history proper (versus chronicle) and the model of explanation to be used in historiography.

Few men are so instructive upon this point as is Douglass C. North, one of the founders of the new economic history and an explicit advocate of the Popper-Hempel model of explanation. His latest book is an attempt to make the economic history of the United States history proper in contrast to his predecessors in that subject. First, he severely restricted the scope of the book to two basic topics, economic growth and income distribution, as the title, *Growth and Welfare in the American Past: A New Economic History*, indicates.[22] After maintaining that for theoretical reasons these are the two main issues in economic history, he then goes on to state his methodological position very explicitly.

In order to talk meaningfully about growth and welfare, it is necessary to use economic theory and statistics. It is impossible to analyze and explain the issues dealt with in economic history without developing initial hypotheses and testing

[22] Douglass C. North, *Growth and Welfare in the American Past: A New Economic History* (Englewood Cliffs, N.J., 1966).

them in light of available evidence. The initial hypotheses come from the body of economic theory that has evolved in the past 200 years and is being continually tested and refined by empirical inquiry. The statistics provide the precise measurement and empirical evidence by which to test the theory. *The limits of inquiry are dictated by the existence of appropriate theory and evidence.*[23]

The statement and scope of subject leaves no doubt as to North's position on the nature of explanation and the type of history he would write. For him, economic theory provides the covering laws and statistics supply the new descriptions.

Try as hard as he may, however, North neither excludes all chronicle nor does he show that the Popper-Hempel model is sufficient to explain history even in a subject grounded on good theoretical foundations. The failure to excise chronicle demonstrates in my opinion the insufficiency of the covering-law model to be both the sole goal and the sole method of historiography. Even though North concentrates only on those problems in United States economic history concerning growth and welfare, he still framed these problems according to the received record of chronicle compiled by those men he would so scornfully replace. True, he rephrases the questions used earlier in the discipline, and he suggests new answers, but the basic problems continue to be set by the structure of the chronicle of American economic history. This structure lays down the statements about the phenomena to be explained even on the second level of explanation in terms of initial and subsequent conditions, and therefore his book contains an implicit chronicle. In addition, no reader will be convinced that the theories of economic growth and welfare are sufficiently developed or as precise in their implications as

[23] *Ibid.*, 1–2, his italics.

North seems to accept or at least sometimes implies. Certainly he has not covered in his book all that is usually considered American economic history.

The failure of North's extreme attempt to eliminate chronicle and to employ covering-law theory shows the limits and the possibilities of second-level explanation in historical synthesis at the present moment. To the extent that he did explain, or even illuminate, past economic phenomena by theory drawn from economics, he did achieve the second level of explanation and write history proper. To the extent that the theory used was not sufficient to explain the totality of phenomena called American economic history, he must omit part of the past as known or not rise above chronicle. If the latter failure is due to lack of adequate economic theory, North can hope to write a better history in the future. If, however, that theory can never be developed for all the phenomena of history as reconstructed, then he is limited to chronicle at best, and therefore so are the rest of us who would analyze the past.

Why the limits of historical explanation exist in the way that they do can be shown quickly by reference to Table 11–1, the chart on the analytical aspects of time in the previous chapter, which is reproduced here for convenience. Repetitive sequences regardless of duration and

Table 11–1

DURATION OF TIME	SEQUENCE OF EVENTS	
	Repetitive	Nonrepetitive
Short term	Process	Accident
		Series of events
Long term	Process	Trend
		History

even complexity of composition are discoverable through comparison and amenable to the formation of generalizations about them. In fact, that is why they are denominated processes. Even though some nonrepetitive sequences may be explained by causal statements of some kind or by other methods of explanation, they are classified as nonrepetitive because they are not explainable by natural or social theory at least as currently constituted. Phrased more technically, the sequences are phenomena studied under two different types of descriptions, one of which can be explained and the other of which can be only partially explained on the second level of "why" questions. Thus we can study processes in history but not history as process, despite attempts to the contrary, and so long as we cannot do that, then we will have theory in history but no theory of history as an analytical time-whole. And to that extent historiography must be chronicle as well as history proper.

Explanatory forms exist to cover various historical phenomena whether unique or recurrent, specific or general, concrete or abstract, but there is no one form of explanation that comprehends history as a time-whole. This statement is as true for small time-wholes as for larger ones. The problem is as paradoxical whether the author is writing about the past of a small town for a few years or the rise and fall of empires and civilizations. Causality, statistical probability, teleological and functional explanations, or any law, theory, or concept will help explain phenomena, recurrent or nonrecurrent, of long or short duration, but no one kind of explanation exists for the holistic treatment of time as historians wish to treat that dimension of human existence. Therefore the historical analyst cannot produce a synthesis in which chronicle and history proper coincide fully, because of the gap between the generalizations we have available at present and the generalizations we need. Historians can and will in the foreseeable future be able to describe more on the first level of questions than they can explain upon the second level.

If the distinction between description and explanation in the manner of chronicle and history as defined here, like that between the specific and the general, the unique and the recurrent, is a matter of perspective on data because of the analyst's purposes,[24] then it becomes evident why the goal of the historian to explain time as an analytical whole is an attempt to reconcile the irreconcilable. In effect, the historian tries to view reality under two mutually exclusive perspectives at the same time. As a result he cannot operate on only the second level of historical explanation, much less use only one model of explanation on that level. Hence the only common overall framework the historian can use to order his data is chronological placement upon an absolutely measured time scale. And this chronological framework introduces a structure into the discipline that necessitates both levels of questions and answers, hence both chronicle and history proper.

Other disciplines might select their data only from repetitive, generalized sequences so as to foster the development of explanations upon the second level of why questions, but the temporal assumptions of historians forbid this easy way out of the problem of explanation. No matter how historical analysts might try to avoid chronicle and concentrate on history proper, their assumption of time as an analytical whole forces them to frame their hypotheses according to the statements established by the chronicle. Even for those new economic historians who

[24] I beg the question whether we can equate the second level of historical explanation with the general and recurrent and the first level with the unique and specific. Although all are a matter of analytical perspective, they may not all be classifiable on the same categorical basis to form one dichotomy only.

would most blatantly disregard the chronicle side of historiography, the holistic time assumption still means that the structure of their analyses is set by the description of their subject matter. Thus the chronicle of American economic history placed the framework of Douglass North's latest book beyond the reach of even modern economic theory. His concern with chronicle, minimal as it was for a history, indicates both his difficulty in combining the many aspects of time simultaneously and the limits of producing explanations only upon the second level, no matter what the intention or desire of the analyst.

Confusion between these two levels of questions and answers and/or combination of them on the part of historians may account partially for some of the philosophers' disagreement over the nature of historical explanation. Most written histories contain mainly the type of questions and answers denominated chronicle here. Seldom do historians ask or answer implicitly, let alone explicitly, questions on the second level. If they ask the latter level of questions, they more frequently than not substitute literary devices for true explanation, such as covering law. Skillful exposition and even evocative prose conceal the lack of answers upon the second level and sometimes even upon the first level. Yet even a literary chronicle must encompass some forms of explanation at least implicitly. No wonder some philosophers believe that historians produce some form of explanation, although quite unlike that used by natural scientists. That some historians have used implicitly and all could use explicitly covering laws, trivial or otherwise, proves to other philosophers that historical explanation is but a poor species of what natural scientists do so much better. Thus philosophers on both sides of the argument can find proof for their contentions about the nature of historical explanation.

A BEHAVIORAL APPROACH
TO HISTORICAL ANALYSIS

If this surmise is correct, then we have clarified the relation of the philosophers' conceptions of explanation to the historians' ideas of goals. The historian must use both levels of questions depending upon what he wishes to understand. Questions of who, what, when, where, and how produce one level of historical explanation; questions of why-who, why-what, why-when, and so forth, produce another level of historical explanation. On either level of explanation, the historian may use whatever logical forms of explanation apply to his purposes, whether causality, statistical generalization, functional, teleological, or genetic explanation, or any laws, theories, or concepts available. Hence in speaking about historical explanation we must distinguish between (1) levels of explanation depending upon the kinds of questions asked, and (2) forms of explanation depending upon the type of connection asserted and the logic thereof, because levels and connections occur in no one-to-one relation between the level of questions asked or the form of logical connection employed.

Differentiating the levels of historical explanation according to the questions asked clarifies but does not solve the ultimate and basic problem of the role of explanation in historical synthesis. Fundamental problems remain: How should historians unite the two levels of questions and answers so as to achieve as much as possible the historian's goal of treating time as

an analytical whole? Written history must be chronicle and history proper, but in what combination? If the historian's goal in regard to time forces the use of a combination of explanatory forms, then what must this combination aim to achieve? Does historical synthesis involve a logic of eclectic explanation in the end that is different from that of the natural and the social sciences? Lastly, does this new stress upon explanatory precision in historical synthesis necessitate new forms of historical exposition unlike the classic narrative?

The analysis of the role of explanation in historical synthesis that produced these inquiries also, of course, points to some of their answers. What the historian desires is not a new form of explanation to be labeled specifically historical explanation, but rather a new model of how to combine those forms he has already. If the historian must use chronicle and history proper in combination, then he can employ all the forms of explanation appropriate to the two levels. If he must combine the two levels in order to treat time as an analytical whole, then his historiography must encompass the explanation of the general as well as the specific, the recurrent as well as the nonrecurrent. For our purposes, these explanatory forms should be used in conjunction with the behavioral categories discussed in this essay.

What the historian ought to combine in his synthesis in order to achieve the holistic study of human behavior in past time as advocated in this book can be sorted into four basic classes.

293

1. General laws of behavior.
2. Social and cultural arrangements.
3. Statements of singular causation.
4. Specific statements of fact.

Insofar as the subject matter is explainable on the second level by universal generalizations or laws about human behavior or natural phenomena, then the historian can and should use covering laws. But much of the subject matter of history is not explainable by universal laws, and these phenomena are of special interest to the historian. Although explanations of such phenomena may not be deduced from general laws, nevertheless they may be explained by the general social and cultural arrangements of the era. Thus specific phenomena would be rendered understandable by general social theory on the second level of explanation, but the specific statements about specific phenomena would not be deducible from the knowledge of the general social theory alone. For example, all groups of men possess culture as we have defined it, but a general conception of culture does not tell us the content of a specific culture. Even singular facts on the first level of historical explanation may be explained upon the second level by statements of causation, probability, teleological or functional explanation, and, if nothing better, genetic sequence. Such an explanation upon the second level uses no covering laws as such or any social- or cultural-

EXPLANATION AND SYNTHESIS
IN BEHAVIORAL PERSPECTIVE

arrangements theory. Lastly, the historian will include in his synthesis data derived from evidence that answers the questions of the first but not the second level of historical explanation. All these elements add up to an historical synthesis and therefore to the logic of it also.[1]

What the historian aims for is an eclecticism of additive explanation so as to produce a whole answer to both levels of questions about a set of phenomena in the past, whether the set happens to be just a day in the life of a famous general or an entire century in the history of a country. In either case, what is chosen as the whole to be understood must be explained insofar as possible by a combination of general laws, prevailing social and cultural arrangements, statements of singular causation, and statements of specific fact not explained on the second level. The historian seeks to add up to a synthetic whole through a combination of a variety of explanatory forms upon the two levels of explanation. Different historical topics would need different proportions of the four elements of eclectic explanation, but the overall logical model of eclectism would be the same in each case. Thus, for example, both a book on the American Revolution and one on the Civil War era in American history would contain general laws about societies in conflict, material on the social and cultural arrangements of the rival parties in conflict, statements about the sequence of events believed causally linked, such as the various legislative acts of the two parties, and specific data believed connected to the out-

[1] Compare my reasoning with Carey B. Joynt and Nicholas Rescher, "On Explanation in History," *Mind*, LXVIII (1959), 383–88, and "The Problem of Uniqueness in History," *History and Theory*, I (1961), 150–62; Alfred Conrad and John Meyer, *The Economics of Slavery and Other Studies in Econometric History* (Chicago, 1964), 15–17; and Quentin Gibson, *Logic of Social Enquiry* (London, 1960), 144–55, 188–92.

break of war, such as the leading men's names or the places involved, the story of Washington or Lincoln, Lexington or Sumter, and so forth—all incorporated into one narrative in each case, but all in different proportions of the elements. Even different books upon the same subject might contain different proportions of the explanatory elements, but the goal of each book would be the same in regard to the nature of explanation provided.

I do not propose here just another version of what historians frequently call a multicausal analysis. Such an approach is usually nothing more than a list of factors presumed connected somehow. Rather, the historian should relate the four basic classes listed above so that he provides, insofar as he can, the necessary and sufficient explanation of both the subsets and total set of phenomena he includes in his synthesis. His eclecticism, in other words, should add up to a dynamic interrelationship of factors, not a mere sequential conjunction of events. Historical synthesis and explanation in this manner would combine both levels of questions and answers in such a way that they were eclectic only in the sense of being analytically disparate and not in the sense of being miscellaneously organized.

The difference a conscious model of explanation, even though eclectic, can make in the analysis of historical events is shown by comparing the usual approaches by historians to the American Revolution and Civil War with the efforts of a political scientist to understand what he calls internal wars. Historians in discussing the causes of these two wars traditionally produce lists of factors either as such in articles and monographs devoted to the topic of causation or scattered about in the narrative of the story of events preceding the outbreak of hostilities. Any survey of the historians' models of explanation for the occurrence of these two events will show almost without exception references to some activities of the decade or two preceding the wars, combined with some exposition of the so-called long-range causes. For the Revolution, the reader gets details of the Stamp Act Crisis, the Boston Massacre, the Boston Tea Party, and so forth, and then one or more trends such as the economic growth of the colonies within the English mercantile system, the evolution of colonial assemblies, the attempted centralization of the imperial administration by London officials, and the developing attitude of American nationality. Likewise, most historians of the Civil War mention such specific events as the Wilmot Proviso, the Kansas-Nebraska Act, and the Dred Scott Case and treat sectional economic, social, and cultural cleavage, and/or the breakdown of the two-party system, and/or the fanaticism of radicals on both sides, and/or something else as the larger causes.[2]

After a survey of the rather motley assortment of interpretations purporting to explain the outbreak of the Civil War, Howard K. Beale concluded pessimistically that historians in the twentieth century had not evolved any interpretations fundamentally different from those of the preceding century. In fact, like their predecessors, they too had failed to make the simplest distinctions to aid in the clarification of their subject.

[2] A recent anthology of essays on the causes of the American Revolution, with bibliography, is George A. Billias, ed., *The American Revolution: How Revolutionary Was It?* (New York, 1965). An interesting article on trends of interpretation is Jack P. Greene, "The Flight from Determinism: A Review of Recent Literature on the Coming of the American Revolution," *South Atlantic Quarterly*, LXI (1962), 235–59. An interesting discussion of Civil War causation from the angle of this chapter is Lee Benson and Cushing Strout, "Causation and the American Civil War: Two Appraisals," *History and Theory*, I (1960), 163–85. The most complete summary of the many approaches taken to the Civil War up to its date of publication is provided by Thomas J. Pressly, *Americans Interpret Their Civil War* (Collier ed., New York, 1962).

A BEHAVIORAL APPROACH
TO HISTORICAL ANALYSIS

(*a*) Most of them, even recent writers, have mixed fundamental forces and trivial incidents rather indiscriminately without proper evaluation. (*b*) Rarely have they differentiated underlying from immediate causes. (*c*) Only a few have distinguished causes of the sectional conflict from causes of secession, or either from causes of the War. (*d*) Even fewer have explicitly faced the question whether the men whose activities they all discuss really influenced history at all. Most historians have given no hint whether choices of men or impersonal determinism, economic or otherwise, brought on the Civil War, or, if both were important, how they were related.[3]

In short, he accuses his fellow historians of lacking the most rudimentary model of explanation in their presumed analyses of the Civil War. Beale himself offers no solution to the problem he sees so well, other than pointing out the need for renewed humility in the face of his sketch of Civil War history. Another historian, Page Smith, casts much the same indictment against those who have interpreted the Revolution since David Ramsay's *History* of that affair in 1789.[4]

Quite another approach to revolution and rebellion is suggested by Harry Eckstein as a result of an investigation into internal wars. That his theoretical framework evolved from a much more comprehensive unit of analysis

[3] Howard K. Beale, "What Historians Have Said About the Causes of the Civil War," in *Theory and Practice in Historical Study: A Report of the Committee on Historiography* (Social Science Research Council bulletin no. 54 (1946), 85. Roy F. Nichols, "The Genealogy of Historical Generalizations," in Louis Gottschalk, ed., *Generalization in the Writing of History* (Chicago, 1963), 130–44, develops this theme in another way. Lee Benson and Thomas J. Pressly, "Can the Differences in Interpretations of the Causes of the American Civil War be Resolved Objectively?" a paper read before the American Historical Association, Dec. 29, 1956 (mimeo.), point out that historians are as careless about analysis of evidence in their models of explanation as they are about the connections they assert.
[4] Page Smith, "David Ramsay and the Causes of the American Revolution," *William and Mary Quarterly*, 3d ser., XVII (1960), 51–77.

than that of the historians can be seen in the very use of the term "internal war." Thus to talk meaningfully about revolution and rebellion, he would urge comparison with mutiny, guerilla warfare, *coup d'état*, or any other "resort to violence within a political order to change its constitution, rulers, or policies."[5] He suggests that the problem of causation be reduced to an analysis of preconditions and precipitants. This analysis should then be attacked in terms of three alternative strategies: Should the analyst emphasize particular conditions or general social processes, structural or behavioral hypotheses, the characteristics of the insurgents or those of the incumbents?

In some ways the distinction between preconditions and precipitants would seem at first glance to be the old one between long- and short-range causes in new guise. Further investigation, however, shows quite a different model of explanation at the base of his distinction than that of the historians. The precipitants do include what historians call the immediate causes or occasions of the internal war, but the preconditions are not long-range causes at all. The preconditions make possible the action of the precipitants, but they are also the results of long-range causes. The word "precondition" suggests the setting-up of a situation in which one or more precipitants produce a resort to violence. Both preconditions and precipitants are necessary in conjunction for an internal war to occur. Both are therefore immediate causes that work in interaction as a result of what historians call long-range causes, but the new distinction presents an opportunity to weigh and organize the connections between long- and short-range causes in ways that the old distinction did not.

[5] Harry Eckstein, "On the Etiology of Internal Wars," *History and Theory*, IV (1965), 133. He justifies use of the term "internal war" on pp. 133–35.

A BEHAVIORAL APPROACH
TO HISTORICAL ANALYSIS

According to Eckstein, precipitants are usually unique in each case of internal war, but preconditions can be explored in terms of general hypotheses about the psychological, cultural, social, political, economic, or religious aspects of the situation. Thus he quickly differentiates between what must be studied as particular to the situation and where general behavioral knowledge may be used to aid the analysis. The distinction between precondition and precipitant therefore further aids the historian by specifying when he may use general theories in his explanations as opposed to when he must use specific statements of cause or, in the terms of the previous chapter, when he may operate upon the second level of questions and answers as opposed to the first.

Given Eckstein's distinction between precondition and precipitant, he can only study preconditions in general, and therefore his strategies of approach to human behavior apply only to that aspect of internal war. The first choice of alternatives is between the study of particular conditions and general processes. Should the analyst develop hypotheses about particular social conditions or about characteristics of the overall social processes in the situation? Eckstein elaborates as follows:

In the first case one would relate internal war to particular socio-economic changes, in the second to characteristics of the general phenomenon of social change itself, such as rapid change or erratic change in any sector, or conditions that may result from any social change whatever, such as imbalances between social segments (e.g., between elites of wealth and elites of status) or incongruities among the authority patterns of society.[6]

He opts for the study of social processes as such rather than any particular one so as to bring the overall structure

6 *Ibid.*, 152.

of the situation into focus for the analyst. Thus the historian of the Revolution or Civil War following this advice would not investigate specific economic *or* political *or* social trends as such but rather the state of their interrelationships in order to detect the nature of the disequilibrium that produced the war. The model of explanation therefore stresses attention to the relationship among the variables as well as reformulating the nature of the variables.

300

Another choice facing the analyst according to Eckstein is the alternative between structural and behavioral hypotheses about causes. By structural hypotheses he means the observer's objective definition of the situation; behavioral hypotheses designate the observer's ideas about the actors' attitudes in the situation. He argues that the actors' views of the situation are important in internal wars, because situations said to be objectively similar do not always produce the violence of internal war. Therefore, the structure of the situation must have been mediated by the actors' definition and interpretation. Accordingly, the analyst of the two great internal wars in American history should not maintain that the objective interdependence of the economic, political, and social conditions he sees caused the war as such; only as he reconstructs the situations as the actors viewed them can he begin to attribute causes.[7]

Lastly, he questions whether analysts should neglect, as they often do, the incumbents of the established political structure in favor of the insurgents who wish to gain their demands. Just as important to the outbreak and success of an internal war as the insurgents' power is the incumbents' lack of power. Elite behavior, performance of duties, and general cohesion should be studied not for either the incumbents or the insurgents but for both sides in order to

[7] I have argued this in relation to the causes of the American Revolution in Chap. 7. Compare Lee Benson, "Causation and the American Civil War: Two Appraisals," *History and Theory*, I (1960), 163–75.

A BEHAVIORAL APPROACH TO HISTORICAL ANALYSIS

get a true picture of the possibility of internal war and its outcome. Once again, this model advances us beyond the previous models of explanation by conscious attention to the weighing of the same variables on both sides for war making and war stopping.

Eckstein, in fact, proposes that internal wars be looked upon as more or less probable given the balance between factors promoting war as opposed to those inhibiting war. Obstacles to war include in general the incumbents' use of repression against would-be insurgents, diversions and concessions to draw off the insurgents' attention and their possible following, and the incumbents' access to facilities for countering violence, such as the allegiance of the people and army, the control of communications, or command of the terrain. On the other side, war is more likely if the incumbent elite is inefficient and disorganized, normal social processes are disoriented, the insurgents' use of subversion ("attempts deliberately to activate disorientation, to form new political orientations and to impede the efficacy of elites"[8]) succeeds, or the insurgents' ease of access to facilities is equal to or greater than that of the incumbents. Eckstein does not believe that all these possibilities are equally probable in a given situation. Thus the analyst should not only be able to predict the probability of an internal war but also the nature of that war, because of the differential possibilities in the situation. A full-fledged revolution, for example, is more likely to occur if the two sides have approximately equal access to facilities. In yet another way, therefore, this scheme puts the factors explaining the situation into a dynamically related conjunction to explain not only the causes and likelihood of outbreak but also the form that outbreak will take.

[8] Eckstein, *op. cit.*, 160.

Essentially, Eckstein's scheme seeks to explain why an internal war happens when it does, who was involved and how, and he suggests some hypotheses about why it took the form it did (the what) by an organization of all the variables at the time of upheaval. The historians' so-called long-range causes are combined into one model through the idea of preconditions as well as precipitants, all in terms of the total social situation as perceived by the actors. Thus by one simple model, he supplies a solution to Beale's criticism of traditional Civil War historiography. Through comparison, he has produced a model that can also be used on many types of internal war and distinguishes for the historian how to combine, and even find, specific facts and generalizations. He does leave the historian with the job of still answering why the long-range causes came about to produce a certain set of preconditions.[9]

At the greatest remove from models in current historical practice but with the greatest implications for historical synthesis is the eclectic model of explanation proposed in Neil Smelser's recent book, *Theory of Collective Behavior*.[10] By collective behavior Smelser means uninstitutionalized behavior such as fads, fashions, religious revivals, messianic and utopian movements, as well as revolutions

302

[9] Compare Louis Gottschalk's model in "Causes of Revolution," *American Journal of Sociology*, L (1944), 1–8. For a vivid contrast between a bad and a good comparative model on revolution, compare the attempts of Crane Brinton to be "scientific" in *The Anatomy of Revolution* (rev. ed., Englewood Cliffs, N.J., 1952) with Charles Tilly's much more sophisticated work, *The Vendée* (Cambridge, Mass., 1964). For a discussion of his model—or rather lack of one—by an historian of revolution, see Robert R. Palmer, "Generalizations About Revolution: A Case Study," in Louis Gottschalk, ed., *op. cit.*, 66–76. A good survey by an historian of analytical approaches to revolution is Lawrence Stone, "Theories of Revolution," *World Politics*, XVIII (1966), 159–76. An even better introduction by a political scientist is Chalmers Johnson, *Revolutionary Change* (Boston, 1966).

[10] Neil J. Smelser, *Theory of Collective Behavior*, (New York, 1963).

and riots. Smelser seeks to account for these diverse phenomena by a model of eclectic explanation he calls the "logic of value-added." Although he admits borrowing the basic idea of the model from economic historians Conrad and Meyer, Smelser provides the most ambitious effort that I know of to explain such a wide variety of social phenomena by a version of eclectic explanation.

Rather than merely providing a list of supposed causes or factors, Smelser organizes his factors into a set of determinants that in combination, he hopes, provide a sufficient explanation of a given phenomenon in his study. As he says,

The key element in this [form of explanation] is that the earlier stages must combine *according to a certain pattern* before the next stage can contribute its particular value to the finished product. . . . Many determinants, or necessary conditions, must be present for any kind of collective episode to occur. These determinants must combine, however, in a definite pattern. Furthermore, as they combine, the determination of the type of episodes in question becomes increasingly specific, and alternative behaviors are ruled out as possibilities.[11]

In other words, he does not envisage a genetic sequence of occurrences recited chronologically but a particular combination of events occurring perhaps over different lengths of time suddenly joining together to produce the phenomenon to be explained. The cause is not one but all the constituents in combination and that combination occurring in a specific sequence of additive mixture.

In order to explain collective behavior according to his logical model, Smelser needs two analytical categories. He must classify all social action, and he must supply a typology of the sequence of determinants. Like his book on the English textile industry, Smelser's categorization of the

[11] *Ibid.*, 14, his italics.

components of social action are an elaboration of Parsons' scheme. The four basic components of social action are

304

(*a*) values, or general sources of legitimacy; (*b*) norms, or regulatory standards for interaction; (*c*) mobilization of individual motivation for organized action in roles and collectivities; and (*d*) situational facilities, or information, skills, tools, and obstacles in the pursuit of concrete goals.[12]

The components are said to be arranged in hierarchical order of decreasing generality and comprehensiveness, and each component is divided into seven levels also in hierarchical order. According to this scheme, situational facilities or role mobilization and their subcategories may change without affecting norms or values, but a change in values and norms must perforce affect roles and facilities and their subcategories. Collective behavior may be directed to changing values, norms, roles, or facilities.

To classify social action is necessary but not sufficient to account for collective behavior, however, so he develops a theoretical sequence of determinants to show how the components fit together to produce a craze, a riot, a revival, or a revolution. The sequence begins with (1) "structural conduciveness." Are certain aspects of the cultural and social situation conducive to uninstitutionalized behavior? Conduciveness is necessary but not sufficient, so he includes the closely related (2) "structural strain," or some kind of problem as perceived by the participants in terms of their personal expectations and cultural standards that cannot be solved by normal institutionalized behavior. Strain and conduciveness do not provide an interpretation or a solution, so he adds (3) "growth and spread of a generalized belief." As he says,

[12] *Ibid.*, 9.

Before collective action can be taken to reconstitute the situation brought on by structural strain, this situation must be made meaningful to the potential actors . . . in a generalized belief, which identifies the source of strain, attributes certain characteristics to this source, and specifies certain responses to the strain as possible or appropriate.

Then with the addition of (4) "precipitating factors," and (5) "mobilization of participants for action," in which the "behavior of leaders is extremely important," we have a full-fledged instance of collective behavior. Yet such behavior occurs within (6) "the operation of social control," for he maintains,

In certain respects this final determinant arches over all the others. Stated in the simplest way, the study of social control is the study of those counterdeterminants which prevent, interrupt, deflect, or inhibit the accumuluation of the determinants just reviewed.

According to Smelser's logic, all determinants must occur together, although not in chronological order of his arrangement, in order to produce collective behavior that "short-circuits" normal processes for the resolution of problems within a society. Collective or uninstitutionalized behavior by his definition is therefore the "action of the impatient" to reduce strain.[13]

No one determinant produces any one kind of movement, but only the total combination results in any movement and that on various levels. The variety of collective behavior that results from a given series of determinants depends upon the level of the component of social action in which there is structural strain. After Smelser's exposition of his rather elaborate theoretical framework, he devotes a lengthy chapter or two to each variety of

13 *Ibid.*, 15–17.

movement: the panic or craze on the facilities level, the hostile outburst on the role level, norm-oriented and value-oriented movements upon the two most inclusive levels.

To summarize the application of Smelser's scheme as he develops it in hundreds of examples is far beyond the scope of this chapter. Rather let us examine his scheme on the level of value-oriented movements. Although this is the most comprehensive level of action, it is also the easiest to discuss and understand. Revolutions and rebellions occur upon this level of social action, but we will not continue to use the American Revolution and Civil War as our example. Such an example would be valuable for analytical continuity, but the task of application would require one or two chapters at least. Therefore, for the sake of brevity, let us switch to American Indian messiahs and their followers.[14] The level of the movement is determined by the nature of the strain and the ability to resolve it. Structural strain and structural conduciveness are interrelated. One deals with the difficulties perceived in the social environment, and the other deals with the possible alternatives, or with the lack of them, to do something about the perceived problems. Thus the question becomes upon what level—values, norms, mobilization, or facilities—do the participants perceive their problems and upon what level do they wish or must they use means to solve these problems? In a value-oriented movement, all other alternatives for reconstitution must be closed but the most basic, that of values.

Many American Indian tribes, for example, under the sting of military defeat and control and placement upon

---

[14] On my attempts to reconcile this theory and history in ethnohistory, see my article, "Faith and Factionalism Among the Senecas: Theory and Ethnohistory," *Ethnohistory*, XII (1965), 99–112.

reservations, possessed no means other than value trans- formation as an out, for their usual facilities (surely the customary knowledge and skills were no longer adequate), the usual mobilization (they were prevented from punish- ing the white persons considered responsible for the state of affairs), and the usual norms (they could not change the rules of the game they were forced to play) were inade- quate. These tribes were suddenly placed in a situation where a complete change of the male role in war, hunting, and governing was called for by the dominant society. Through governmental agent and missionary, the dominant society demanded new knowledge and techniques, new roles and new organizations, new rules for living, and even a new value system so the Indians could live like white middle class American farm families.

As Smelser points out, strains occur in clusters, and no one strain leads to one type of social movement. But all analysts agree that the consolidation of control over an Indian tribe represented by reservation formation consti- tutes a stressful situation that promoted messianic move- ments to reformulate values. Added to this is the strain induced by missionization, particularly in the area of values, for that is the target of missionary effort. Finally, governmental repression makes alternative responses other than basic value changes impossible. So the factors of strain and conduciveness combined to promote a value-oriented movement in an Indian tribe.

In addition to structural strain and conduciveness, a generalized belief must crystallize that will identify the source of the problem as perceived by the actors and posit certain seemingly appropriate solutions in terms of value orientations. The messiahs' *Weltanschauungen* qualify as such generalized beliefs. The set of beliefs defined evil and envisioned secular and religious regeneration. To most

Indian messiahs, the bad plight of their fellow tribesmen could be traced to a departure from traditional religious practices and the adoption of certain white vices such as drinking. They usually urged a combination of traditional Indian religious beliefs and practices with some ideas and practices borrowed from Christianity as the new religion of the demoralized tribe.

Thus the messiahs presented value orientations for the demoralized Indians. The views they offered fulfill Smelser's list of functions of a generalized belief: they reduced the ambiguity of a stressful situation by explaining and proposing a solution; they short-circuited the normal process of slowly recasting problems at a higher level of social action and solving them at a lower level by creating a belief that does both at once; and lastly, they mobilized individuals for action by creating a common culture within which leader and followers could act together. In the Indian tribes I have studied, though, it seems that while strains were felt by all in a tribe, the adoption of solutions, hence perception of solutions, differed according to factions. The resolution of this problem of differential perception is probably a matter of psychological study no longer available to us.

Into the complex of strain, conduciveness, and crystallization of a generalized belief, Smelser adds a precipitating factor that "creates, sharpens, or exaggerates a condition of strain or conduciveness" and, as such, "links the generalized belief to concrete situations, and thus brings the movement closer to actualization."[15] In this sense the placement of the tribes under American military control upon a reservation is a condition of strain, but the coming of the government agents or the missionaries is the precipitating

[15] Smelser, *op. cit.*, 352.

*A BEHAVIORAL APPROACH
TO HISTORICAL ANALYSIS*

factor. Their entrance adds on the last proverbial straw in the situation that gave rise to the prophets. The very presence of agents and missionaries marks the wishes of the dominant American society in the new situation. They focus attention on the necessity of a confrontation upon the level of values because they demand such a sweeping change in Indian life.

The stage is set for the additional determinant of the mobilization for action, in which leaders play such an important role. Leaders of value-oriented movements must be, of necessity, charismatic leaders. They must seem out of the ordinary and linked to the supernatural because they appear in their views to reach to the very depths of a society's values. They must seem superhuman in order to envision the reconstruction of an entire social order and in order to receive the total commitment they demand of their followers. It is evident that Indian messiahs fulfill these qualities of a charismatic leader.

The type of movement that issues from such leadership and even the nature of the leadership must vary according to the social control exercised by the parent society. The response of the parent society will determine how it becomes institutionalized as well as whether it even gets started. The relatively inflexible position of the state and Federal governments for permanent repression of the customary Indian warfare and for ever greater consolidation upon smaller reservations has been pointed out frequently, but equally important, it seems to me, was the lack of physical coercion beyond these demands. In other words, the Indians had leeway within this framework of pacification and landsales. Although they were no longer permitted to kill the agents of the alien culture, they were not forced to heed their requests to farm, to read, or to pray. Annuity allocation, missionary example, and the

EXPLANATION AND SYNTHESIS
IN BEHAVIORAL PERSPECTIVE

government agent's harangue were used, however, to change aboriginal society in the direction of middle class white agrarian society. Thus the dominant society set the contact conditions. In light of this policy, it would seem that the strain would be greatest after initial military defeat and placement upon reservations. Messianic movements would be natural in these circumstances, but whether they would be peaceful or hostile would depend on further governmental control. Perhaps the amount of previous acculturation would also account for the difference between the peaceful outcome of a movement like the Handsome Lake Religion as opposed to the hostile outbursts in the latter part of the nineteenth century.

So, in like manner, Smelser's theoretical scheme of determinants may be applied upon each lower level of social action. In each successive case of a component, those components above it in the hierarchy remain unaffected while those below are changed until at last the level of facilities alone is changed but all above remains unchanged. Revolutions and Messianic movements change norms, roles, and facilities, but a panic or craze may occur without affecting any level but that of situational facilities. A panic or craze may herald a more inclusive movement, but they as such do not cause the alteration in the upper levels.

By adding specific data, such as the names of Handsome Lake, the Prophet, or Wovoka, such tribes as Seneca, Shawnee, or Paiute, and a dated history of events to Smelser's scheme for analyzing a value-oriented movement as outlined above, we get a complete model of eclectic explanation. Smelser accomplishes this rather extraordinary feat for a variety of hitherto seemingly unique and inexplicable phenomena by starting with a theory of the social whole built upon Parsonian foundations. This whole includes both general laws and social and cultural arrangements. To this he adds a theory of timing in an analytical but not concrete sense; his timing sequence is not necessarily the actual chronological ordering of action. To this framework may be added the specific causal statements and the specific statements of facts needed to provide a complete narrative of a set of historical events. Both the general and the specific, the unique and the recurrent, are embraced in one fused network of analysis and description.

311

The logical structure of eclectic explanation propounded here and exemplified in one possible way by Smelser's work is a hideous hybrid from the viewpoint of the logician, but it is the only possible, and therefore sensible, one for the historian, given his overall goal about time and the reconstruction of past reality. The historian uses the same logical forms of explanation as other analysts but in such a combination as to produce the answers to questions he wishes to explore upon both levels of historical explanation. Insofar as he can, he should explain upon the second level by whatever form necessary, but to explain only upon that level is impossible and to explain even upon that level in terms only of covering laws is even more difficult—if it is possible to conceive of varying degrees of impossibility.

To adopt even this model of eclectic explanation for historical synthesis poses certain grave problems given the current condition of social theory. The most obvious and first great problem in this eclectic explanation is, What is the whole? What determines a synthetic whole? How does the historian know when his explanation is complete? If no procedures of explanation exist upon the second level for the fourth element of specific facts, how does the analyst know which facts relate to the phenomena studied? The whole is determined by selection from the chronicle of history, but just how does the analyst know if he has explained even eclectically the phenomenon if he has no overall guiding theory to determine limits? If the historical analyst can explain by means other than mere statement of the chronicle, he should try to do so, but to the extent the chronicle seems relevant, he must include it in its bald form. In this regard the historian is probably no worse off than sociologists and economists in their studies of social change and economic development. Theories exist for parts of social change and economic development, but no overall theory yet exists. Insofar as those theories do apply, then social change or economic development is explainable, but the whole of these two topics are not explainable by a set of theories, let alone one theory. So these analysts like those of history must seek wholes as large as can be handled by present theory and then group these together on the basis of the chronology of the subject chosen.[16]

An allied but somewhat different problem facing the advocate of eclectic explanation is the difficulty in determining the amount and significance of the various elements that in combination are said to comprise the totality of the eclectic explanation. How does the analyst determine what the proper proportion of the various elements is to explain a synthetic historical whole, if he does not know what constitutes the whole in any case? Without an overall theory he cannot measure the amount of inputs. A physicist can determine the vectors of force that caused a physical object to move, for example, but can the historian do the same to explain why the times changed? If the historian does not understand why the whole social change occurred, how can he measure the components of that explanation? Once again the historical analyst is in the same posi-

[16] Wilbert Moore, "A Reconsideration of Theories of Social Change," *American Sociological Review*, XXV (1960), 810–18, argues against the possibility of only one overall theory of social change.

A BEHAVIORAL APPROACH TO HISTORICAL ANALYSIS

312

tion as the sociologist who would study social change, and both must resort to the art of intuitive judgment to compile the factors of explanation. At best, they can estimate the force of various factors through comparison. Both historian and social-change theorist can help each other with data and theory on this problem.[17]

Thus structural-functional theory made possible Smelser's eclectic explanation by providing an understanding of both the social totality and the relative factual inputs. Although in most cases theorists do not believe they have reached the theoretical codification postulated by Smelser, still his approach, the pitfalls aside, indicates the theoretical foundations necessary for comprehensive eclectic explanation as well as the goal of such explanation and how its logic can work. To produce such explanation demands (as Smelser's work shows by commission and omission) meticulous attention to what is to be explained and what entities in combination explain that which is to be explained. In both instances, the behavioral orientation advocated in this book promotes an awareness of the problems of wholes, of shortcomings of procedure, and of the possibilities of social theory and concept in the explanation of past human behavior. Such an approach to historical explanation necessitates a different kind of attention to the framing of questions and the researching of their answers than has previously characterized most historical writing.

In this regard the new economic historians are in the vanguard of the profession. More than any other historical analysts, they have borrowed theory from a social science, one of the most theoretically sophisticated of all, in order

---

[17] The logical possibilities of cumulative causation for eclectic historical explanation are argued by Ernest Nagel, *Structure of Science: Problems in the Logic of Scientific Explanation* (New York, 1961), 582–92, and Gibson, *op. cit.*, 190–92.

to achieve a new explanatory precision in their field. Thus their methods of analysis are instructive to other historians who would seek the same goal in writing more history properly. Even if their resources in theory and statistical data are greater than those for other historians, still their general procedure is applicable to all historical analysis.[18]

The first thing demanded for the new history is a new attitude toward data. Techniques of quantification must be substituted whenever possible for impressionistic surveys of materials. Data hitherto considered unquantifiable are now counted. Even for recalcitrant data, Conrad and Meyers of the slavery-profitability controversy point out the possibility of a quasiquantitative method called Baysian statistics that enables decisions based upon qualitative judgments about the likelihood of simple yes or no answers.[19] Although some evidence may never be treated quantitatively, the historian can at least make conscious allowances for these cases and so achieve greater precision than otherwise. By having an explicit yardstick against which to measure his qualitative data, the historian is in a better position than he thought at first he might be. In the end, however, the attitude toward data is more important than any quantifiability of it in promoting greater explanatory precision.

Much more important to historical analysis than statistics is the framing of questions to ask of the material, or hypotheses, if you will. Quantification is no substitute for a carefully thought-out set of questions. In fact, I would

[18] The best among many discussions of methodology in the new economic history are Robert Fogel, "Discussion," *American Economic Review*, LIV (1964), 377–89; Conrad and Meyer, *op. cit.*, 3–30; George Murphy, "The 'New' History," *Explorations in Entrepreneurial History*, 2d ser., II (1965), 132–46; and Jonathan Hughes, "Fact and Theory in Economic History," *ibid.*, III (1966), 75–100.
[19] Conrad and Meyer, *op. cit.*, 31–40.

A BEHAVIORAL APPROACH
TO HISTORICAL ANALYSIS

argue that counting far too often replaces cerebration in the recent adoption of social science fads by historians. If the method of explanation depends upon the type of description, as Danto argues, then carefully framed questions promote greater explanatory precision, as North points out. Good questions promote greater testability, and greater testability leads to better historical explanation on all levels. Well-framed hypotheses, then, may to some extent ameliorate the lack of precise data in the goal of more rigorous historical analysis. Certainly comparison among similar phenomena, even unaided by statistical methods, still accomplishes a great deal without such precise measurement.

Since the framing of questions depends to a great extent upon the theory, the historian should become better acquainted with the social sciences. Although other social scientists have not achieved the conceptual utopia of economists, there still exists in those fields much more theory or at least well-framed generalization than most historians are aware of for their purposes. Even rudimentary concepts in the social sciences possess important implications for the more rigorous analysis of history, as we have frequently seen in this book. If nothing more, the historian's concern for explanatory precision will point out the limits of social science theory when applied to past behavior and thereby lead to its less temporocentric formulation. Without some generalization, trivial or otherwise, the historian cannot advance from chronicle to history.

In all these cases of data-handling techniques, of framing hypotheses, and of theoretical foundations, historians in fields other than economic history are not as badly off as most of them believe. Although they cannot hope to emulate the precision or elegance of their colleagues in economic history, they can follow their example to the extent possible given the nature of their data and the theory at their disposal. Historians will write better history if they achieve greater explanatory clarity, even if they do not reach the prescriptive desires for strict scientific explanation of Popper and Hempel.

To achieve even the halfway point advocated here demands that historical analysts know the criteria for explanation as expounded by contemporary philosophers. Conscious methodological assumptions frequently questioned, fully explicit rules of verification, knowledge of types of explanatory forms, and a command of logic are all tools in the bag of an historian who attempts to write history for modern men. In the end, a change in attitude toward what he is seeking to do advances the historian farthest along the road from chronicle to history. Greater consciousness of the problems of explanation will make the historian more aware of the limitations of theory, and so he will suspect the too-easy adoption of social science fads at the same time as he will employ that theory that proves useful to his work and contributive to historical understanding.

Certainly explanatory precision and an emphasis upon the second set of questions are the hallmarks of the behavioral movement as a whole in all branches of the social sciences, and they should be for history also.[20] The behavioral orientation demands a stricter approach to explanation in order to apply it at the same time as it aids in that task on both explanatory levels. The specific behavioral approach advocated in this book aids the historical analyst both in asking and answering both sets of questions about past behavioral phenomena and in formulating explanation

[20] David Easton, *A Framework for Political Analysis* (Englewood Cliffs, N.J., 1965), 1–22, talks about behavioralism in general very briefly and its implications for political science at greater length.

on both levels. The observer-actor and internal-external distinctions are so fundamental that they apply to both levels. The levels and categories of historical analysis outlined in Chapter 3 develop these distinctions upon the first level of explanation in order to answer the questions of who and what behaviorally. The possible behavioral explanations for these topics on the second level are covered for individual persons in Chapter 2 and for groups in the chapters on society and culture. The problem of organizing both levels of explanation as a totality in relation to human behavior is the subject of the chapters on models and systems and part of the chapter on time.

Use of a behavioral approach does not preclude concern about maintaining rigorous explanatory criteria, nor is it a substitute for explanation. Rather, it is a guide to finding better explanation in relation to human behavior. In this sense, this book is no substitute for volumes on the logic of explanation. In fact, the approach advocated in this book should urge the reader to acquire a knowledge of explanatory criteria in order to write better history. If a behavioral approach requires more precise explanation, so more rigorous explanatory criteria applied to historical writing will demand a more explicit and complex behavioral approach. At the same time, precision in logic will reveal the limitations of a behavioral approach and the possibilities of historical understanding.

This quest for explanatory precision and rigorous behavioral analysis raises many questions about the nature of exposition in historiography. Must written history cease being literature as the classical narrative was and develop new forms of expression? Is the new history incompatible with the old literary model? Can explanation and exposition still be fused in narrative form as hitherto it was supposed to be? Does behavioralism imply a new kind of historical exposition? We shall discuss these questions only insofar as they constitute a problem for historical explanation and synthesis from a behavioral viewpoint.

The relationship between explanation and exposition is of necessity a close one. The nature of the presentation of the facts and their explanations will directly affect the nature of the exposition. At the same time, the nature of the exposition will determine the obtrusiveness or unobtrusiveness of the explanation, if it allows explanations to be offered at all. Whether the explanations are stated boldly and baldly or hidden in narrative or even omitted is determined by the nature of the exposition. Although the latter two courses are possible, the former is preferable in my opinion. Since all historiography must encompass explanation of some kind, the clearer such explanations are, the more historical understanding will be promoted.

In the classic historical narrative, there was no conflict between literary exposition and historical understanding in the minds of the writers. Explanation insofar as historians sought it was intertwined in a narrative that evoked empathy, recounted the chronicle, and partially accounted for that chronicle, all at the same time. In such exposition, the two levels of explanation were confused, if the second level was considered at all. Gaps in explanatory connections were gracefully bridged or hidden by literary devices, and so artistic exposition became in a sense a substitute for rigorous analysis. Such a procedure is now intolerable in a day of stricter criteria for explanation.

But what form of exposition is needed to present this new history? Should historians write only monographs that seek explanations of specific topics? Certainly, they cannot write works of theory and explanation upon the second level alone, because their assumption of time as an analytical whole forbids such an easy way out of their expository dilemma. To the extent that chronicle cannot be explained upon the second level, then narration must still be used in historiography, but even narration must assume a new form in light of our advanced behavioral knowledge.

Because views on man, singly and collectively, have changed so much in the present century, modern novelists have long attempted to escape nineteenth-century narrative forms, and so their efforts offer a clue to possible new kinds of historical exposition. Twentieth-century writers have attempted to escape the restrictions of time as chronological sequence and the identification of author and subject. In the works of innovative novelists, plot began to reflect the multiple viewpoints of many human consciousnesses and many different time scales rather than the first- or third-person narration of sequential events on a single time line. As a result of these innovations, the artistic unity of the novel seemed shattered for a while. In the hands of James Joyce and William Faulkner, the novel form even seemed to disappear entirely, but now we realize that they merely expanded literary horizons by adopting a more complex view of human reality.[21]

If storytelling has changed so radically, then should not history telling also change? The multiplicity of human consciousness that plays a part in the life of past men called history must be represented in the historical narrative if it would be true to current knowledge of behavior and contemporary standards of explanation. The older omniscient viewpoint adopted by the great literary historians of the past must be superseded by a multiple viewpoint in new

---

[21] A concise treatment of the changing nature of the novel during recent times is David Daiches, *The Novel and the Modern World* (rev. ed., Chicago, 1960). The historical background of the narrative form as such is given in Robert Scholes and Robert Kellogg, *The Nature of Narrative* (New York, 1966).

EXPLANATION AND SYNTHESIS
IN BEHAVIORAL PERSPECTIVE

expository form. Just as novelists discovered new forms of exposition through patient experimentation, so too historians who would relate chronicles must search for new ways of telling their stories.

Perhaps the whole argument about the necessity for new narrative forms can be presented by analogy with the change in painting between the last and our century. If Clio had sat for her portrait in the middle of the nineteenth century, she would have been painted as a romantic but nevertheless simple three-dimensional maiden in the manner of Bouguereau or, better, Ingres. Today we would commission, at the least, Picasso for her picture. In fact, his *Girl Before a Mirror* could be the exact portrait we would demand. In that well-known picture, Picasso simultaneously combined views of her internal state with different external views of the girl, although these aspects could be seen in reality by one person only at different times, and all with the girl viewing her own reflection in a mirror. If this book had as frontispiece the portrait of Clio that inspired its contents, it would be this work of Picasso, because it represents so accurately the complexity I espouse for historical writing. Like Picasso, historians must simultaneously present in their syntheses the many viewpoints present in past time with the external actions they produced and how they were consequently seen by the actors at that time and viewed by observers later. In a sense, this aspect of the painting is a pictorial representation of Chapter 3. As with the girl watching her reflection in the mirror, so too the historian must constantly reconsider his own assumptions in analyzing the past and be aware of the explanatory connections he asserts. Just as Picasso distorted the seeming unity of perception to represent reality as experienced by modern man, so the historian of today must present his syntheses in as complex a manner as possible within a behavioral frame. Just as he must derive facts by attention to the behavioral complexity of past life, so he must synthesize those facts in new ways so as to portray accurately that behavioral complexity. Only by exploring new forms of exposition can the historian write history complex enough to satisfy the dual goal of accurately analyzing the past and producing a work appealing to the complicated consciousness of the modern reader.

*EXPLANATION AND SYNTHESIS
IN BEHAVIORAL PERSPECTIVE*

INDEX

327

Economic history, 190–92, 285–87, 314

Economic interpretation, 52, 56–57

Economic Interpretation of the Constitution, An (Beard), 56–57

Economics, 172, 181, 209
   cultural approach to, 154–55, 157–59
   development theory of, 312
   historical explanation of, 285–87, 289–90, 313–14
   loose functional analysis of, 196–97
   mechanistic approach to, 175
   social basis of, 83
   study of, time and, 212–13
   systems analysis of, 190–92
   vocabulary of, 2–3
   See also Feudalism; Imperialism; Industrialism; Mercantilism; Slavery

"Economics of Slavery in the Ante-Bellum South, The" (Conrad and Meyer), 190–91, 314

Edwards, Jonathan, 236

1812, War of, 73, 160

Eisenstadt, Schmuel N., *Essays in Comparative Institutions*, 255

Emerson, Ralph Waldo, *Politics*, 126

Empire, defined, 149

Empirical systems, 173, 198

England, 115, 219, 235, 241
   in American Revolution, 232
   industrial growth in, 199–204, 238, 257
   party system in, 261

English Yeoman Under Elizabeth and the Early Stuarts, The (Campbell), 219

Equilibrium, 238
   of systems, 176–78, 181–83, 187, 195, 206
   varieties of, 212–13

Erikson, Erik H., *Young Man Luther*, 58

Essays in Comparative Institutions (Eisenstadt), 255

Ethnocentrism, 144–45, 261–62; *see also* Temporocentrism

Ethnographic semantics, defined, 148

Evaluation, *see* Values

Evidence, *see* Historical evidence

Existential category, 121–22, 125, 137

Expected group behavior, 99–100, 107–15, 241
   evidence of, 108–9

Explanandum, defined, 270

Explanans, defined, 270

Explanation, *see* Historical explanation

Explicit cultural patterns, 133–35, 145

Exposition, 317–21

Facilities, situational, 304, 306–7, 310

Factual synthesis, 143

Faulkner, William, 216, 319

Federalist papers, 152

Feudal Society (Bloch), 258

Feudalism, 82, 94, 257–60

First New Nation, The (Lipset), 113n

Fleming, Donald, 147

329

331

Marx, Karl, 97, 274
May, Ernest, 165–67
Meadows, Paul, 40
Meaning, *see* Definition; Terminology
Meaning of History, The (Marrou), 272*n*
Mechanistic model, 175–76, 180–83, 186–87
  for economic analysis, 192–93
  historian's choice of, 188–89
Medieval history (Middle Ages), 82, 94–95, 228; *see also* Feudalism
"Men of Little Faith" (Kenyon), 152
Mentifacts, 84, 120
Mercantilism, 135–36
Merritt, Richard L., 232–33
Merton, Robert, 193–98
  "Paradigm for Functional Analysis in Sociology," 193–96, 207
Messianic movement, 306–10
Meyer, John R., *see* Conrad
Miller, Perry, 235–38, 240–41
Mobilization of participants, 305–9
Models, 30–31, 169–88
  defined, 170
  equation of theory, system and, 170, 173–74
  organismic vs. mechanistic, 175–83, 186–87
  See also specific models
Moral judgment, 55, 160–61
  in chain of being, 132
  by historians, 15, 24
More, Thomas, 94–95
Mores, 102–3
Motivation, 18, 33, 50, 55–63, 193
  conscious and unconscious, 67

as core of social science, 7–8
  group, 65
  mobilization of, 304
  in social psychology, 31
  two theories of, 58–59
Multicausal analysis, 295
Murphy, Gardner, 32
Myths, 122–25, 220, 282
  ideology vs., 137–41
  Smith's definition of, 123–24

Napoleon I, Emperor of the French, 25, 266
Narrative history, 271–73, 277–78
  chronicles as, 282, 284
  news forms of, 317–20
Nationalism, 97, 115–16, 232–33
"Natural" history, 147
Necker, Jacques, 163
Negroes, *see* Slavery
Neo-Platonists, 131
New economic history, *see* Economic history
New England Mind: From Colony to Province, The (Miller), 236
New England Mind: The Seventeenth Century, The (Miller), 236
Newton, Isaac, 215
Nomothetic-idiographic dichotomy, 245–46, 248, 264
Normal norms, 100, 104–5
Normative category, 122, 125–26, 137
  in chain of being, 132
Normative norms, 100, 104–7, 207
Normative rules, *see* Cultural norms
Norms (standards), 102–7, 125–28, 137, 206–7

333

335

337

Wallace, Anthony F. C., *Culture and Personality*, 89–90, 172–73

Walsh, W. H., *An Introduction to the Philosophy of History*, 224

War of 1812, 73, 160

Ward, John H., 126–27

Washington, George, 217, 295

Watson, John, 28

Weber, Max, 154, 197–98

Wedgewood, C. V., 276

West, the, 109–10, 152; *see also* Frontier

"What Historians Have Said About the Causes of the Civil War," (Beale), 297

Whewell, William, 224

White, Andrew Dickson, 217

Wholes, problem of (holism), 169–88, 204–10, 288–94

in eclectic explanation, 311–12

historian's emphasis on, 265–69

loose functional analysis and, 198

organismic approach to, 175–80

periodization and, 227–28

systems analysis of, 175, 188–90

time sequence and, 234, 238

See also Synchronic analysis

Williams, Raymond, *Culture and Society, 1780–1950*, 147–48

Words, changing meanings of, 147–51

World War I, 15

World War II, 15

Young Man Luther (Erikson), 58

DATE DUE

3/4			
MAY 16 1974			
NOV 11 1974			
GAYLORD			PRINTED IN U.S.A.